International environmental diplomacy

International environmental diplomacy

The management and resolution

of transfrontier environmental problems

Edited by

John E. Carroll

Professor of Environmental Conservation
Deparment of Forest Resources
University of New Hampshire

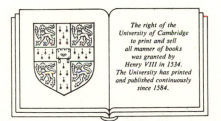

The right of the
University of Cambridge
to print and sell
all manner of books
was granted by
Henry VIII in 1534.
The University has printed
and published continuously
since 1584.

Cambridge University Press

Cambridge
New York   New Rochelle   Melbourne   Sydney

Published by the Press Syndicate of the University of Cambridge
The Pitt Building, Trumpington Street, Cambridge CB2 1RP
32 East 57th Street, New York, NY 10022, USA
10 Stamford Road, Oakleigh, Melbourne 3166, Australia

First published 1988

Printed in Great Britain by
the University Press, Cambridge

British Library cataloguing in publication data
International environmental diplomacy: the
management and resolution of transfrontier
environmental problems.
1. Environmental policy 2. World politics
—1975–1985
I. Carroll, John E. (John Edward), 1944–
333.7'2 HC79.E5

Library of Congress cataloguing in publication data
International environmental diplomacy.
Includes index.
1. Environmental law, International 2. Diplomacy.
I. Carroll, John E. (John Edward), 1944–
K3585.4.15726 1987 341.7'62 87–5159

ISBN 0 521 33437 3

GO

Contents

Contributors

John E. Carroll
Department of Forest Resources, University of New Hampshire,
Durham, New Hampshire 03824, USA

Lynton K. Caldwell
Institute of Advanced Studies in Science, Technology and Public Policy,
Indiana University, Bloomington, Indiana 47405, USA

Erwan Fouéré
Deputy Head, Delegation for Latin America, Commission of
the European Communities, Apartado 67076 Las Americas,
Caracas, Venezuela

Allen L. Springer
Department of Government and Legal Studies, Bowdoin College,
Brunswick, Maine 04011, USA

Albert E. Utton
School of Law, University of New Mexico, Albuquerque,
New Mexico 87106, USA

Konrad von Moltke
Environmental Studies Center, Dartmouth College, Hanover,
New Hampshire 03755, USA

Patricia Birnie
Department of Law, London School of Economics, Houghton Street,
London WC2A 2AE, UK

Lars Björkbom
Swedish Ministry for Foreign Affairs, Political Department,
Section V, Box 16121, S–103 23, Stockholm 16, Sweden

Michael S. McMahon
Benesch, Friedlander, Coplan & Aronoff, 1100 Citizens Building,
850 Euclid Avenue, Cleveland, Ohio 44114, USA

Armin Rosencranz
The Pioneer Foundation, PO Box 33, Inverness, California 94937, USA

Göran Persson
Swedish National Environmental Protection Board, Box 1302,
5–171 25 Solna, Sweden

Douglas M. Johnston
Faculty of Law, Dalhousie University, Halifax,
Nova Scotia B3H 4H9, Canada

Sato Nurmi
Ministry of the Environment, Kakukatu 3, 00531 Helsinki 53,
Finland

David Edwards
Environment Programme Section, Marine Environment Division,
International Maritime Organization, 4 Albert Embankment,
London SE1 7SR, UK.

1

Introduction

A transboundary environmental problem arises when all or most of the benefits of any pollution-emitting activity accrue to one nation, while all or most of the costs of that activity accrue to the nation across the border. It is the existence and the location of the border, therefore, and the imbalances or asymmetries in costs and benefits that result between two (or more) nations, which defines the existence of a transboundary environmental problem, and not necessarily the actual environmental impact of the activity in question. And, indeed, since perception equals reality in the context of politics and diplomacy, if people of a nation perceive (believe) that damage is being done to them, a transboundary environmental problem exists, regardless of whether or not there is real environmental damage or cost. Perception thus becomes reality. Likewise, if transborder damage goes unrecognized by the populace affected, then there is generally no transboundary environmental problem. The conduct of international environmental diplomacy represents an attempt to resolve such transboundary/transnational environmental problems to the satisfaction of the governments concerned.

There has been a long history of localized rather site-specific transboundary environmental problems in the border regions of many nations, probably from as long as boundaries have existed. There is nothing particularly unusual about them except that they happen to occur along or near international borders and have an effect on the nation across the border. Many such problems have had long and complicated histories, which were much exacerbated by their transborder nature. Such incidents never exerted much impact on the status quo of the nation in which they occurred since, although rarely resolvable, they could often be managed or contained, or sometimes even ignored (for long periods and sometimes indefinitely). Europe in particular is rife with such site-specific cases, given the proximity of so many nations to international borders, as well as the long history of industrial development on that continent.

Many of the problems that have been contained are viewed as success stories in national capitals, simply because they did not damage bilateral diplomatic relations. However, they are viewed as success stories much less often by the people in the border regions who live in their shadow and must suffer their effects. Nor are they viewed as success stories by environmentalists more broadly concerned with ecological destruction. Be this as it may though, there are indeed among them a few real success stories from the point of view of both environmental clean-up and amicable transnational relations, especially if the terms of success are defined narrowly.

In the late 1970s, through both the broad dissemination of scientific findings and the vociferous complaint of the people of Sweden, Canada and other nations, the world first became aware of the growing concern over a phenomenon called acid rain. With this concern and interest came the knowledge that serious and complicated transboundary, transnational environmental problems of a size and complexity not before seen would characterize an ecologically uncertain future and could further becloud already inscrutable international diplomatic relationships.

With the advent of acid rain, the era of very large-scale international environmental problems began, and with it came the first real necessity for the exercise of international diplomacy. And with the advent of acid rain, the entire situation has become uncontainable and unmanageable in both North America and Europe, given the numbers of people and economic interests affected the vastness of the regions involved (with both emittor and receptor regions being far removed from the international borders and located deep within the territory of the nations concerned); the complexity associated with multiple pollution sources and multiple pollution effects; and the complexity of the science involved. Upwind–downwind relationships, within and between and among nations, are exacerbated in complex ways.

These factors are much greater in both magnitude and complexity from any transboundary environmental problems which have gone before: they introduce a new breed of transboundary environmental problem and a new challenge for environmental diplomacy. Acid rain constitutes only the beginning of this range of broader and infinitely more insidious transnational environmental problem, which must perforce include ecological decline of the world ocean; both pollution and abnormal warming of the world atmosphere; and the movement in the atmospheric and aquatic commons (and interchangeably between the two) of all manner of border-crossing toxic substances from humankind's industrial production and behaviour and lifestyle. Indeed, many now believe that transborder toxic pollution, both air and water, will soon supersede in political and economic importance the now much better known problem of acid rain. Atmospheric warming through the 'greenhouse effect' (the CO_2 issue from fossil-fuel burning and forest removal) will force its way onto the international environmental and diplomatic agenda before too long.

Hence the public issue of international environmental diplomacy is arriving on the scene with a vengeance and deserves significantly greater attention than it has heretofore received. This book, representing the work of fourteen European and North American leaders in this field, is an attempt to stimulate that attention.

The book is divided into five parts, each containing chapters addressing different aspects of the subject.

In Part One, four chapters present a framework for international environmental diplomacy as it has existed and exists in industrialized nation-states.

In Chapter 2, Professor Lynton K. Caldwell addresses the changing institutional structure of international cooperation. Professor Caldwell, who has authored many well-known books, articles and papers on various aspects of both international environmental policy and US domestic environmental policy, and has been closely associated with the initiation and continuing development of national environmental policy and environmental impact strategy in the US, is concerned with the paradoxes of international environmental cooperation and with the institutional infrastructure required to deal with those paradoxes, through the stages of initiation to negotiation, from ratification to implementation, and to the conduct of that implementation through various kinds of international institutions. Professor Caldwell is particularly concerned with the growing role of non-governmental organizations (NGOs) in the process, and with the decreasing significance of boundaries both between official and unofficial status, and between governmental and non-governmental institutions. He predicts the broadening of the structure of international environmental cooperation and an increase in the operational responsibilities of environmental agencies in the international sphere.

In Chapter 3, Erwan Fouéré, career diplomat with the European Community (EC), formerly of the EC environmental secretariat in Brussels and, at the time of writing, with the EC Latin American delegation in Caracas, is a negotiator and practitioner of international environmental diplomacy. Mr Fouéré addresses emerging trends in this field from both a European and Latin American perspective. He measures the intent and promise of the 1972 Stockholm Declaration on the Human Environment against the lack of response by governments in the ensuing years to the meaning of that declaration, and discusses the global interrelatedness of actions and its implications that, as economic and ecological interdependence increases, the ability of governments to deal unilaterally with the problems on a national scale will diminish, making transborder cooperation a necessity if problems are to be resolved or avoided. He describes some success but much fundamental failure, leading to the state of the global environmental problematic of today. This failure has been caused by the difficulty of reaching scentific consensus on issues and of balancing short-term costs and long-term benefits; and the problem of effectively implementing legally-binding commitments entered into internationally. Mr. Fouéré addresses as well the perspective of developing countries and the interrelationships of environmental protection, development assistance and economic development. Like Professor Caldwell in the preceding chapter, diplomat Fouéré also presents and discusses the increasingly important role of NGOs in achieving resolution of international environmental problems.

In Chapter 4, Professor Allen Springer of Bowdoin College (USA) provides an analysis of Stockholm Principle 21 and its relationship to the US environmental policy and to international law. Following an historical description of the situation extant in government prior to the time of Stockholm and the origin and nature of Principle 21, he inquires whether the US under the Reagan Administration is reneging on its Stockholm commitment, especially in the context of US withdrawal from a position of leadership on environmental issues, a leadership it had sought at Stockholm. Professor Springer discusses the value of international law from what he sees as an American attitudinal perspective; the small role that international law has played in US domestic legal proceedings; state environmental responsibility and a procedural approach thereto; a private law approach; and the role and continuing relevance of traditional international environmental law, with recommendations for which US policy should remain or become once again more responsive.

Professor Albert Utton of the University of New Mexico (US) addresses in Chapter 5 problems and successes of international water agreements using the US–Mexico bilateral water relationship, about which Professor Utton has researched and written extensively over many years, as a case example. The US–Mexico border region provides one of the few examples in the world of a 'First World–Third World' interface and bears witness to the peculiar kinds of often extreme imbalances and thus extreme problems which can affect the people living in that kind of meeting place of nations and peoples. Professor Utton discusses the range of transboundary environmental problems in this region from surface water quantity (apportionment) and quality (salt pollution, from irrigation and evaporation in this very dry region), sewerage discharge, etc. to the emerging serious problems of transborder ground water depletion and contamination. Both economic and physical approaches are used to describe the legal situation in the two major drainages, the Colorado and the Rio Grande, and as well in many of the minor drainages, some of which represent more extreme problems, albeit in a more local context. The chapter treats three selected case studies, and concludes with a warning of impending problems associated with greatly increasing population and economic activity in this water-scarce region.

Part Two presents three chapters on legal and diplomatic resolutions in international environmental diplomacy.

Professor Konrad von Moltké, widely known for his European transboundary environmental work with the Institute of European Environmental Policy in Bonn and currently associated with Dartmouth College and the Conservation Foundation in the US, focuses in Chapter 6 on international commissions and their role in the implementation of international environmental law. He describes the misfit between environmental phenomena and institutional arrangements to deal with them, and looks at the advantages and disadvantages of existing institutions as compared to the creation of new ones. After describing a number of such institutions (commissions and the international conventions enabling them to come into being), Professor von Moltké concludes that environmental issues are fast becoming the third major pillar of the emerging international system, alongside security and economic issues, and that this pillar is worth a great deal more examination and attention than it has yet received.

In Chapter 7, Professor Patricia Birnie of the law faculty of the London School of Ecoomics (UK), distinguished scholar of international law recognized for her work on whaling conventions and commissions specifically and international environmental law generally, discusses the role of law in solving certain environmental problems. Professor Birnie first distinguishes between law and diplomacy, and then surveys means of international law-making; the old legal order; newly emerging principles and approaches; concepts of common space and common heritage; new uses of old means of law-making; institutions; matters of responsibility, liability and compensation; enforcement, penalties and sanctions; dispute settlement; and the various ways that society has responded to the new approaches. Professor Birnie concludes that the main role of law is the avoidance and minimization of disputes by establishing the framework for the building of a legal order within which activities which might adversely affect the environment take place only within a regulated and monitored regime. She also finds that the role of law in dispute-solving could be enhanced if states were more willing to establish and use binding dispute settlement procedures, but recognizes that at present they are not so willing.

Swedish diplomat Lars Bjorkböm in Chapter 8 examines the resolution of environmental problems through the use of diplomacy. Like diplomatist Fouéré and many of the academic scholars represented in this volume, he recognizes the necessity of accepting the central role of environment in many coming diplomatic challenges. Mr Bjorkböm observes that the handling of environmental issues entails special difficulties in that environmental problems are dimensions of human activities in most sectors of society and governance and do not constitute a sector of their own, whereas most national governments have organized themselves in sectoral structures, thereby isolating environment and relegating it to an independent unrelated status which it does not enjoy in reality. Mr Bjorkböm focuses upon the issue of SO_2 and his country's considerable experience with it as a transboundary air pollution issue, indeed, as a leader among nations in attempting to rectify this problem. He observes from this experience that many venues and paths have to be used, non-governmental and as well as governmental, to bring a problem to the attention of national decision-makers as well as the international community. Mr Bjorkböm cites the considerable challenge presented by the need for coordination in the environmental field. And, like Professor von Moltké, he establishes the linkage between enviroment and national security, discussing why environment has been given such low priority within diplomatic problem-solving in the past and explaining why it must ascend in priority if national security is to be preserved, given the crucial linkage between environmental degradation and social, economic and political destabilization. He concludes that governments must perceive more clearly the role that forceful efforts to redress the ongoing environmental destruction could play in preventing the development of international crises that will become more difficult to control and contain.

Part Three deals with the case of acid rain, perhaps the single greatest transboundary environmental issue to bring about truly transnational environmental diplomacy.

Professor John E. Carroll explains in Chapter 9 why acid rain has become such a serious bilateral environmental problem in North America between the US and Canada, focusing on the inherent imbalances and asymmetries between these two nations which virtually ensure the existence of a difficult-to-resolve transboundary problem. Possible remedies are suggested, and linkages between this and other serious North American continental environmental problems are discussed.

Attorney Michael McMahon in Chapter 10 states the acid rain case in North America as it would be presented by emitters of SO_2 and NO_x and by regions, such as the American Midwest, that are dependent on such emissions. He discusses the significant reductions in SO_2 emissions made by the US during the 1970s prior to the advent of the acid rain issue but in response to concerns over site-specific near-ground SO_2 pollution. He focuses upon the American utility industry in particular and analyzes each of the arguments made by proponents of reduced emissions. He provides a detailed treatment of the US Clean Air Act, describing its significance and its environmental impact thus far. Mr McMahon also re-examines early claims about acid rain and scentific imperatives for reduced emissions, and takes a close look at Canada's interest in acid rain legislation, its bilateral offers to the US, its unilateral plans to reduce emissions, and in particular its failures in reducing its own emissions, in keeping its own house in order, as it were. Mr McMahon concludes that acid rain will remain an intractable issue in North America and that US SO_2 emitters and regions (i.e., utilities and Midwestern states) will continue to face the consequences of not being able to demonstrate to a broad audience the efforts that have been taken to date and that will be taken in the future to control SO_2 emissions. He calls for a continued questioning of the credibility of Canadian acid rain requests in light of that nation's own regulatory actions, and suggests ways in which the issue may come to be resolved.

In Chapter 11 Armin Rosencranz, noted writer on topics of international environmental policy and diplomacy, provides an extensive political analysis of the acid rain controversy in Europe and North America. He uses as a framework the various national responses to the Convention on Long-Range Transboundary Air Pollution signed at Geneva in 1979. The behaviour and response of Poland and the UK, both very considerable emitters of SO_2, are given detailed attention, as are those of the European Community and the US. Mr Rosencranz recognizes, as do other contributors to this volume, that the precedent established in the international response to today's comparatively straightforward acid rain issue will set the tone for crucial efforts to head off other international environmental problems in coming years, for it is acid rain more than any other such transboundary environmental issue which has captured public attention.

In Chapter 12 Göran Persson of Sweden's National Environmental Protection Board presents a scenario for progress toward resolution of the acid rain problem. Mr Persson tackles the question of how much emissions must be reduced to avoid acidification of surface and ground water, and soil and forest damage, before outlining the answer developed after considerable scientific research by his government and that of neighboring Norway. He discusses the inadequacy of countermeasures at the receiving end and the availability of technical solutions, and answers three arguments commonly used by large emitters: (1) if abatement of SO_2 and NO_x were embarked upon, it is impossible to measure its effectiveness; (2) abatement technologies are improving and we need wait only a few years to have more cost-effective solutions; and (3) the costs of abating pollution are greater than the damage done to the receptors. After putting these arguments to rest, Dr Persson concludes that Europe must be regarded as one common airspace in which uniform rules governing emissions must apply and that the measures taken should make reduction of sulfur emissions from oil and coal-burning their first aim.

Part Four comprises three chapters dealing with the case of marine pollution as a challenge to the international oceanic commons.

In Chapter 13, Professor Douglas Johnston of Dalhousie University (Canada) describes an unusual framework for analyzing the success achieved and problems encountered in international marine pollution agreements. Professor Johnston, a distinguished professor of international maritime law who has written extensively on law of the sea and the international coastal zone management, has developed a classification scheme which provides a clear method of understanding the often very unclear field of general law-making conventions affecting the high seas; global marine pollution conventions; regional marine pollution arrangements; intergovernmental liability and compensation schemes; and general maritime safety conventions. After distinguishing five different sources of marine pollution, Professor Johnston sketches six 'family portraits' to illustrate how the various global and regional conventions and arrangements operate in practice. In attempting to evaluate the record of environmental diplomacy in this field, Professor Johnston concludes that the process of marine pollution diplomacy may be more important than the product, and that a clearer evaluation of that process may emerge from a study of the input (i.e. what goes into the making of these conventions and arrangements) rather than from a textual analysis of the output. And, since technical elites control the highly technical input necessary to marine pollution diplomacy, effective marine pollution diplomacy depends on the ability of these technical elites to de-politicize the process. Professor Johnston contends that the primary emphasis in the field of marine pollution diplomacy should now be placed on the integration of existing treaty-based arrangements at the regional level, rather than on the resort to new global treaties.

In Chapter 14, Ms Satu Nurmi of Finland's Ministry of the Environment presents an extensive treatment of issues and problems in the protection of the marine environment, using the Baltic Sea as a case study. She describes the Baltic Monitoring Program (BMP) organized by the Contracting Parties to the Helsinki Convention; discusses the main sources and forms of pollution in the Baltic, and problems in their control and abatement; effects on marine life; and management options and problems. Ms Nurmi concludes that regional cooperation is the best and most efficient way of dealing with enclosed or semi-enclosed seas, and that multi-national control has resulted in better compliance with environmental objectives, which quite often benefit areas beyond national jurisdictions.

In Chapter 15, Mr David Edwards, Head of the Environment Programme Section of the Marine Environment Division, International Maritime Organizatioan (IMO) in London, comprehensively reviews the status of implementation and development of regional arrangements on cooperation in combating marine pollution. Included in his chapter are tables categorizing all the regional arrangements extant throughout the world, while the text details the main elements of the arrangements, various regional, subregional and bilateral contingency plans and anti-pollution manuals; a detailed review of each arrangement region by region; a discussion of those elements of regional arrangements which are amenable to harmonization; an identification of sources of technical assistance on developing national and regional contingency plans; and a response to major marine pollution incidents which are beyond regional capabilities. Mr Edwards concludes by describing the obvious differences between those agreements involving the more-developed and better-equipped countries, and those in which developing countries predominate and cautions that in the case of the latter there is a real risk that the agreements will remain as yet another example of the triumph of hope over experience.

Chapter 16, the concluding chapter, seeks to discover the perhaps not so complicated underlying roots of the numerous and seemingly complex problems identified and described in the fourteen preceding chapters. The reader is asked to ponder the trade-offs stated or implied in the variety of alternatives presented in those chapters by their authors, authors who are both students and practitioners of international environmental diplomacy.

Part I

*The framework of
international environmental
diplomacy in the industrial world*

2

Beyond environmental diplomacy: the changing institutional structure of international cooperation

Lynton K. Caldwell

Arthur F. Bentley Professor of Political Science Emeritus, and Professor of Public and Environmental Affairs Indiana University

In a world governed by nations, the disposition and ability of national governments to make and honor agreements are fundamental conditions for international cooperation. New problems of cooperation for national governments and for international diplomacy have been posed by the emergence of environmental issues on the agenda of international affairs. The scope and scale of many environmental issues transcend the traditional boundaries of national interest and responsibility. Governments are being asked to cooperate in the implementation of international agreements in which national interests may be regarded as unclear or as adversely affected by a proposal. Perceived differences in national interests are the primary obstacles to all international cooperation. In international efforts requiring sustained coordination some nations may refuse to participate or may cooperate ineffectually. Moreover, the disposition of nations to cooperate may vary with changes in governments of the day, as demonstrated in policy reversals by the government of the US during the early 1980s. For the effective implementation of many international cooperative agreements, institutional arrangements beyond direct administration by national governments have been required. These international institutions now encompass a diversity of

concerns other than environmental, some of which, notably in relation to
maritime commerce and infectious disease, predate the environmental
movement. But the complex transnational character of many environmental
problems presents special difficulties in a world governed upon the premises
of exclusive national sovereignty.

A paradox of international environmental cooperation

National governments are characteristically reluctant, and seldom
able on their own motion, to initiate proposals for international environmental cooperation. Yet effective international cooperation for environmental protection requires action or abstinence by national governments.
Negative inclinations toward positive commitments are not unique to
environmental issues, but are strongly characteristic of them. Such issues
tend to extend geographically beyond any one nation's frontiers and beyond
the lifetime of political office-holders and their constituents. National
political leaders are therefore unlikely to see much advantage in the serious
pursuit of international environmental cooperation unless their own national
(and personal) interests are involved. Without a national constituency,
governments are unlikely to give serious or sustained attention to international issues.

The reasons that persuade governments to negotiate international
environmental agreements and to make formal commitments to cooperate
are not necessarily those that determine whether, how, or when governments
will act. Why do governments enter into international agremeents which
subsequently they fail to implement? Several reasons are apparent. *First*, the
officials or agencies that negotiate agreements are not always those auth-
orized to implement them. Negotiators and implementors may respond to
different constituencies. *Second*, a government may never have been sincere
in its apparent commitments; its intentions regarding implementation may
never have been serious. It may have been responding to current fashions in
international politics or may have endorsed a policy primarily to demonstrate
solidarity with allied nations. *Third*, its intentions may have been genuine,
but its administrative capabilities insufficient to carry out its obligations.
Fourth, the negotiating government may fall from power and its successor
may be unwilling or unable to honor its commitments.

Few if any public or international issues are more extensive and intrusive
than those described as 'environmental'. Not only are environmental issues

difficult to circumscribe conceptually, they are no less difficult to classify for legal or administrative purposes as the exclusive concern of particular governmental agencies. It is difficult to foresee where commitments to environmental protection may lead; hence political caution. Expansion of knowledge regarding the causes and effects of an environmental problem and experience in endeavoring to cope with it may lead policymakers into confrontation with an unforeseen number of collateral issues, some of which may be politically sensitive. Demographic and economic behaviors may be found to be critical factors in environmental problems. Matters hitherto regarded as strictly national and, as with population growth non-governmental and private, may be found to require modification if problems beyond the national borders are to be solved. For example, burgeoning population growth and a resultant clearing and cultivation of agriculturally marginal land on eroding slopes in mountainous regions may lead to siltation and flooding of downstream rivers in neighboring countries. Land development and deforestation in Nepal has been alleged to have increased the severity of floods in India and Bangladesh. Even as in Haiti and El Salvador, when direct environmental effects are largely confined to the country in which they were created, the resulting improverishment of the people and impairment of the economic infrastructure such as roads and dams may aggravate social and political instability, making more difficult its participation in all forms of international cooperation.

International environmental cooperation is thus confronted by a paradox which although not unique to it, is characteristic of the kind of issues in which the effects of national policies transcend national boundaries. For cooperation to be international, it must occur between or amongst nations. But no nation is able unilaterally to administer international activities, and concurrent action by nations may require coordination and direction that they cannot individually provide. Each nation may undertake its share of the action provided the action can be apportioned by national jurisdiction. For environmental phenomena, division of responsibility may be only partially feasible (as with point source pollution), or may not be practicable for such purposes as protection of migratory animals, long-range atmospheric transport of pollutants, or for policies relating to international common spaces, notably the high seas and deep sea bed, extra-terrestrial space, and Antarctica.

All governments, moreover, are far from equal in their ability to participate in cooperative programs. Many of these programs require advanced technoscientific capabilities that only a few nations possess. Many states can neither contribute skilled personnel to cooperative programs nor effectively administer their obligations on home territory. Financially the nations are extremely unequal. And as previously observed, nations may be unequal in their dedication to the objectives of environmental cooperation, and those differences may not only be marked amongst governments, but also within governments and may vary over a period of time.

The paradox then is that international cooperation is impossible without national concurrence, but mere concurrence as a formality is insufficient to insure that effective cooperation will occur. Something more than national governments is needed to attain the objectives of international environmental cooperation. The need has been answered in various ways through institutional structures capable of operating with limited autonomy apart from the governments that created them. In many cases this autonomy is closely checked by national authority, but in others something that may be called transnational environmental administration has become possible. For environmental issues, as with other areas of international relations, the structure of international cooperation has been changing.

Initiation to negotiation

To understand the structural arrangements for undertaking international environmental efforts, knowledge of the circumstances leading to international action is necessary. The emergence of an organized international environmental movement and a collateral growth of knowledge regarding the courses and consequences of environmental problems have generated an evolutionary progression in international institutional development. In some cases, of which organizations for international rivers and lakes offer numerous examples, initial purposes and functions have been expanded and even superseded by new activities requiring enlargement of autonomy, personnel and funding. This growth of 'extra-national' organization and management is seldom favored by external affairs officers of national governments. The foreign office is often a persistent opponent of such expanded autonomy, opposition in which the military agencies of governments frequently join, depending upon the relationship between particular environmental commitments and national defense. These agencies are seldom initiators of international cooperation other than in formation of political alliances. They are the logical redoubts of chauvinism and their administrators are seldom equipped by knowledge or inclination to consider ecological or environmental issues in other than strategic terms. Departments of commerce, and agriculture have often expressed reservations or opposition with regard to environmental commitments perceived as prejudicial to national economic interests. And some forms of environment-related cooperation, as in the international fisheries commissions, have served more to accommodate mutual short-term economic interests than to protect an international natural resource.

Foreign offices may nevertheless pursue environmental issues through diplomatic channels when domestic sentiment strongly favors governmental action and national political leaders try to position themselves on the positive side of public opinion. Personal interest and sympathy at the highest social or political levels may influence the responsiveness of government agencies to particular issues beyond what they would do on their own initiatives. At the least, positive attitudes toward international environmental cooperation associated with persons of high status and visibility such as Indira Ghandhi or the Duke of Edinburgh help to warm the 'climate' of international cooperation and reinforce the legitimacy of the environmental cause.

Initiatives for international cooperation on environmental issues have almost invariably arisen outside governmental bureaucracies. They have seldom originated within the hierarchy of major political parties. Proposals and pressure for cooperative action characteristically have originated with groups of persons organized to promote some common purpose and to persuade governments to act on its behalf. From a long list of possible examples, the following illustrate a characteristic sequence of events.

On 10 March 1902 at Paris 11 European nations signed a treaty concerning the Conservation of Birds Useful to Agriculture. This diplomatic event was the outcome of 35 years of effort to obtain an international convention for the protection of birds and animals useful to agriculture, initiated in 1868 by an assembly of German farmers and foresters. Diplomatic negotiations, initially to develop a network of bilateral agreements, were carried on primarily by Austria-Hungary, France, Italy and Switzerland. The Swiss in 1872 proposed an international regulatory commission, but the other governments concerned were not interested in a new institution that might compromise their sovereignty. International Ornithological Congresses in 1891, 1893, and 1900 kept the issue alive and, in 1884, set up in Vienna an International Ornithological Committee which continued to press for international action. Finally in 1902 an international convention was drafted, following a joint Austrian–Italian declaration in 1887 committing the respective governments to 'strict and comprehensive legislation for bird protection'. In fact the declaration was not implemented by action, although it provided a basis for negotiating the treaty of 1902. This early example of interaction between non-governmental organizations and governments has become the normal pattern of interaction across a broad spectrum of public issues. International congresses or conferences have become regular although discontinuous components of the structure of international cooperation and have been especially important for the initiation of environment-related agreements.

A differing example of changing emphases in continuing negotiation is the Convention between the US and other powers providing for the preservation and protection of Fur Seals (signed 7 July 1911). The history of this convention exemplifies the practical necessity of providing for the continuation of cooperative action beyond diplomacy. The treaty of 1911 was responsive formerly to the fur trade and to a belief within the signatory states that unless intergovernmental agreement to restrain and control the taking of seals was achieved, the species would soon face extinction. The treaty has been periodically renegotiated and renewed without significant changes. But today the harvesting and distribution of fur seal pelts is being challenged by a number of environmental and animal protection organizations so that implementation under present premises may be forced back to negotiation of the demand now being voiced that the slaughter of 'excess' population for commercial purposes should cease.

Environmental issues are seldom wholly unlike other international issues with implications for domestic policies, but their implementation is often more difficult than is their negotiation as formal conventions. Where no supervisory institution has been provided, independent of the regular bureaucratic hierarchies and with a special charge to implement, cooperation by signatory states has tended to be perfunctory. Treaties for protection of migratory wildlife, notably of birds, have been only moderately effective. Those treaties have seldom contained provisions for safeguarding animal habitat and food supply, provisions that would impinge upon national economic interests. Similarly, the 1975 Convention on Wetlands of International Importance appears to have provided only minimal protection for migratory waterfowl. Draining of wetlands, clearing of forest cover, irrigation and cultivation of drylands, and pre-emptions of the food supply of larger birds and mammals have followed from national economic development policies which governments have generally been unwilling to modify for environmental reasons.

Where the territorial sovereignty of nations is not directly challenged, organized environmental groups, often collaborating across national boundaries, are in better position to protest against national policies which they regard as environmentally destructive. Economic interests have historically been organized and have interacted with governments to advance their objectives. The rise to influence of environmental organizations with international concerns has been a relatively recent development. Non-governmental organizations now provide a continuity in international environmental policy not obtainable through periodic international conferences.

Where people have been free to organize for the advancement of common interests and to interact with government on their behalf, the number and strength of these non-governmental organizations (NGOs) has grown prodigiously. The expansive growth of communication and transportation technology has, in effect, shrunk time and distance almost everywhere. Resources of money and appropriately skilled personnel have increased the ability of NGOs to influence the policy agendas of governments and to follow through to obtain action. Possibly no other area of non-governmental effort to influence government has a broader popular base. Moreover, recognition of common interests among environmental groups has led to the formation of networks for communication and coordinated action. The exceptional extent of the involvement of environmental NGOs in international environmental affairs has given a qualitatively distinctive character to this aspect of international relations. The organized environmental movement has become truly global.

In 1980, the Environmental Liaison Centre in Nairobi, established by NGOs to facilitate their cooperation with UNEP, reported that of the more than 1000 organizations represented at the Centre 'half were from the less developed countries'. A much larger number of environmental NGOs are not affiliated or directly associated with the Centre. Many are represented through federative organizations such as the International Union for Conservation of Nature and Natural Resources (IUCN). In 1982, on the tenth anniversary of the United Nations Conference on the Human Environment, a Centre report estimated the presence of 2230 environmental NGOs in developing countries, of which 60% were formed during the preceding decade. In the developed countries 13000 environmental NGOs were reported, of which 30% had been formed during the same period.

In the initiation of proposals for international environmental cooperation
the NGOs now play a regular and significant part. Even when a proposal
appears to originate in a chief of state (such as the World Charter for Nature
with President Mobutu of Zaire), NGOs provide the energy and perseverance needed to carry it through negotiation to formal agreement. There are
many points of interaction between NGOs and governmental authorities at
which proposals are initiated and developed. For example, the World
Charter for Nature originated at a Triennial Assembly of the IUCN hosted
by the government of Zaire. The IUCN is the best example of the
intermeshing of governmental and non-governmental organizations concerned with environmental problems and has been, in cooperation with the
World Wildlife Fund, a major agent for the initiation and promotion of
treaties and other international agreements. The General Assembly of the
United Nations, the Economic and Social Council, the General Conference
of UNESCO, and the Board of Governors of UNEP are also major forums
for exchange of views and initiation of international action on numerous
environment-related issues.

These collective or collaborative interactions are now the principal
mechanisms for the initiation and formulation of proposals for international
environmental efforts. Particular individuals may take a lead in catalysing
cooperative effort and keeping the negotiating process on track; Stepjan
Keckes played such a role in the UNEP Regional Seas Programme, and
Carlos Benvenides for the Peru–Bolivia program to protect the endangered
vicuna. Other examples could be cited, but invariably active organized
support must be mobilized to move governments and intergovernmental
organizations to action. Thus international environmental diplomacy differs
greatly from popular images of formal protocol-conscious closed-door
negotiating. De facto there has emerged a qualitatively new institutional
structure for initiating and negotiating international environmental relationships.

Ratification to implementation

The signing of a treaty customarily completes the first phase of a
formalized effort toward institutionalized international environmental
cooperation. Agreement has been reached amongst the negotiating parties,
but no objective has as yet been realized in the environment. Diplomacy now

moves to respective national capitals in which forces of inertia or resistance may be entrenched. A signed treaty presumably represents the professed intent of signatory governments; but governments, particularly democratic ones, are complex and their authority sometimes divided, as in the US between executive and legislative branches. Treaties negotiated under the authority of the President of the US do not bind the nation until ratified by a two-thirds majority of the Senate. Treaties are everywhere negotiated by representatives of the governments of the day, but in the phases of ratification and implementation other agencies of governance enter the process – notably parliaments and bureaucracies. Years may pass before a signed treaty receives the number of ratifications sufficient to put it into effect.

Several factors may defeat or delay ratification. Other issues of higher priority may displace consideration of a treaty on political agendas, especially where no immediate national exigency is felt. Delay tends to work against ratification, providing time for mobilizing opposition. During an interval of delay political control of governments may change, as happened in the US after the negotiating but before the formal signing of the Convention on the Law of the Sea in 1981. Bureaucratic departments and ministries whose orientation is essentially national frequently object to treaty provisions that they regard as prejudicial to their missions. As previously noted, agencies for agriculture, commerce, natural resources development, and military defense have frequently opposed national environmental commitments that would, or might, compromise their objectives or operations. The US Navy, for example, objected to restrictions relating to whaling, alleging the need for whale oil for certain types of lubrication. And state and provincial fish and game departments in Canada and the US opposed provisions in the Convention on International Trade in Endangered Species (CITES) that would have restricted the activities of fur trappers. Budget and treasury officials tend to be especially unenthusiastic about appropriations for international organizations and programs where there is no directly visible domestic economic payoff.

Outside government, private manufacturing and commercial interests have opposed international agreements that would impose trade restrictions either in relation to prohibited product under the CITES or would require changes in their customary methods of operation. Furriers and Aleut natives have opposed the termination of treaty provisions allowing the 'harvesting' of North Pacific fur seals. Difficulties arise as for example in the importation to the US of shells of species of turtles which although on the list of endangered species have in fact been bred in captivity for commercial purposes and have not depleted wild stocks. Because there is no discernable difference between the shells of wild and captive-bred turtles special certification would be necessary to legalize importation. But legality may turn on interpretation of the language of a treaty, and adversely affected interests in such cases may attempt to influence its implementation.

In efforts to implement international commitments the role of NGOs has become a regular and anticipated part of the action. All of the larger environmental NGOs with international missions monitor the administration of treaties and other international agreements. They report regularly to their memberships and to elected officials on observed performance, and may identify failures or insufficiencies in program implementation. NGOs not only provide surveillance on implementation by governments in their home countries, but collectively form a network able to monitor all or most of the governments involved, including those governments or their nationals not parties to a treaty but acting contrary to its provisions as, for example, states such as Angola not party to the International Whaling Convention but possibly affording a base for so called 'pirate' whalers.

Formal or informal interventions by NGOs with political and administrative authorities are the more frequent method of NGO participation in the implementation process. But where governmental action appears to ignore or contravene international obligations as perceived by NGOs stronger measures may be taken. How strong and in what form depends upon the tolerance of a national government or judicial system for opposition and the degree of NGO dedication to a particular cause. The principle of conventional international law that no nation should permit its territory to be used to harm its neighbors has been invoked on other than environmental issues, but as nations have pushed development projects to accommodate economic and population growth, environmental consequences and controversies have increasingly followed. NGOs have no standing in the World Court, but may bring pressure upon governments to seek remedy through the Court as, for example, in the efforts by Australia and New Zealand to restrain nuclear testing in the South Pacific by the French government. Where they have obtained standing in national courts, environmental NGOs and ad hoc environmental coalitions have engaged in lawsuits to restrain governmental action in transboundary environmental disputes. The bilateral Boundary Waters Treaty of 1909 has been invoked in litigation over projects in Canada and the US that have been alleged to contravene its terms, as for example in the controversy over the Skagit–High Ross Dam.

Finally, direct action has been employed by NGOs when other methods appear to have been ineffective. NGO-sponsored boycotts against products of Japanese origin were attempted without much success in efforts to retaliate against continued commercial whaling defended by the government of Japan. The NGO Greenpeace has used less peaceful methods of intercepting acts at sea that although legal are highly objectionable to its membership. In 1985 a direct confrontation by Greenpeace with French military authorities, intended to prevent nuclear tests in the South Pacific, resulted in a major diplomatic incident involving the sinking of a Greenpeace ship by French intelligence agents. Angry remonstrance by the government of New Zealand to France and the forced resignation of several high-ranking French officials was diplomatic fallout from the projected nuclear tests which France, having declined to ratify the Partial Nuclear Test Ban Treaty (1968) regarded as within its sovereign right.

Environmental NGOs also observe and report upon the performance of intergovernmental organizations, especially those associated with the United Nations system. UNEP is the only UN agency solely concerned with the full range of environmental problems. But many of its UN Specialized Agencies have major environment-related issues and collectively are the principal actors in the implementation of international environmental cooperation. The environmental programs administered through the UN system are numerous and diverse to a degree precluding their description here. Amongst the Specialized Agencies the greater number of environment-related programs are carried on through the Food and Agriculture Organization (FAO), the International Maritime Organization (IMO), the United Nations Educational, Scientific and Cultural Organization (UNESCO), the World Health Organization (WHO), the World Meteorological Organization (WMO), and the World Bank and associated development banks. NGOs with international concerns are eager to obtain consultative status with UN organizations. The significance of their status in program implementation is not readily apparent. The influence of NGOs is more probable in the stages of program formulation and planning where – in conjunction with the official representatives of member governments – it may be considerable. NGOs are represented in force (usually in parallelling forums) at major UN conferences and at assemblies of the Specialized Agencies where international programs and proposals for new international agreements frequently originate.

The role of these unofficial components of the structure of international environmental cooperation has been emphasised here because, *first*, it has been absolutely essential to most international environmental action, and *second*, it is much less visible than action by the national and intergovernmental bureaucracies that actually administer international environmental programs. The nature and extent of NGO influence on international environmental policy has not received comprehensive or detailed study. The cost of such study would be considerable and is not likely to be borne by any of the conventional sources of research funding. The case for the importance of NGOs in the structure of international cooperation therefore rests primarily upon influence, documented in their own reports.

Implementation through international institutions

Two conditioning aspects of international environmental cooperation have now been emphasised.

First, there is the paradoxical circumstance that today only sovereign states can collectively establish the cooperative relationships necessary to resolve many transnational environmental problems, and yet for that cooperation to succeed, some part of national sovereignty or of political freedom must be surrendered. Nations have been reluctant to concede this surrender, and their representatives have often insisted upon an unalienable right to administer environmental affairs in accordance with exclusive national priorities. Commitment to this exclusive sovereign right caused the eight signatories to the development focused Amazonian Treaty of Cooperation to abstain from voting in the UN General Assembly on the World Charter for Nature.

Second, international cooperation is today strongly influenced by non-governmental organizations operating across political and bureaucratic boundaries and forming networks of influence on policy decisions. This influence bears directly upon national governments and intergovernmental organizations and has worked toward the institutionalization of international cooperation. The viability of many international institutions would be doubtful were it not for the presence of NGOs behind them. These NGOs are numerous and diverse including philanthropic, scientific, educational, reformist, and economic associations and multinational corporations. But they no more than national governments can unaided attend to the business of continuing international environmental protection efforts. And so, like governments, they have sought the creation of multinational institutions to carry on missions that are beyond their competence to manage unilaterally. These are the official international environmental agencies and programs.

Paralleling this official part of the total structure the unofficial non-governmental part of the structure continues independent but often coordinated activities. Although extra-national and non-governmental this unofficial structure has a public and official character in that its purposes correspond to those of national and intergovernmental agencies. Because of its diversity of form and function, this informal part of the structure is not easy to describe. It might be argued that no general non-governmental structure exists, although international environmental cooperation is significantly mediated by a diverse and inchoate group of agencies having no official status. This argument however, misses the functional relationships among these NGOs and the interactive network that they form on many environmental issues. Not all organizations in the network interact or interact directly. Some develop serious differences in policy and tactics. There is nevertheless a significant degree of communication and the coordinative effort between the principal environmental NGOs and the UN Specialized Agencies and with representatives of the environmental agencies of national governments.

Amongst these organizations, personal acquaintances develop and the viability of the institutional network is enhanced because it incorporates an interpersonal network of people who have met at international conferences, on negotiating teams, and on fact finding missions, served on the same committees, and collectively have developed competence in cross-cultural cooperation. International environmental activists are a widely travelled group, many having direct knowledge of environmental conditions in various parts of the world. There is also some interchange amongst the personnel of environmental NGOs and of intergovernmental environmental programs with movement in both directions. Such interchange seems likely to faciliate communication between the official and unofficial sectors of the total international structure. This personal factor should not be discounted, for it is through people that institutions actually work.

Persons associated with these environmental organizations both officially and unofficially learn through experience what is required to deal effectively with the transnational problems. Although learning is an individual process, learning can also be shared. Through persons working together in international environmental efforts, ideas and experience have been interchanged, including differences of opinion. A result has been collective or social learning. Where transnational environmental problems have increased or grown more evident, and where need for expansion of existing authorities or for new initiatives can be established, governments have conceded more authority and resources to international organizations. For example, growth in functions and status has characterized the history of the International Joint Commission of Canada and the US and may in part be attributed to the considered experience of former commissioners. The Lake Chad Basin Commission in Africa and numerous bilateral and multilateral river basin authorities elsewhere have acquired expanded functions as new needs have become apparent. Of course not all international environmental bodies succeed in their missions, some decline and others are narrowly confined by their parent states. Yet those that address major transnational problems tend to become stronger in proportion to their demonstrated effectiveness.

In the long view there appears to be an inevitability in the growth of international organizations in an increasingly interdependent world. The case for transnational environmental organization has to this extent overcome mutual antagonisms and suspicions amongst the Mediterranean and Baltic states. The UNEP Regional Seas Programme illustrates world-wide recognition that important national needs – or rather the needs of people in sovereign states – cannot always be served unilaterally by national governments. Antagonistic cooperation has become a practical option for governments whose hostilities do not preclude recognition of mutual interests. Thus the Mekong River Basin Commission continues to function, and the Kuwait antipollution treaty for the Persian Gulf is still in effect, amidst disorders of international war.

In international diplomacy, even as in national affairs, the de facto boundaries between official and unofficial status are changing and even losing traditional significance. The actual structure of public environmental action has become more extensive and complex than is commonly appreciated. Governance and transnational negotiation are no longer exclusive prerogatives of official governments, but now include intergovernmental international agencies and a diversity of non-governmental organizations.

With time and experience the structure of international environmental cooperation will be defined in broader terms, and the operational responsibilities of environmental agencies, now minimal, will doubtless be increased. If there is to be global government at some unspecified future time it will probably evolve in this way. The political and governmental models of the past can hardly be expected to serve the needs of a world of new knowledge and new necessities. We are probably at a relatively early stage in the growth of transnational institutions for the administration of transnational environmental programs. We can see the general trends, but the ultimate outcome of these developments cannot be foreseen.

References

Detailed documentation for the foregoing paper may be found in three of my recent publications, as follows:

The Structure of International Environmental Policy, *Journal of Public and International Affairs* (University of Pittsburgh) **5**, (Winter 1984): 1–5.

International Environmental Policy: Emergence and Dimensions. Durham, North Carolina: Duke University Press, 1984.

US Interests and the Global Environment: Considerations for United States Policy. Muscatine, Iowa: The Stanley Foundation, 1985.

3

Emerging trends in international environmental agreements

Erwan Fouéré

Deputy Head, Delegation for Latin America
Commission of the European Communities

Man is both creature and molder of his environment, which gives him physical sustenance and affords him the opportunity for intellectual, moral, social and spiritual growth. In the long and tortuous evolution of the human race on the planet a stage has been reached when, through the rapid acceleration of science and technology, man has acquired the power to transform his environment in countless ways and on an unprecedented scale. Both aspects of man's environment, the natural and the man-made, are essential to his well-being and to the enjoyment of basic human rights, even the right to life itself.'

Par. 1, Declaration on the Human Environment, Stockholm, June 1972

I commence by quoting from paragraph one of the Declaration on the Human Environment, adopted at the UN Conference in June 1972. The Declaration and the 26 Principles adopted at that Conference were to inspire and guide the peoples of the world in the preservation and enhancement of the human environment.

A visitor from a distant galaxy (let us call her Princess Lea of Star Wars fame), observing the discussions from the sidelines would no doubt have been struck by the demonstration of enthusiasm and hope which was prevalent in Stockholm in 1972, and would have left feeling content that the world was going to deal with its problems in a sensible manner. The Stockholm Conference, the first real attempt on a global level to set down basic principles and agree on new forms of world cooperation, was the culmination of a major effort on the part of many nations and committed individuals, inspired by the rallying call of such pioneering leaders as Barbara Ward and René Dubos for 'the care and maintenance of a small planet'. If the environmental dangers then seemed to loom large, so too did the promise of global cooperation to counter them.

If that same visitor from her distant galaxy were to stop by and pay a second visit to planet Earth 13 years later, she could be forgiven for thinking she had returned to the wrong planet. As she surveys the scene she would quite rightly ask herself what happened to all those promises and lofty principles to which the world community of nations solemnly commited itself. Were the principles no longer valid; had the world leaders made a mistake? Or could it be that the leaders had not kept their promises and had not lived up to their commitments?

This second reaction is as we know closer to the truth. The Stockholm principles are as valid today as they were 13 years ago. The series of UN conferences that followed Stockholm had a more or less common pattern – governments agreed on the nature of the problem and agreed on the solutions. But their actions did not always match their promises.

Now the situation has deteriorated even further – there are far greater and more complex problems which require action often at far greater cost than if previous action had been taken at the right time. The current pattern of development is affecting all elements of the natural environment and is disregarding the delicate balances between them – from birds, whales and trees to human beings. Environmental degradation and social injustice, like conservation and development, are two sides of the same coin.

Yet never before has awareness of the importance of the natural world surrounding us and of the fragility of its human and natural resources been more acute than at this period in time. As our understanding of environmental issues deepens, we have come to appreciate the extraordinary interdependence and fragility of that tiny part of our planet in which life is possible. A few thin metres of soil, a few miles up into the sky and a similar depth down into the ocean, encompasses virtually the whole of the biosphere in which we and other living things survive.

We have come to realize the basic and indestructible links between what humans do in one part of the world and what they do in another. The evidence is there continually to remind us of this fact – whether it be the untreated seaborne wastes of one country or the toxic fumes from an industrial complex, it is neighbouring countries which suffer the consequences. A few greedy nations can overfish the sea's wealth and deprive others of subsistance hunting needs and valuable foodstocks as well as much needed income. The greed of a few other industrialised nations for high quality wood is causing the destruction of vast tracts of tropical rain forest in Asia and Latin America with as yet unquantified effects on global climate and atmospheric patterns, and making even more desperate the search for fuelwood by poor families in many parts of the world. How many would believe that in an average Indian village, a woman now has to walk 1400 km a year just to collect fuelwood. In developing or newly industrialised countries such as Brazil the scale of damage from misguided development programmes (involving prestigious capital intensive projects) is multiplied ten times over with repercussions far beyond Brazil's borders. How many of us can really visualize an agricultural development programme which covers almost the size of France, involves the destruction of pristine tropical moist forest with an enormous variety of fauna and flora, including many unidentified and unstudied species, and the forced resettlement to a totally alien environment of roughly 8000 Indians belonging to 34 native tribal groups? Yet this is what is happening today, in spite of the World Bank decision to block a $500 million loan because of the negative environmental consequences. And last year in the same country, the completion of a vast hydro-electric scheme has flooded an area the size of Luxembourg, destroying in the process over 13 million m^3 of high quality timber.

We perceive a constant theme throughout this debate: the global interrelatedness of actions, with its corollary of global responsibility. The frequent references made on an international level to 'the world of interdependence in which we live' reflects our global system with complex linkages not just between countries, but between various component parts of the system, whether they be political, economic or environmental.

A major implication of this is that, as economic and ecological interdependence increases, the ability of governments to deal unilaterally with problems on a national scale will diminish. More and more, economic, social, energy and other problems with an environmental or ecological basis within countries will prove *resolvable* or *avoidable* only through increased cooperation among countries.

When one considers the capacity we now possess for mutual destruction and the easy availability of the means of violence, we realize the premium that must be put on somehow making this interdependence work.

A noted contemporary Irish writer and wit, Flann O'Brien, would have described this complex state of affairs as a 'conundrum of inscrutable potentialities'. Not to be left undaunted he would have, with his perennial bicycle, proceeded to scrutinize, like a doctor his patient.

What would he have discovered?

He would have discovered that in spite of some progress having been made, the response from governments has in general been far from satisfactory. Whether because of lack of political will, or lack of resources, or simply because they have been daunted by the very complexity of the situation, governments have yet to show that degree of determination and will to cooperate which is so necessary if the problems are to be dealt with adequately. The increasing tendency of governments and elected leaders to delay the implementation of much-needed long-term solutions to many of the economic, social and human resource issues has led to short-term improvised decision making, best described as crisis management. Governments have often found it more convenient to hide behind the scientific uncertainty of certain environmental issues in order to avoid agreeing on the taking of decisions of a preventive or even curative nature. This of course has had automatic repercussions on an international level, as typified by the acid rain issue to which I shall return later. In developing countries, the situation is even more complex. There the problems relate primarily to the undermining and destruction of the renewable resources of soil, forests, plants and animal life which provide the principal basis for their development. This is largely due to the inappropriate nature of many development efforts, often supported, I might add, by financial contributions from multilateral and bilateral aid agencies from the industrialised North; it is also due, in particular in many of the newly industrialised countries, to the very low priority yet attached to what one would call environmental security.

Flann O'Brien's diagnosis would not have been entirely of the doomsday variety however. Where progress has been made, it has been not insignificant when one compares the present situation with 13 years ago.

When one considers for example, the starting-off point of the European Community's action programme in the field of the environment, one cannot but be impressed with the progress that has been made, particularly when one takes into account the unique and binding nature of the Community's decision-making process and the very different approaches to environmental protection pursued by the 12 Community member states. In the 12 years since the adoption of the first action programme, over 100 legislative measures, covering reduction of air pollution, water pollution, waste management, protection of wildlife and natural habitats, have been adopted. During this time the approach to environmental policy has also changed. Twelve years ago it was regarded as a desirable but optional extra that could be afforded when economic conditions were favourable but had to be set aside when times were hard. Now the emphasis is on prevention, which is if anything far cheaper than the curative approach. Environmental policy can now only be seen as a structural policy at the very heart of the whole web of the Community's social and economic policies. The message from the present Community environmental action programme is clear: that sound environmental policies are not only vital in themselves but are an essential part of sound economic development, and that they must prevent problems arising rather than aim at clearing them up afterwards. It has already been well demonstrated that such policies can and have played an important role in promoting economic growth and stimulating jobs.

The fact that environmental issues are now a regular feature on the political agenda of summit meetings underlines, if indeed there was a need to do so, that much remains to be done, however, and that a more determined and vigorous approach is required. It also serves to emphasise the environmental dimension of many of today's problems, such as unemployment, and the contribution that environmental measures can provide to solving them.

In parallel with action within the Community, the international level has witnessed the adoption of several measures directly related to environmental protection, ranging from general environmental standards and guidelines, and codes of conduct, to binding agreements and conventions. Indeed, Community-wide legislation has at times stimulated agreement on an international level, as was the case with its legislation controlling the marketing of chemical substances which contributed to agreement within the OECD on several measures aimed at harmonising chemical control policies.

The slowness with which at times these measures and legal instruments are adopted internationally underlines the complexity of the task, however. Many of the agreements or conventions are arrived at after arduous negotiations, aimed at finding compromise solutions based on differing political and economic motives of the states concerned. Often the real solution to the environmental problem has been identified, but the need for compromise coupled with hard political and economic facts, has sometimes resulted in a side-stepping of the more adequate solution and the adoption of a half measure which does not solve the core of the problem being addressed.

There are three main underlying factors which have affected and continued to affect our capacity on an international level to adequately and effectively address the key issues on the environmental agenda:

(i) the difficulty of finding accurate scientific data on global environmental issues and long-term trends upon which a consensus among the scientific community on their nature, cause and consequence can be reached;

(ii) the difficulty of carrying out cost–benefit analyses of proposed environmental measures and balancing mathematically the short-term costs on the one hand and the long-term benefits on the other;

(iii) the problem of effective implementation of legal instruments, commitments entered into internationally, especially by those countries which have yet to establish an environmental protection infrastructure as part of national government policy.

As will be illustrated in succeeding paragraphs, considerable advances on the three fronts will *have* to be made in order to achieve the political consensus necessary for promoting more vigorous and innovative forms of international cooperation.

The Final Act on Security and Cooperation in Europe, or Helsinki accord as it is generally known following its signature by 34 nations from east and west Europe in that city on 1 August 1975, was notable for its attempt to bridge the gap between East and West. As the Irish Foreign Minister, Mr Peter Barry, said at the ceremony in Helsinki in August 1985 marking the tenth anniversary, 'the Final Act, while not a binding legal instrument, was to have served as both a code of conduct to guide relations in Europe and a programme of action'. Perhaps because of the sensitive and complex security, political and human rights issues involved as well as the fact that the

Final Act has a moral rather than legally binding nature, implementation of the various parts of the Act has been far from satisfactory.

A partial exception has been the environmental chapter from which a number of initiatives have emerged, mainly thanks to efforts deployed within the UN Economic Commission for Europe. Some would consider that this is because environmental protection has generally been regarded, perhaps erroneously, as a politically-neutral area of public policy, and that it continues to attract extensive bipartisan support from public opinion. A contributing factor is the opening it gave the Soviet Union and other East European countries to have attention focused on possible cooperation in these issues in order to reduce the attention and pressure for cooperation on the other more controversial issues (human rights for example). Whatever the reason, the subsequent years after the signature of the Act saw a number of positive developments, in particular the initiation of negotiations for the conclusion of a convention on an issue which continues to dominate the international diplomatic agenda at least in Northern Europe and North America: acid rain.

The Convention on long-range transboundary air pollution was signed in Geneva in November 1979 by all signatories of the Helsinki Act, plus the Community. The Convention was the product of hard-fought negotiations, with on the one hand the Nordic countries, affected by the acid rain phenomenon (over 70 % originating outside of the Nordic region) calling for stringent and binding controls of SO_2 pollution from power plants and other major sources throughout Europe, and on the other, countries such as the Soviet Union, Poland, West Germany and the UK, some of the major polluters, refusing to take part in any convention requiring a percentage reduction of SO_2 emissions or imposing a ceiling which would prohibit increases in national pollution levels. They claimed that more research was required before the relation between cause and effect could be effectively proved.

Eventually the Nordic countries settled for a less ambitious Convention lacking any specific abatement requirements.

Following the entry into force of the Convention in 1983 and new evidence emerging of the increasing effects of acid precipitation on soil, forests and the aquatic environment, the roles of some of those more reluctant countries were reversed. West Germany, one of the major polluters, after witnessing the devastation from the effects of acid preci-pation of the Black Forest, a major recreation area, joined the Scandinavian cause. Now in July of this year in Helsinki, at the third session of the executive body established to implement the Convention, 21 countries, including seven from the EC, signed a Protocol to the Convention. This Protocol provides for a reduction of at least 30 % in the annual total emissions of SO_2, to be achieved by 1993 at the latest, taking 1980 as the reference year.

The Community itself was not able to sign the Protocol, because the EC Council of Ministers has not yet been able to adopt the draft EC directive aimed at limiting emissions from large combustion plants. Three EC countries have refused to go along with the additional measures of control over SO_2 emissions proposed by the Commission, claiming that they are not justified on the basis of scientific data currently available, even though data is now available which shows that in some parts of the Community the acid input to the environment is about twice as large as the environment's capacity to neutralize it. The concerns of some of these countries over the costs involved are certainly legitimate. But as the member of the EC Commission responsible for the environment, Mr. Clinton Davis, said at a symposium in Strasbourg:

> I am absolutely convinced that acid rain is one of those cases, identified by the European Council, where environmental protection can contribute to improve economic growth. Measures drastically to reduce emissions will of course impose costs. The costs of electricity will rise. But the benefits to other sectors of our economies – in terms of damage costs avoided – will certainly be very large.

Here you have a perfect example of the first two of the three underlying factors I mentioned above. Such difficulties are only too prevalent in many other issues of the current international environmental agenda, such as protection of the ozone layer for which a Convention was signed in Vienna just over six months ago, and the measures aimed at protecting endangered species being discussed in the International Whaling Commission, for example.

They lie at the root cause of the slow pace with which such issues are dealt with on an international level. The state of scientific knowledge very rarely enables unequivocal conclusions to be drawn about the measures needed. While it is certainly true that we are unlikely ever to have a perfect understanding of most environmental issues, it would be unwise to use this as an excuse for delaying agreement on any form of action. If governments wait for scientific near-certainty, it will often be too late for them to act at all. An added factor in making the process of achieving a political consensus (on what measures should be taken) even more difficult is the increasing tendency of a number of countries to question the validity of long-term trends in global environmental issues as predicted in several authoritative reports and studies. The need for sound environmental data and a coordination of environmental indicators for purposes of comparative analysis is well recognised; the task of putting together reliable data on the condition of the world's natural resources, as well as a credible analysis of possible future trends which will stand up to the severest of critics, should be one to which the recently established World Commission on Environment and Development should devote particular attention.

Just as difficult is the quantification of costs involved in implementing certain environmental measures and the benefits accruing from such implementation. The problems involved in carrying out cost–benefit analyses of environmental measures related to the need, specifically in the present difficult economic situation, often makes it difficult to show as convincingly as possible how short-term costs are justified by long-term benefits. While it may be relatively easy to put a price tag on specific measures to reduce SO_2 emissions from large combustion plants (the increase in consumer electricity bills, for example), it is far more difficult to quantify the long-term benefits to the economy, to the overall human environment and to society at large. It is interesting to note in this context that in the countries of the Community, a Eurobarometer 1983 Opinion Poll showed that 60 % of the people consider environmental protection measures more important than measures to control prices. Public opinion is still very much supportive of strong environmental action, with governments often lagging behind.

The third factor, that of implementation, is even more complex because it involves questions of sovereignty and national sensitivity. Yet upon it depends the effectiveness of a particular measure and overall and uniform progress towards solution of the problem being addressed.

The EC has developed a sophisticated verification procedure in the implementation by member countries of the decisions adopted on a Community level, which involves the European Court of Justice. Rare are the international agreements or conventions, meanwhile, which provide for sanctions to be imposed for non-implementation.

The problem of implementation is particularly acute in the developing countries, which very often lack the environmental, legal and institutional framework, not to mention the expertise required in implementing various agreements entered into.

A good example is provided by the CITES Convention. Negotiated in 1973 and entered into force in 1975, its objective is the protection of a large number of species of wild fauna and flora threatened with extinction, by means of restricting and subjecting to strict control the international trade in animals and plants belonging to these species and the products derived therefrom. According to the extent of the threat, the endangered species are included in Appendices I, II and III to the Convention. Trade in these species where permitted is subject to the issue of permits or certificates by the Contracting Parties. The Convention provides for the appointment of competent management authorities to issue these documents. All of these measures and procedures presuppose an already established expertise in the national administration, particularly the ability of customs officials to be able to identify goods from species for which trade is prohibited, as well as the ability to know for which products an export licence may be issued.

At the last meeting of the Contracting Parties in Buenos Aires, the delegate from Bolivia, whose country had ratified the Convention already in 1979, was made to respond to accusations that his country was not respecting the conditions under which export licences could be issued. The Conference even went as far as adopting a resolution whereby it was stipulated that export permits issued by Bolivia would *not* be honoured if, after a period of 90 days, it had not adopted measures to ensure full conformity with Convention rules. The Bolivian delegate responded that his country simply did not have the technical know-how or expertise required to ensure respect for Convention rules. A number of developed countries plus the Community (which will provide a contribution of between US $30 000 to 40 000) subsequently agreed to provide technical assistance including training programmes for customs officials to enable Bolivia to conform with the Convention. The fact that it took six years to appreciate these deficiencies reflects the seriousness of the problem.

This example underlines two factors:

(i) The incorporation of selective 'sanctions' for non-conformity in conventions is good practice;

(ii) Conventions should provide for technical assistance and training

programmes to be financed by the industrialised countries or
multilateral aid institutions for the purposes of assisting developing
countries in establishing the infrastructure and expertise which
implementation of the Convention requires.

Another dimension of the implementation effort is the question of
sufficient funds being made available to cover running costs as well as
projects. On occasion secretariats are established, but are expected to
operate on a shoe-string budget. One recent example is the Caribbean
Convention negotiated in the context of UNEP's Regional Seas Programme.
Although it involves 28 countries plus the Community, the Convention's
Trust Fund for the 1986–87 biennial comes to just under US$1.3 million
with France contributing 25 % of the Fund, while the US contribution is nil.

On a much wider plane, these examples highlight the social, human and
environmental problems of the developing countries, where they are already
serious enough to deny many millions of people basic needs for food, shelter,
health and jobs.

The words of Indira Gandhi at the 1972 Stockholm Conference ring as
true today as in 1972: 'that the environmental problems of developing
countries are not the side effects of excessive industrialisation but reflect the
inadequacy of development'.

Present development trends in the developing countries, many of which
stem from consumption patterns as well as economic and trade policies of
the industrialised North, are placing unbearable strains on the natural
resource base and threatening the environmental security of these countries.
Because they often lack the infrastructure and capacity to evaluate, as well as
a sufficiently acute awareness of, environmental priorities, these countries
are increasingly at the receiving end of goods and products whose use is
either prohibited or severely restricted in the exporting country.

The use of chemical pesticides in developing countries provides the most
alarming example. In these countries, pesticides bring a promise of higher
yields, of more food for the hungry and of freedom from diseases spread by
insects. But pesticides also bring a new hazard into the lives of agricultural
workers. There is growing documented evidence of severe poisoning and
even death to many thousands of these workers because of uncontrolled use
of pesticides hazardous to health. The countries of Central America, where
cotton growing is a major activity, provide a typical example. Cotton is
notoriously susceptible to pests and accounts for more than a quarter of

worldwide insecticide use, according to a 1983 OXFAM Report. By the early 1970s there were 8 important pest species identified in Central American cotton fields and spray applications were reaching 40 per season, as opposed to 7–10 in the 1950s.

The problem is not only the type of pesticides freely available, but also the way they are used. Try asking a poor agricultural labourer, living in a remote area without electricity or other conveniences, to follow typical instructions one finds on labels of the pesticide containers: 'Store in a cool, dark and dry place', 'use rubber gloves and face masks', etc. Very often, you will find that in any case he cannot read.

This state of affairs imposes a heavy responsibility on exporting countries, many of whom are EC member countries, to follow strict regulations governing the export of hazardous substances so as to protect the importing nations from the health and environmental hazards involved.

Apart from the EC, several attempts have been made, in the OECD, and UN ECOSOC, all so far inadequate, to establish guidelines or a code of conduct to be followed by exporting countries. The latest efforts are within the current annual Conference of the FAO in Rome. The minimum obligations which exporting countries should assume are adequate notification procedures to the importing countries. But far more will be required in the longer term, such as technical assistance for the establishment of a pest management infrastructure in these countries. We will also need far greater cooperation from business and industry, who are in the final analysis the main actors in this area. They are in fact the principal agents through which environmental correction and prevention must take place.

The problems of the developing countries lies not just in the agricultural area, but also in the uncontrolled expansion of cities and urban centres.

Owing to the combined effects of massive rural to urban migration and natural population increase among urban residents, developing countries cities grow at an annual rate of 4 %. According to the latest figures from HABITAT, the present urban ratio of 31 % in developing countries will increase to somewhere between 40–50 % within 15 years. We are talking about the creation during the next 15 years of 120 cities the size of New York, most of which will be concentrated in the developing world.

The urban increase is by no means a new phenomenon. In the late 1940s, Mahatma Ghandi was prompted to say, in response to a remark about the fast disappearance of wild life, 'Yes, it is decreasing in the jungles, but is increasing in the cities'. Now the problems have gotten worse; some of the world's largest cities have reached a virtually unmanageable size, where social conditions have become dehumanised and have resulted in worsening crime, urban degradation and uncontrolled pollution.

Acid rain is now a phenomenon not just confined to the industrialised North; it is a cause of increasing anxiety in Latin America and Asia, according to a recent Earthscan report. More people converging on these cities means more cars and the expansion of urban residential areas into outlying industrial zones, one of the reasons for the larger number of people killed by the Union Carbide gas explosion in India, as well as the oil explosion in Mexico in 1984. Such increasing concentration of population in one area coupled with an often highly centralised administrative system is also a recipe for worsening the effects of natural disasters, such as the recent earthquake in Mexico City. One positive factor to emerge from this otherwise human tragedy is that a public debate has been launched on the imperative need for a more rational urban planning and a far more decentralised approach in government organisation.

All of these problems presuppose an enormous and far greater effort than heretofore from developing and developed countries alike, particularly the latter. The industrialised world is slowly and belatedly coming to understand that the conservation and wise management of natural resources must be a prime objective of its effort both public and private to aid and encourage sustainable economic development in the developing countries. The World Conservation Strategy launched in 1980 by the IUCN and UNEP underlined that conservation and development are and must be, convergent and not conflicting goals. The key concept in trying to make common cause between development aims and conservation in the developing countries is *sustainability*. Only the promotion of sustainable economic development, one that provides people with the opportunity to earn a decent livelihood in a non-destructive manner, will ensure the greatest benefits to this generation while maintaining their potential to meet the needs and aspirations of future generations. The only kind of development that can be sustained is the kind that uses these resources without destroying the resource base.

For this to work it requires also the participation of the developing countries themselves. In Latin America, for example, a far greater awareness of these issues would greatly contribute to the search for effective long-term solutions.

There are already many joint initiatives and conventions on the Latin American statute books, but most have remained a dead letter. The Amazon

Pact, signed by eight countries in 1978, is one example. The aims of the Pact are limited enough as it is – exchange of information, pooling of scientific expertise, etc. But if you add to this the fact that the foreign ministers, who according to the terms of the Pact, should meet regularly, have only met twice since 1978, one can consider the Pact as at best providing a framework within which action can be progressively developed. Governments of the Continent have still to reach the stage where environment and resource issues become as in Europe a regular feature on the diplomatic agenda. Unfortunately, more priority and time during meetings between Latin American leaders is devoted to settling long-lasting border disputes, of which there are many. Yet what better way of creating a climate conductive to a diplomatic negotiated settlement between the parties in dispute than to promote bilateral and regional cooperation on those environmental and resource issues most of which are situated in border areas anyway – the Amazon River should be a uniting force between those countries through which it flows.

Non-governmental organisations (NGOs) have, with a perseverance and dedication which has often been the cause of both irritation and admiration among governments, provided some unique examples of how these problems can be addressed. They have sown the seeds of public awareness, which should eventually persuade those more reluctant governments to stand up and take note of what is happening.

In Central America, NGOs have been particularly effective. This is a region buffeted by political and social conflict of immense proportions, with an average of over 70 % of the population living in rural areas. The tensions within the region have generated an additional burden on the economic and natural resource base. There is estimated to be over half a million refugees spread throughout the region. NGOs have even been able to operate in areas where governments have no control and a state of lawlessness prevails.

Central America is an area where the development of a harmonious relationship between human populations and their natural resource base must be recognised as a critical and even decisive factor in bringing about political, economic and social stability.

This and the priority to be given to development programmes which are economically sustainable in the long run is recognised within the region itself; a large part of the draft Act for Peace and Reconciliation prepared by the Contadora Group of countries is devoted to the economic and social efforts required. Until such time as the economic and social conditions – the root causes of the conflict in the region – are addressed, the resulting tensions and climate of mutual suspicion will continue and reduce any chances there are of reconciliation and regional integration in the area.

This is the essence of the Community's involvement in the area, as demonstrated by the signature just two weeks ago at the Foreign Ministers Conference in Luxembourg of a cooperation agreement between the EC and the countries of the region.

The President of the World Commission on Environment and Development said recently that 'the present global environment and resource problems require new forms of international cooperatioan'. This is particularly true when one considers some of the major issues looming ahead, where we will need to ensure that the necessity to maintain the delicate balances of the planetary environment and arrive at the kind of environmental security on which future development depends, will dominate over the short-term gains which many will be tempted to fight for.

I can safely predict that one future battleground will be *Antarctica*, with its vast deposits of highly prized minerals and probably the last untouched natural wilderness of the world. The 1959 Antarctic Treaty signed by 12 states will shortly be coming up for review. The problems which arose over the signature of the Law of the Sea Convention give an indication of the kind of problems we will be confronted with in relation to the Antarctic.

A precedent of sorts was established for the discussion of resource questions when the Convention of Antarctic Marine Living Resources was adopted in 1980, which established measures for controlling the use of resources in the area, notably the abundant stocks of krill. But the Convention lacks an effective control mechanism, and the powers of the body established to implement the Convention are indeed limited: decisions are reached by consensus, and any party that feels unable to adopt a particular recommendation has only to give notice within 90 days.

In the battle of control of resources that will no doubt emerge, let us hope that the nations concerned will remain inspired by the words of the Malaysian Prime Minister at the UN in 1982:

> 'The days when the rich nations of the world can take for themselves whatever territory and resources they have access to are over. Henceforth, all the unclaimed wealth of the earth must be regarded as the common heritage of all the nations of this planet.'

This is the principle which should inspire future deliberations. It should be the message which should guide the actions of our governments both on a national and international level. In so doing we should be recognising, as did the ancients in India and China centuries ago, that one can take from the Earth and the atmosphere only as much as one puts back into them.

Europe has a major role to play in such future efforts. It should build on those significant achievements it has helped to promote in these last years, and take a leading role in pushing through more innovative forms of international cooperation.

Let me conclude by quoting an old Kashmiri proverb which reflects in a sense the essence of our joint efforts: 'We have only borrowed the world from our children – one day we will have to restore it to them'.

4

*United States environmental policy
and international law:
Stockholm Principle 21 revisited*

Allen L. Springer

Department of Government and Legal Studies, Bowdoin College, Brunswick

Introduction

A needed reassessment of US international environmental policy may be underway. The tragedy at Bhopal, India, has raised again the difficult question of what restraints, if any, the US ought to place on the overseas operations of its companies and their subsidiaries. House Democrats have held hearings to discuss a range of concerns about the commitment of the present administration to international environmental protection programs.

What seems to be missing both in the defense of current policies by administration officials and in the attacks of their critics is a serious attempt either to relate American policies to standards of international law or to examine ways in which courts and arbitral tribunals can be used more effectively. To some extent this may reflect renewed American skepticism about the relevance of international law and legal institutions generally in the wake of the United States' refusal to defend itself against Nicaragua before the International Court of Justice and the unhappiness of many Americans affected by the Court's decision in the Gulf of Maine boundary delimitation case.[1] It may also be a reaction to perceived limitations of the body of international law that relates specifically to the environment. Whatever the reason, the failure to appreciate the importance of placing US environmental policy in a larger legal perspective could undermine the US's position of leadership in the environmental field just as effectively as the reluctance of the Reagan administration to fund the activities of the United Nations Environment Program and other multilateral environmental programs. More importantly, it could hamper the development over the long term of a stable, effective system for protecting environmental interests and preventing and resolving environmental disputes.

This paper examines the relevance of international law and legal institutions in the current debate about the shape and direction of US environmental policy. It begins by reviewing the status of international environmental law in the late 1960s and the importance of the 1972 Stockholm Conference on the Human Environment. After a brief look at some of the most contentious decisions of the Reagan Administration, it then sets forth some of the ways in which law and legal institutions can further international environmental goals. I hope to suggest that, despite the shortcomings of a body of law still at an early stage of development, US interests can best be protected by policies that recognize the continuing importance of Principle 21 of the Stockholm Declaration and other rules and procedures of international environmental law.

US environmental policy and the Stockholm Conference

The pre-Stockholm situation

Environmentalists of the late 1960s had reason to be concerned about the limitations of international efforts to protect the environment. International law seemed particularly primitive compared to progressive developments in national legislation, of which the US National Environmental Policy Act of 1969 was the most prominent example. Traditional customary international law actually gave license to damaging behavior through principles such as 'freedom of the seas' and 'exclusive jurisdiction' over national territory. The US contribution to this legal heritage was hardly encouraging. In 1895, Attorney General Judson Harmon dismissed Mexican opposition to US plans to divert waters of the Rio Grande by claiming that the US had the legal right to use rivers within American territory as it pleased, regardless of the effects on Mexico.[2] Although the infamous 'Harmon Doctrine' had fortunately been undermined by the evolution of twentieth-century riparian rights theory, it served as a warning that political boundaries could present serious obstacles to effective environmental protection.

The US also unintentionally helped to illustrate the limitations of international environmental law in 1969 when it sent the icebreaking tanker *Manhattan* through waters along Canada's northern coast toward the oil fields of Prudhoe Bay. Fearing the potential threat to Canada's arctic resources from large-scale oil shipments through this ecologically vulnerable region, the Canadian parliament extended Canada's arctic maritime jurisdiction and claimed the right to impose national anti-pollution standards on ships up to 100 miles from shore. The Canadian government simultaneously amended its International Court of Justice (ICJ) declaration to deprive the Court of jurisdiction should the controversial measure face legal challenge, a move defended by Prime Minister Pierre Trudeau because there 'is as yet little law and virtually no practice' to control marine pollution.[3]

Environmentalists may have been too quick to discount the potential value of past state practice in the struggle against environmental degradation. Agreements such as the 1902 European Convention Concerning the Conservation of Birds Useful to Agriculture and the 1911 Fur Seal Convention reflect a long history of concern for migratory wildlife and living marine resources although both conventions admittedly focus primarily on the problem of overexploitation rather than pollution.[4] More directly relevant is the practice regulating international waterways provided by bodies like the Rhine and Danube river commissions. Though created in the nineteenth century by states with a different sets of priorities, they have been called upon to respond to twentieth-century environmental challenges.[5] The 1909 Boundary Waters Treaty between the US and Canada was particularly noteworthy in its insistence that all boundary waters 'shall not be polluted on either side to the injury of health and property on the other'.[6] The International Joint Commission established to help implement the agreement still plays an integral role in Canada–US environmental relations.

The rare use of courts to resolve environmental disputes seemed another sign of the limited value of international law. It would be a mistake, however, to overlook two important decisions by international arbitral tribunals whose rulings helped to clarify and to encourage the further development of the rules of state environmental responsibility. These rulings also illustrate some of the limitations of traditional state practice.

The US was a party in what is still the leading case in international environmental law: the 1941 *Trail Smelter Arbitration*. The tribunal investigated and accepted as well-founded complaints that a smelter in British Columbia had caused damage in the state of Washington. In ruling that no state had the 'right to use or permit the use of its territory in such a manner as to cause injury by fumes in or to the territory of another or the properties or persons thereof',[7] it awarded compensation for some of the damage the US had suffered and ordered changes in the plant's operation to limit harmful emissions. Less positive was the tribunal's unwillingness to permit 'minor' matters to disrupt bilateral relations. The complaint had to be 'of serious consequence and the injury established by clear and convincing evidence'[8] before it merited international action, at least by an adjudicative body. Intervention before the plant was built and the damage done would thus have been premature, even if it constituted a far more practical and cost-effective way to prevent or at least control a potentially harmful activity. By providing compensation only for 'tangible injury translatable into provable monetary damages,'[9] the tribunal also effectively placed some important, if unquantifiable, US interests, including unexploited forests and wildlife, as well as aesthetic values, beyond the protection of international law. Finally, by basing the US right of diplomatic protection on the damage done to its 'territory . . . or the properties or persons therein', the tribunal highlighted another major problem with traditional rules of state responsibility: the difficulty of taking action to respond to the pollution of areas beyond the territorial jurisdiction of any state.

The *Lake Lanoux Arbitration* of 1957 was established by Spain and France to respond to Spanish objections that French plans to divert waters of a transboundary water system without Spanish consent violated an 1866 treaty and principles of customary international law. While rejecting the Spanish argument as permitting an unreasonable veto for the lower riparian, the tribunal also made clear France's duty to take Spanish interests into account and Spain's right to intervene in the planning process even before the diversion took place and the damage was done.[10] Had the project threatened to cause 'definitive pollution' of the river or to otherwise 'injure Spanish interests . . . Spain could then have claimed that her rights had been impaired'.[11] This project was acceptable because both the quantity and quality of the water entering Spain would be unchanged and the tribunal was spared the difficult task of balancing what could have been the competing, though 'legitimate', interests of the two nations.

Environmentalists of the late 1960s thus found what seemed an inadequate legal framework through which states could respond to pressing international environmental problems. What 'pro-environmental' principles had evolved, concepts such as 'good neighborliness' and 'equitable utilization', lacked the required precision and were easily circumvented in a system lacking strong, centralized structures for interpreting and applying legal rules. More specific treaty law existed in areas such as marine pollution. Unfortunately, the standards imposed usually were not particularly restrictive, often more a political reaction to catastrophic accidents rather than a rational basis for effective pollution prevention. Slow ratification processes and non-participation of key countries further limited their effectiveness. Even where the rules were clearer and when transgressors could be identified, international environmental law seemed to lack remedies sufficient to deter potential polluters or to compensate injured parties after-the-fact.[12]

The Stockholm Conference and Principle 21

The US's enthusiastic support for the Swedish proposal to convene a global conference to discuss the 'problems of the human environment' had little to do, however, with the state of international environmental law. Genuine concern in Washington about the deteriorating quality of the environment was certainly a major factor. It was taken for granted that the US should play a key leadership role in responding to the threat of pollution, not simply because of its superior understanding of the problem, but also because, as Senator Claiborne Pell put it, 'while we are only 6 % of the world's people, we actually produce 40 % of the world's pollution'.[13]

Yet love for the environment and a sense of guilt for past polluting activity only went so far. Very close to the surface was the fear that tough national pollution control measures would place US companies at a competitive disadvantage in international markets.[14] To protect US economic interests, members of the Senate called upon US representatives to the Stockholm Conference to 'advocate and support multilateral accords . . . enforceable by the United Nations or multilateral economic sanctions'.[15]

On an institutional level, environmentalists argued that what was needed was a powerful international organization modelled on the US Environmental Protection Agency and with sufficient legal personality to bring suits in national and international courts on behalf of global environmental interests. Some, like George Kennan, argued that such an agency, though needed, was a political impossibility within the UN and encouraged the US government to focus its energy on other like-minded Western nations. Run by scientists and other apolitical individuals, a proposed International Environmental Agency would devise international environmental standards and use its scientific prestige to encourage eventual global acceptance.[16] The Nixon Administration favored the creation of a voluntary $100 million environmental fund, to which the US was prepared to contribute up to 40 %, but preferred a less ambitious institutional arrangement under the purview of the UN's Economic and Social Council.

For governments not yet ready to accept the equivalent of an EPA on the national level, an international version was a non-negotiable proposal, probably even among the US's Western allies. Developing countries, however, were particularly wary of such grandiose plans and feared the possible impact of the industrialized world's new environmentalism on their fragile economies.[17] In 1971, Maurice Strong, the Secretary-General of the Stockholm Conference, brought together an expert group at Founex, Switzerlannd, to air Less-Developed Countries' (LDC's) concerns and to explore the relationship between environmental protection and economic development. The Founex Report,[18] though reassuring the LDC representatives and instrumental in encouraging their active participation at Stockholm, dashed any lingering American hopes of achieving agreement on the need for uniform global pollution standards. What had once been viewed as a global meeting to discuss problems of primary concern to developed countries rapidly evolved into an often heated dialogue between North and South. The battle over what became Principle 21 of the Stockholm Declaration on the Human Environment was particularly intense.

Though Principle 21, like the rest of the Stockholm Declaration, technically is not binding, it does represent an effort to express the basic rule of state responsibility for environmental protection. The debate at Stockholm centered on the apparent conflict between the still controversial concept of 'permanent sovereignty over natural resources', of such importance to delegates from developing countries, and the responsibility of states to prevent extraterritorial damage, a principle that environmentalists saw as fundamental to any global program to combat pollution. The resulting formulation is a triumph of diplomatic compromise.

> States have, in accordance with the Charter of the United Nations and the principles of international law, the sovereign right to exploit their own resources pursuant to their own environmental policies and the responsibility to ensure that activities within their jurisdic-

tion or control do not cause damage to the environment of other States or of areas beyond the limits of national jurisdiction.[19]

Set forth in this important principle is the dual relationship between the state and the environment within its territory. With the state's right to manage its resources free of outside interference comes the duty to ensure against extraterritorial environmental damage. Principle 21 remains within the *Trail Smelter* tradition by adopting a 'strict liability' approach. One need not prove 'culpable negligence' or demonstrate some other fault on the part of the state to engage its responsibility. Yet Principle 21 differs from the more restrictive holding of the *Trail Smelter Arbitration* in several important ways. First, it holds the state responsible for all 'activities within its jurisdiction or control', not simply those within its territory, a provision that could, for instance, extend state responsibility to the overseas activities of its national corporations or even, under some circumstances, to the overseas behavior of non-nationals. Second, while *Trail Smelter* held that Canada was liable for damage to US territory, Principle 21 makes clear the state's duty to protect 'common areas' beyond the limits of national jurisdiction. Finally, the kind of 'damage' the state is expected to prevent is not limited by such threshold-defining adjectives as 'serious'.[20]

Principle 21 does not make clear what 'state responsibility' actually entails, either in terms of the actions states are expected to take to prevent pollution or the nature of their liability should extraterritorial damage occur. Political differences at Stockholm made any greater specificity impossible.[21] Given the reluctance of states thus far to commit themselves to general rules of state environmental responsibility, the true meaning of Principle 21 (and, indeed, its legal status) must develop through customary state practice. Nonetheless, it represents an important articulation by the international community of perhaps the most fundamental rule of international environmental law.

Developing countries also made sure that the United Nations Environment Program (UNEP) that ultimately emerged from the conference would be a coordinating and catalytic body, rather than the powerful advocate of environmental values desired by environmentalists. UNEP would monitor changes in the global environment through the Earthwatch Program and use the modest Environment Fund called for earlier by President Nixon to help existing Specialized Agencies devise appropriate responses to threats UNEP identified.[22]

The Stockholm Declaration contained language that US negotiators might have preferred to change and UNEP as it ultimately emerged was a somewhat different institution than either Administration officials or US environmentalists had initially envisioned. Despite this, US support was never seriously in doubt. After the conference, President Nixon declared that the US had 'achieved practically all of its objectives at Stockholm' and termed UNEP 'an important step which had our full support'.[23] Over the next ten years, the US contributed over $70 million to UNEP operations.

Reneging on the Stockholm commitment?

The thirteen years since Stockholm have brought many changes to the international community's program of environmental protection. Regional organizations, for example, now play a far more important role, a trend recognized by UNEP in its creation of the very successful Regional Seas Program.[24] Within UNEP, there appears to be a far greater degree of consensus about the scope of the problems faced than at Stockholm. Developed nations now accept a broad definition of the 'human environment' that takes into account many problems of primary importance to developing countries. LDC representatives have also come to appreciate more fully the need to deal directly with the negative environmental consequences of economic development. The hostile rhetoric of past Governing Councils has thus given way to what US officials now consider a 'generally businesslike, harmonious atmosphere'.[25]

Perhaps the most striking change, however, has been the apparent withdrawal of the US from the position of leadership on environmental issues it so actively sought at the Stockholm Conference. Ronald Reagan, who had campaigned for the presidency on a platform of reduced governmental interference in the marketplace, brought to Washington individuals whose commitment to environmental protection was questionable, at least as defined by previous administrations. Critics were quick to point to one of Reagan's first actions as President, the decision to repeal Jimmy Carter's Executive Order strengthening governmental controls over the export of hazardous substances, as evidence of a new anti-environmental attitude in Washington.[26]

Of perhaps greater concern to members of Congress, however, were Administration attempts to slash the US contribution to UNEP by as much as 70 %. Congressional pressure has prevented any reductions in the $ 10 million given by the US to support UNEP's annual budget, but it has not been an easy process. Nor has the Administration looked with particular favor on funding for other multilateral environmental programs. Although a signatory of the 1983 Cartagena Convention for the Protection and Development of the Marine Environment of the Wider Caribbean Region,[27] and a seemingly enthusiastic supporter of the Regional Seas Program, the US has refused to contribute the relatively nominal sum of $ 500,000 proposed as its voluntary share of the Caribbean Trust Fund. Given the importance of the region to the Administration and the fact that the Action Plan brought together in a cooperative venture countries as diverse as Cuba, Nicaragua, El Salvador and Honduras, Congressional critics called the decision short-sighted.[28] The Administration was also faulted for its decision to cut by one-half the US contribution to UNESCO's Man and the Biosphere research program.[29]

Some Administration officials have been criticized for their alleged inability to appreciate the seriousness of international environmental problems. In 1982, Richard Funkhauser, director of the EPA's Office of International Activities, faced tough questioning from members of the Subcommittee on Human Rights and International Organizations of the House Committee on Foreign Affairs about the EPA's opposition to an Organization for Economic Cooperation and Development (OECD) draft report on global environmental issues.[30] Funkhauser's proposed reply to the report had suggested a new title, 'OECD Globaloney', and compared it to 'earlier "gloom and doom" publications which are currently under scientific challenge'. Funkhauser cited as an example the *Global 2000* report commissioned by the Carter Administration and hailed by environmentalists as an important assessment of the environmental challenges faced by the nation.[31] The Administration's delayed response to acid rain is also seen as indicative of its limited recognition of important environmental threats.

Administration officials argue vehemently that what has changed is not the US commitment to protect the environment, but the perception of the best means by which to do so. The US policy and budgetary response should be determined not by a sense of guilt, as implied by the rhetoric of 1972, but by a careful analysis of the costs and benefits of proposed regulatory actions. Officials have also raised a familiar theme in insisting that the US has been bearing more than its fair share of a budget that may have encouraged UNEP bureaucrats to undertake programs beyond the organization's appropriate scope.[32] The Reagan Administration has insisted that UNEP remain a catalytic, rather than an 'action-oriented' agency[33] and work to consolidate and rationalize the environmental activities of UN and Specialized Agencies, rather than embark on 'bold, new environmental ventures'.[34] The goal of environmental protection, it is argued, can be furthered more effectively by concentrating limited funds on bilateral aid programs administered by the Agency for International Development.[35] Equal significance is attached to making better use of 'free market' mechanisms to encourage appropriate behavior by would-be polluters, instead of relying on governmental regulation.[26] The US has argued for an increased role for private industry in international environmental protection programs and thus strongly supported the 1984 World Industry Conference on Environmental Management.[39]

Critics remain unpersuaded; many continue to view the central problem as a lack of appropriate environmental commitment by top Reagan officials. Thomas Stoel, Director of International Programs of the Natural Resources Defense Council, has been particularly critical of Anne Burford, formerly head of the EPA, as a key figure in the regressive policies adopted in the early days of the Administration.[35] Richard Funkhauser was also attacked by Stoel as one of the 'ideologues within the Administration [who] have largely prevented meaningful action' by more environmentally conscious State Department officials.[39] Without support at EPA, 'the leadership and sense of urgency displayed by the previous administration has been replaced in most . . . areas of international environmental activity by a low key and often passive attitude by most of the leaders of the present State Department'.[40]

While generally supportive both of AID's bilateral assistance programs and of UNEP's interest in making better use of industry expertise, Administration critics argue that the US has surrendered its leadership position in the environmental field by moving away from its support of multilateral environmental protection programs. House Democrat Don Bonker, a member of the US delegation, criticized the US position at the 1982 Nairobi UNEP conference marking the tenth anniversary of the Stockholm Declaration, alleging that the 'US was generally considered to have reneged on its long-standing commitment to and leadership in global environmental affairs'.[41] Coming at a time when the Reagan Administration had put the US on record as opposing the World Health Organization's code of conduct on infant formula and was pulling back from the law of the sea negotiations, the positions adopted by the US delegation at Nairobi were seen as 'but another step in a trend away from supporting multilateral cooperation to resolve common problems'.[42] While this could result in some loss of prestige for the US government, more important was the potential impact on the global environmental protection movement, since no country appeared ready to step in to take up this crucial role.[43]

To respond to the Administration's apparent neglect of the country's global environmental interests, critics have called upon Congress to assert itself internationally as it once did on a domestic level with the 1969 National Environmental Policy Act. Needed are said to be new legislative initiatives to control hazardous exports, to ensure that international lending agencies promote environmentally sound development projects, and to provide US agencies with the capacity, once again, to take the lead in responding to global environmental problems.

The value of international law

US attitudes

While this exchange has raised important questions about the direction of US international environmental policy and the best means to achieve US objectives, there has been little discussion of the legal dimensions of that policy. The US has generally been supportive of treaty-making efforts in the environmental field. In the case of some problems, such as acid rain and ozone depletion, the Reagan Administration has tended to resist the conclusion of specific agreements as long as there remains doubt among scientists as to the extent of the threat faced and the most appropriate regulatory measures.[44] Where legal undertakings are needed, US officials seem more comfortable with general 'umbrella' agreements than with detailed statements of US obligations, and have generally avoided compulsory dispute settlement procedures.

The reluctance to treat environmental issues as legal questions has not been confined to the Reagan Administration and seems to stem from a more basic fear that to inject law into otherwise friendly relations amounts to hostile behavior.[45] A pragmatic, problem-solving approach is preferred, both to minimize disruptions of 'more important' areas of US foreign policy and to isolate issues of more manageable proportions. It also permits maximum flexibility for diplomats, whose primary responsibility is, understandably, to avoid or resolve quickly unwanted disputes rather than to protect environmental interests. Continuing concern about the inadequacy of existing rules of international environmental law and the alleged slowness and primitive nature of international adjudicative and arbitral proceedings have contributed to skepticism about the relevance of international law in environmental disputes.

Nowhere is this attitude more evident than in the US's bilateral relationship with Canada. Both US and Canadian officials have usually gone out of their way to avoid the allegedly contentious process of asserting their countries' sovereign rights in the many environmental disputes that have arisen along their extensive boundary. The International Joint Commission, first intended to serve primarily as a judicial institution, has never been permitted to exercise the adjudicative powers given to it by the Boundary Waters Treaty.[46] The decision to submit the Gulf of Maine boundary dispute to a chamber of the International Court of Justice thus represents an important aberration from normal practice. Unfortunately, the outcome, which some observers saw as an unhappy compromise between the Canadian and US positions, may not encourage either state to repeat the experience.[47]

While the reluctance of nations to frame their environmental relationships in legal terms is understandable, and often quite appropriate,[48] there are several distinct ways in which international law can contribute to the goal of environmental protection.

The role of international law in domestic proceedings

International law has a relevance in domestic courts and administrative proceedings that is often overlooked. Particularly in the US, with its long tradition of judicial independence, federal and even state and local judges take seriously both the explicit international undertakings of the US government and customary international law. The problem is to convince a party with standing to invoke these rules of international law, normally a state rather than a private individual, that it is in its interest to do so. Foreign governments are seldom anxious to appear to be interfering in the internal affairs of another sovereign state, particularly through the assertion of legal rights. While this attitude is understandable, evolving patterns of transnational relations and, at least in some areas, the decreasing significance of political boundaries suggest that more direct participation of foreign diplomatic officials in national judicial and regulatory proceedings may help prevent unnecessary disputes.

This would seem to be the case in the debate that began in 1973 over a plan by the Pittston Company to use Canadian waters to transport crude oil to a proposed oil refinery in Eastport, Maine.[49] The idea was opposed by the Canadian government and, after more than ten years of regulatory proceedings on the local, state and federal levels, the company finally shelved the project. Early in the regulatory process, however, Maine's Board of Environmental Protection (BEP) was required by Maine law to decide whether the Pittston Company had secured the right to transport oil to the refinery, an issue in which Canada's legal right to prohibit passage was a central concern. The BEP was more than receptive to Canadian input, but the Department of External Affairs chose to stay aloof from the proceedings. Only a vaguely worded Canadian statement delivered by State Department representatives (who immediately dismissed it as mistaken) made its way to the BEP hearings. The BEP and later the EPA thus were forced to sidestep this crucial aspect of the proposal. Bodies like Maine's BEP can play a useful role in preventing transboundary environmental disputes, but only if diplomatic officials are prepared to take better advantage of their procedures and perhaps confront at an earlier stage and in an unfamiliar setting questions of international law.

A procedural approach to state environmental responsibility

A second development in international environmental law builds upon the legal tradition of the *Lake Lanoux Arbitration*. Unlike *Trail Smelter* and Stockholm Principle 21, which emphasize the state's substantive obligation to prevent, and if this fails, to make reparation for extraterritorial environmental damage, the *Lake Lanoux* case focuses on the procedural expectations of international environmental law: what steps the state should follow to ensure adequate protection of external interests. Seen as a more positive approach to the problem than is provided by traditional regimes of liability and compensation, the search for rules of 'dispute avoidance' has attracted the attention of a number of specialists in international environmental law.[50]

Among the obligations most often mentioned in this connection are the duty to evaluate the proposed extraterritorial impact of activities planned within the state's jurisdiction, the duty to inform those who may be affected of the possible results, and the duty to engage in consultations at an appropriate level to minimize the deleterious effects of the project. A number of international agreements, like the 1974 Nordic Convention on the Protection of the Environment,[51] include specific provisions enumerating these responsibilities and a reasonably persuasive argument can be made that the 'good neighborliness' doctrine of customary international law makes them binding on all members of the international community.

For the US, long a leader in the field of environmental impact assessment, this approach may provide fewer objections than traditional liability regimes. US law already requires federal agencies to prepare impact statements for projects with international impact and, as the Eastport experience illustrated, the EPA takes potential extraterritorial damage into account in its regulatory proceedings.[52] As a member of the OECD, the US has agreed to the non-binding 'Principles Concerning Transfrontier Pollution', which advocate not only impact assessment, but 'early' notification and 'diligent' consultation.[53] In 1978, the US Senate unanimously endorsed a treaty under which all signatories would agree to a program making such procedures mandatory.[54] This approach deserves further consideration.

A private law approach

A third development in international environmental law is the increased emphasis being placed on the role of foreign private claimants in national judicial and administrative proceedings.[55] Private parties are seldom as reluctant to intervene abroad as are their home governments, particularly when they feel directly threatened or injured. By permitting foreign nationals effective recourse at the national level, unwanted international disputes may be avoided or at least delayed as allegedly injured parties pursue 'domestic remedies'. Yet effective recourse is often difficult to find abroad given such common obstacles as standing requirements and the governmental claim of sovereign immunity. There also may be little incentive to provide foreigners unilaterally with rights a country's own nationals do not enjoy abroad.[56]

The 1974 Nordic Convention contained the first of what will likely be a number of reciprocal 'equal access' agreements. Under the convention, a signatory must ensure that nationals of the other parties are permitted the same access to its courts and administrative proceedings enjoyed by the state's own citizens. Extraterritorial injury is to be considered as significant as damage to national territory and, when compensation is sought, it 'shall not be judged by rules which are less favorable to the injured party than the rules of compensation of the State in which the activities are being carried out'.[57]

In 1979, the American and Canadian Bar Associations called for a similar agreement between the United States and Canada as one of the two recommended treaties emerging from a joint study of US/Canadian dispute settlement.[58] In addition to providing equal rights of access and compensation, the agreement includes a prior notice provision when there is a 'significant risk of pollution' to transboundary interests.[59] Recent efforts of the Uniform Law Conference of Canada and the National Conference of Commissioners of Uniform State Laws of the United States have helped secure the adoption of the ABA/CBA-drafted Transboundary Pollution Reciprocal Access Act by a number of individual states and provinces.[60]

These attempts to provide equal access are clearly in the interest of private litigants threatened by transboundary pollution. Treaties mandating equal access on a reciprocal basis might also be useful, if more difficult to negotiate, with other bilateral and multilateral partners. Nevertheless, the limitations of this approach must be recognized. By leaving intact the state's sovereign immunities, equal access agreements do little to promote governmental, as opposed to private responsibility for polluting activities. There are also many instances of transboundary pollution where it would be difficult to link the damage done to specific private interests. Furthermore, the equal access approach guarantees only nondiscriminatory application of whatever national and local environmental standards exist; it does not ensure a greater degree of environmental protection and does nothing to make more uniform the varied national standards that have angered US companies. Finally, by focusing attention on the state's procedural obligations, it could undermine the more truly substantive elements of state responsibility embodied in such principles as strict liability for extraterritorial pollution.

The continuing relevance of traditional international environmental law

These new and evolving forms of international environmental law all have something to offer and deserve consideration by those responsible for the formulation of US policy, just as they must recognize the substantial contribution made by 'non-legal' diplomatic and managerial approaches. Yet, even the often-maligned rules and procedures of traditional international law, as expressed in the *Trail Smelter* case and Stockholm Principle 21 and applied and developed by formal judicial institutions, have an important role to play in the struggle to protect the global environment.

Much has changed since the late 1960s. Vague rules of customary and treaty law have been sharpened and tightened by increasing state practice and improved scientific understanding of the negative effect of pollution. Innovative developments in judicial institutions, such as the adoption of a chambers procedure by the International Court of Justice, have made the traditional, if infrequent practice of third party dispute settlement potentially less ponderous and unpredictable. Recent ICJ decisions, including the ruling in the Gulf of Maine case,[61] also suggest an increasingly pragmatic attitude among international judges toward the need for a workable settlement to the dispute before them.[62]

There are at least three areas of traditional international environmental law to which US policy should remain or become more responsive.

First, the US should stay at the forefront of multilateral efforts to create international environmental protection standards.[63] Even those who generally oppose a legal approach to international environmental problems seldom object to the use of treaties and other binding instruments. There is the legitimate question of timing; a premature agreement could cast in legal concrete understandings that may be altered by time and new scientific information. General 'umbrella' agreements, such as those employed so successfully by the Regional Seas Program and later used in the 1985 Vienna Convention for the Protection of the Ozone Layer, are an effective, non-threatening way to encourage legal cooperation between states with significant political differences and/or very different views of the most appropriate way to respond to particular pollution threats. It is important, however, that momentum not be lost in the search for the more precise legal obligations provided by the protocols attached to these conventions. Critics of current Reagan Administration policy should see the advantages of developing a firmer set of international linkages to help protect against further erosion of the US's Stockholm commitment. The US should also continue its support for the work of the International Law Commission and UNEP's 1981 Montevideo Programme for the Development and Periodic Review of Environmental Law in developing a clearer understanding of the types of activities the state is expected to control, the most appropriate procedural means to do so, and the implications of a failure to discharge this responsibility.

Second, despite the prevailing political climate and some current unhappiness with the ICJ, the US should consider seriously the advantages of returning to its traditional support of compulsory dispute settlement, at least in the environmental area. Multilateral agreements that create significant obligations for the signatories are strengthened by the greater predictability and sense of commitment that the potential resort to binding third-party settlement can provide. There has been sufficient experience with international arbitral and adjudicative proceedings, particularly in Western Europe, to permit the creation of reasonably efficient procedures that can still screen out patently political or unfounded claims.

Finally, and perhaps as a first step toward a more general acceptance of compulsory environmental dispute settlement, US officials should look again at the second proposal by the American and Canadian Bar Associations: an agreement to arbitrate, through an ad hoc three-person tribunal, 'any question of interpretation, application or operation of a treaty in force between them, which has not been settled within a reasonable time by direct negotiation or referred by agreement of the Parties to the International Court of Justice or to some other third-party procedure . . .'.[64] Arbitration would be mandatory only where the dispute raised questions of treaty law, but the US and Canada could agree to submit any dispute to this process,[65] and, also by joint agreement, request an advisory opinion of the tribunal.[66]

There is much to be said for this proposal. As a compulsory procedure, it could encourage diplomats to focus on transboundary pollution threats before the momentum that so often builds around major development projects makes dispute resolution more difficult and before the costs to private parties become excessive. Even if used only by joint agreement, a predetermined arbitral process would be far easier to set in motion once a dispute arises. As experience with arbitration increases confidence in the procedure, innovations such as allowing unilateral requests for advisory opinions, perhaps even by state and provincial governmental agencies, might be introduced.[67]

The proposal also raises serious questions for both Canada and the US. Some are of a constitutional nature; others relate more to the fear of injecting increased and premature litigiousness into a bilateral relationship that, for all the occasional tensions, has remained remarkably close. As a practical matter, separating treaty from customary law would likely be far more difficult than the draft agreement implies.[68] Given dissatisfaction in the US with the *Gulf of Maine* decision and the ICJ proceedings instituted against it by Nicaragua, as well as the possible implications of compulsory arbitration in the more controversial area of trade relations, there would likely be little support for the proposal at this time.

These problems can be addressed in the right political climate. There are definite advantages for US international environmental policy of a system that could interpret and, in the process, help to develop the rules of state environmental responsibility if, at first, only on a bilateral level and only through the interpretation of treaties. Acceptance of even a modified form of the ABA/CBA arbitration proposal would be a useful step toward reasserting the importance of Stockholm Principle 21 and emphasizing that state protection of the environment is not a political preference but a legal duty.

Notes

1. See A. Springer, *Resolving US–Canadian Environmental Disputes: The Role of Adjudication in the Gulf of Maine Dispute*, at 7–9 (Sept. 20, 1985), (a paper presented to the Association for Canadian Studies in the United States, Philadelphia, PA).
2. 1 Moore, *International Law Digest* 654 (1906).
3. P. Trudeau, *Notes for an Address to the Annual Meeting of the Canadian Press*, Toronto (Apr. 15, 1970), in 9 *ILM* 600 (1970), quoted in Bilder, 'The Settlement of Disputes in the Field of the International Law of the Environment', 1975 *Recueil des Cours* I:139, at 195.
4. See generally, Caldwell, *International Environmental Policy: Emergence and Dimensions* 28–36 (1984), and Lyster, *International Wildlife Law* (1985).
5. See generally, Bourne, 'International Law and Pollution of International Rivers and Lakes,' 6 *UBC L. Rev.* 115 (1971); and Gaja, 'River Pollution in International Law', 1973 *Recueil des Cours* I;354.
6. Treaty Relating to Boundary Waters and Questions Arising Along the Boundary Between Canada and the United States, January 11, 1909, United States–Canada, in 12 Bevans, *Treaties and Other International Agreements of the United States of America* 322 (1968–1976).
7. Trail Smelter Arbitration (US v. Canada) 3 *UNRIAA* 1905, at 1965 (1949).
8. *Id.*
9. Rubin, 'Pollution by Analogy: The Trail Smelter Arbitration', 50 *Or. L. Rev.* 259, at 272 (1971).
10. '(T)he upstream State . . . has the obligation to take into consideration the different interests at stake, to strive to give them all satisfaction compatible with the pursuit of its own interests and to demonstrate that . . . it has a solicitude to reconcile the interests of the other riparian with its own.' Spain v. France, 12 *UNRIAA* 281 (1957), digested in 53 *AJIL* 156, at 169 (1959).
11. *Id.*, at 160–1. It should be recognized that unclear in the decision is whether these rights existed as a matter of customary international law or flowed from the 1866 treaty. The generality of the tribunal's ruling on this point thus can reasonably be questioned.
12. See, Springer, *The International Law of Pollution: Protecting the Global Environment in a World of Sovereign States* 31–4 (1983).
13. UN Conference on the Human Environment: Preparations and Prospects: Hearings Before the Senate Committee on Foreign Relations, *92nd Cong., 2nd sess.* 17 (1972) [hereinafter cited as UN Conference Hearings].
14. See International Cooperation in the Human Environment through the

United Nations: Hearings Before the Subcomm. on International Organizations and Movements of the House Committee on Foreign Affairs, *92nd Cong., 2nd sess.* 4–25 (1972).

15. UN Conference Hearings, *supra* note 13, at 54.

16. Kennan, 'To Prevent a World Wasteland: A Proposal', **48** *Foreign Aff.* 401 (1970).

17. See generally, Springer, 'International Aspects of Pollution Control,' in *International Handbook of Pollution Control* (E. Kormondy (ed.), forthcoming).

18. 'Founex Report on Development and Environment: A Report Submitted by a Panel of Experts Convened by the Secretary General of the United Nations Conference on the Human Environment', June 4–12, 1971, in **586** *International Conciliation* 7 (1972).

19. 'Report of the United Nations Stockholm Conference on the Human Environment', *UN Doc. A/Conf.* 48/14, at 2, Principle 21 (1972), in **11** *ILM* 1420 (1972).

20. See Springer, *The International Law of Pollution, supra* note 12, at 82–3, 124, 134.

21. See generally, Sohn, 'The Stockholm Declaration on the Human Environment', **14** *Harv. Int'l. L. J.* 485 (1973).

22. See generally Caldwell, *International Environmental Policy, supra* note 4, at 36–72.

23. 'Review of the Global Environment 10 Years After Stockholm: Hearings of the Subcomm. on Human Rights and International Organizations, House Comm. on Foreign Affairs', *97th Cong., 2nd sess.* 15 (1982) (quoted by Senator Claiborne Pell) [hereinafter cited as Review of the Global Environment].

24. See A. Springer, *Pollution and the Global Environment: A Regional Initiative*, at 21–30 (April 14, 1984) (a paper presented to the New England Political Science Association, Newport, RI).

25. 'US International Environmental Policy: Hearings of the Subcomm. on Human Rights and International Organizations of the House Comm. on Foreign Affairs', *98th Cong., 2nd sess.* 25 (1984) (statement of Bill Long) [hereinafter cited as US International Environmental Policy].

26. See 'Review of the Global Environment', *supra* note 23, at 259–62 (testimony of S. Jacob Scherr).

27. Cartagena Convention for the Protection and Development of the Marine Environment of the Wider Caribbean Region, March 24, 1983, **22** *ILM* 227 (1983).

28. In the words of Senator Pell: 'It is a strange ordering of priorities that this administration should propose hundreds of millions of dollars for the Caribbean Basin initiative and for regional military assistance and yet has failed to come up with a mere $500,000 contribution to the Caribbean Trust Fund. The U.S. failure to contribute to the Caribbean action plan is, even in security terms, pennywise and pound foolish.' Review of the Global Environment, *supra* note 23, at 4 (statement of Claiborne Pell.)

29. *Id.*, at 370.
30. *Id.*, at 290–317.
31. *Id.*, at 473–4.
32. Bill Long of the State Department's Bureau of Ocean and International Environmental and Scientific Affairs (OES) told Congress in 1984 that his office had been 'unable to make the case that the United States was getting $10 million of value out of UNEP', and argued that UNEP could be encouraged to define its priorities more carefully if faced with fewer resources. 'US International Environmental Policy', *supra* note 25, at 55 (statement of Bill Long).
33. See 'Review of the Global Environment', *supra* note 23, at 22 (statement of James L. Buckley); and 'UN Holds Global Meeting', **121** *Sci. News* 358 (1982).
34. 'Review of the Global Environment', *supra* note 23, p. 27 (statement of Bill Long).
35. *Id.*, at 28–30 (statement of M. Peter McPherson).
36. According to Funkhauser, 'The U.S. is committed to the premise that the free market approach can play a constructive role in the protection of the environment, though it may need to be accompanied by complementary government action. Technological innovation and economic incentives are the foundation for the resolution of future environmental problems which so often involve difficult economic development choices. There must be more optimism and credence given to the roles and contributions of science, technology and human ingenuity, in addressing environmental and resource problems.' *Id.*, at 298.
37. *Id.*, at 15–25.
38. 'US International Environmental Policy', *supra* note 25, at 93.
39. 'Review of the Global Environment', *supra* note 23, at 406.
40. 'US International Environmental Policy', *supra* note 25, at 85 (testimony of Robert O. Blake).
41. 'Review of the Global Environment', *supra* note 23, at 492.
42. *Id.*, at 497.
43. *Id.*, at 382 (testimony of Thomas Stoel).
44. See 'Review of the Global Environment', *supra* note 23, at 27 (testimony of James Buckley.)
45. Bilder, 'Settlement of Disputes in the Field of the International Law of the Environment', 1975 *Recueil des Cours* 1:225.
46. Cohen, 'The Regime of Boundary Waters – The Canadian–United States Experience', 1975 *Recueil des Cours* 3:219, at 258–9.
47. See generally, Springer, *Resolving U.S.–Canadian Disputes*, *supra* note 1, at 7–10.
48. See generally, *id.*, at 13–19.
49. See generally, Springer, *The International Law of Pollution*, *supra* note 12, at 185–200.
50. See generally, *id.*, at 141–52.
51. Nordic Convention on the Protection of the Environment, February 19, 1974, **13** *ILM* 591 (1974).

52. See Springer, *The International Law of Pollution, supra* note 12, at 191–3.

53. 'Principles Concerning Transfrontier Pollution', November 14, 1974, in *OECD and the Environment* 54–6 (1976). See generally, McCaffrey, 'The OECD Principles Concerning Transfrontier Pollution: A Commentary', in 1 *Envt'l Pol'y L.* 2 (1975).

54. See 'Review of the Global Environment', *supra* note 23, at 5–11.

55. National courts in the state where the victim of pollution resides may be willing to hear transboundary claims, but it can be very difficult to enforce judgements against foreign defendants.

56. See generally, Kumin, 'Transfrontier Environmental Disputes and National Courts: An Approach for Western Europe' 3 *Fletcher Forum* 24 (1979); and McCaffrey, 'Transboundary Pollution Injuries: Jurisdictional Considerations in Private Litigation Between Canada and the United States', 3 *Cal. Wes. Int'l L. J.* 191 (1973).

57. Nordic Convention, *supra* note 51, at 592.

58. *American Bar Association–Canadian Bar Association, Settlement of Disputes Between Canada and the United States (1979)* [hereinafter cited as ABA/CBA Report].

59. *Id.*, at 40–56.

60. See generally Rosencranz, 'The Uniform Transboundary Pollution Reciprocal Access Act', 11 *Envt'l Pol'y L.* 105 (1985).

61. Delimitation of the Maritime Boundary in the Gulf of Maine Area (Can./U.S.), 1984 *ICJ Rep.* 246 (Judgement of Oct. 12), reprinted in 23 *ILM 1197* (1984).

62. See generally, Springer, *supra* note 1, at 19–24.

63. Ideally, these ecostandards should be expressed as treaty obligations but 'potentially mandatory standards', such as those employed by the International Maritime Organization, and 'recommendations' adopted by bodies like the International Atomic Energy Agency, have intrinsic value and can acquire greater legal significance over time. See Springer, *International Law of Pollution, supra* note 12, at 105–9.

64. ABA/CBA, 'Draft Treaty on a Third-Party Settlement of Disputes', in *Settlement of International Disputes Between Canada and the United States, supra* note 58, at xxi. See generally Wang, 'Adjudication of Canada–United States Disputes', 19 *Can. Y. B. Int'l L.* 158, at 175–8 (1981); and McCarney, 'A Proposed Model for Dispute Settlement in North America', 6 *Can.–U.S. L. J.* 89 (1982).

65. ABA-CBA, 'Draft Treaty', *supra* note 58, Art. 2, at xxi.

66. *Id.*, Article 10, at xxv.

67. *Id.*, at 90. For a discussion of how the ABA/CBA system might be useful in two specific environmental contexts, see Springer, *supra* note 1, at 30–1.

68. See generally, Wang, *supra* note 63, at 212–17; Carroll and Mack, 'On Living Together in North America: Canada, the United States and International Environmental Relations', 12 Den. J Int'l L. Pol'y 35, at 41–3 (1982); and Springer, *supra* note 1, at 31–2.

5

Problems and successes
of international water agreements:
the example of
the United States and Mexico

Albert E. Utton

Professor of Law
at the University of New Mexico,
Albuquerque, New Mexico

1   Population and economic growth projections

Catalytic forces which can be anticipated to raise significant natural resources issues in the Mexican–US border region are population and economic growth. This growth can be expected to place increased demands upon land, air, and scarce surface and groundwater resources along much of the nearly 2000 mile border separating the two countries.

Briefly, on the US side we find that the entire southwest is part of the so-called 'sun-belt' area, and population projections are for continued growth along that border. On the Mexican side of the border, Dr Francisco Alba of the Colegio de Mexico reports a national population growth rate of 3.2 % during the 1970s, and estimates a 2.7 % population growth rate for the 1980s. This could mean nearly a doubling of the national population in 25 years. His figures show an even faster growth rate for those Mexican states bordering on the US–Mexico frontier, with a 3.6 % per annum growth rate. Alba speaks of the 'staggering growth' of urban centers in the border area, and he says that much greater population growth in the border area is due 'not only to population growth *per se*, but also to the strong immigration patterns and national economic development policies for the border region.[1]

Much of the expanding population is highly concentrated in border urban areas; eight urbanized municipios account for 80 % of Mexico's frontier population. The distribution of population along the border in the US in 1970 was even more concentrated. Approximately 72 % of frontier population was in the urbanized counties of San Diego (California), Pima (Tucson and Nogales, Arizona), and El Paso (Texas). On the US side of the Rio Grande/Rio Bravo border region, the bulk of the population is in the two extremes – El Paso County, and Hidalgo and Cameron Counties. Population growth projections for selected Texas border cities call for a doubling of the population of many of the border cities, and a tripling or near tripling for the McAllen and Brownsville areas.

Dr. Alba succinctly diagnoses growth factors affecting the border area:

> The dilemmas that are presented are very serious because by the year 2000 migration to the border areas will continue to be affected by the economics of the border. That is, although within Mexico the population growth as a whole may be reduced somewhat, the growth rate at the border areas will continue to be affected by those economic forces and the migratory patterns that derive from them.
>
> We have to consider also that the demographic dynamics have a momentum that is created by the different age structures that are components of the present demographic patterns in Mexico and that a short-term reduction is very difficult because there are certain patterns that really are predetermined.
>
> An annual increase of 3 % in the workforce is already a given because of age structures within the population, and this will continue until the year 2000.[2]

Dr John Hedderson of the University of Texas at El Paso observes that the US side of the Texas border region is 'growing much faster than the rest of the United States, and has for all of this century'.[3] Dr Niles Hansen of the University of Texas at Austin adds:

> In 1975, the birth rates in Laredo, McAllen, and Brownsville were almost twice the national rate. In the United States as a whole, only one metropolitan area (Provo, Utah, 35.1) had a 1975 birth rate higher than that of McAllen. El Paso's birth rate of 21.6 was exceeded only by six non-borderlands metropolitan areas.[4]

In addition, large energy resources are located in the Colorado River

Basin and the development of these energy resources will place substantial additional demands upon the limited water resources of that Basin, which will in turn have transboundary impacts upon Mexico and the US–Mexico border region.

In summary, many of these dramatic projected population and economic increases can be expected to greatly increase the demand placed upon land, air, water, and biologic resources in the border region.

2   Demands on surface water resources

2.1   *Colorado River*

2.1.1   Allotment of water   The 1944 Colorado River Treaty between the US and Mexico quantified the respective shares of the two nations. The share of Mexico was established at 1 500 000 acre-feet per year. This amount of water is to be delivered in accordance with annual schedules formulated by the Mexican section of the International Boundary and Water Commission before the beginning of each calendar year. The schedule for the Mexican allotment includes maximum and minimum amounts to be delivered by the US during particular months. However, in the event of 'extraordinary drought or serious accident' in the US, minimum amounts may be reduced in the same proportion as are consumptive uses in the US. This 'extraordinary drought' provision is the major remaining water quantity issue.

The generality of the 'drought' language could lead to substantial problems in times of water shortage. Cesar Sepulveda observes that these questions 'could seriously affect the relations between the two countries', and goes on to illustrate the concern of Mexico:

> The Treaty of 1944 failed to specify whether the drought could occur in the total region served by a river system or only in a portion of it, and also did not define the intensity nor duration of the drought. Further, no precise measurement is provided. Such imprecisions give rise to many interesting hypothetical questions. For example, if severe drought conditions do indeed exist in the United States during one year, the reduction in consumption would not be immediately calculable, and until such calculations could be made, would Mexico not be entitled to receive her full allotment of water?[5]

A respected American commentator adds '[i]t takes little imagination . . . to foresee conflict if Mexico's deliveries are ever cut . . . ' under the 'extraordinary drought' provision.[6]

2.1.2 Quality of water On the other hand, the water quality problem has been a prime irritant to the peaceful relations of the two countries, and is one that both will have to watch closely. The two nations have struggled with this problem through a series of interim agreements which culminated in Minute 242, a binational agreement to constitute a 'permanent' solution to the salinity problem. Minute 242 was signed on August 30 1973 by Ambassadors Herrera of Mexico and Friedkin of the US. Its most important provision is that the salinity of the water at the Morelos Dam shall be no more than 115 parts per million (ppm) plus or minus 30 ppm above that of the salinity at the Imperial Dam. This, in fact, means that the farmers in the Mexicali Valley of Mexico will be irrigating with water which is no more than 115 ppm plus or minus 30 ppm higher than the salinity of the water which their US neighbors in the Imperial Valley across the international boundary receive from the Imperial Dam.

In order to reduce the salinity at the Morelos Dam to the 115 plus or minus 30 ppm above the salinity at the Imperial Dam, a reverse-osmosis desalting plant near Yuma, Arizona, and a canal through the Santa Clara Slough to the Gulf of California in Mexico are required. The canal is to carry the brine produced by the desalting plant. All of the construction cost is to be borne by the US.

The other principal elements of the agreement are: 'that the United States will support efforts by Mexico to obtain appropriate financing on favorable terms for the improvement and rehabilitation of the Mexicali Valley'; that each country 'shall limit pumping of groundwaters in its territory within five miles . . . of the Arizona–Sonora boundary near San Luis to 160 000 acre-feet . . . annually'; 'that the United States and Mexico shall consult with each other prior to undertaking any new development of either the surface or groundwater resources, or undertaking substantial modifications of present developments, in its own territory in the border area that might adversely affect the other country'; and that the Minute 242 constitutes a 'permanent and definitive solution of the salinity problem'.[7]

Nonetheless, there is still potential for water quality questions to arise between the two countries. There is a range of potential water quality impacts from energy development in the Colorado River Basin, but salinity is the water quality problem of greatest concern to both Mexico and the US.

The water of the Colorado is the lifeblood of the thirsty south-western US and the Mexicali Valley of north-western Mexico. It presently meets the needs of 15 million people by supplying the water for their cities and irrigating the agriculture, mining, and industrial enterprises within the basin, not to mention the recreational, fish, and wildlife uses of the river. In addition, that basin is being called upon to meet the nation's energy demands. It has been said that the Colorado River Basin is one of the richest storehouses of energy resources in the US. Within the four states of Arizona, Colorado, New Mexico, and Utah, conservative estimates indicate that there are more than 23.5 billion tons of recoverable coal reserves, of which more than half are of the low sulphur variety which is in demand for generation of electricity. In addition, these four states contain nearly 90 % of US uranium reserves, and virtually all of the domestic oil shale reserves are located in Colorado, Wyoming and Utah.

As Professor Lee Brown and associates point out, 'it is an inescapable conclusion that the upper Colorado will play an important role in any US effort to achieve even semi-independence from foreign energy sources'.[8]

Numerous projections of energy-related water consumption in the Colorado have been made. The 1974 *Report of Water for Energy in the Upper Colorado River Basin*, prepared by the US Department of the Interior, concluded that under this set of projections there could be significant shortages occurring in all states on the upper basin except Wyoming by the year 2000. More recent studies have been less pessimistic. The August 1975–76 'Water Assessment' of the US Water Resoruces Council concludes that the projected future modified flow of the outflow point of the region, when compared with the delivery requirements to the lower Colorado region, implies surplus water still available after the year 2000 for upper basin use. The various projections vary as to when a water crunch might arise in the basin. Technological changes in electrical generation techniques, for example, may affect these figures significantly but, whatever the estimate, there is unanimity that significant additional demands for consumptive use will be placed upon the Colorado River for energy developments.

Because Mexico's allocated share of the waters of the Colorado is a prior obligation under the Colorado River Treaty, one would not anticipate water quantity disputes except in the case of an extreme drought which would affect both nations under the terms of the treaty. However, water quality is another matter, and the question of salinity on the Colorado has to be the prime continuing water issue between Mexico and the US.

Bishop, in his study on the impact of energy development on Colorado River water quality, says 'the impacts of pollutants on stream quality levels in the upper Colorado River Basin are potentially significant in areas of intense energy development'. He goes on to state that 'the most pervasive and important water quality problem facing the United States and Mexico is salinity. Since the two countries have agreed under Minute 242 on a salinity level for water delivered to Mexico, an important water quality concern is the effect of energy development on the future salinity levels in the river'.[9]

Various studies have attempted to assess the changes in Colorado River salinity as a consequence of future development, and it generally is agreed that increased energy development will lead to increased consumption and that salt concentrations in the river therefore will rise with accelerated energy development. This increase can be expected because of reduced amounts of water for dilution. Various strategies have been devised to contain salt releases into the Colorado and under Minute 242 the desalting plant at Yuma has considerable capacity for taking salt from Colorado River waters. Water and salt mass balance model studies have analyzed the effect of future development of compact waters in the Colorado Basin for a variety of alternative energy development futures. Bishop concludes that 'the total dissolved solids/concentrations are seen to increase below Imperial Dam even though the total salt load in the river is reduced via water diversion for energy. Thus salinity concentrations are affected more by taking water that serves for dilution out of the river than by the removal of salt load from the water'.[10]

The Yuma desalting plant has substantial capacity for meeting future salinity increases. However, because the projections are for increased salinity concentrations and because the quality of water delivered to Mexico is tied to the quality of water delivered to the Imperial Valley in the US, there has to be a continuing concern about water quality in the Colorado River. This means that any possible effects of future (energy) development will have to be considered in the planning and implementation of programs to meet water quantity and quality commitments to Mexico.

2.2   *The San Pedro, Santa Cruz, New River, and other surface flows*

There are a number of rivers flowing from Mexico into the United States or vice versa which, because of their transboundary nature, raise the potential for competition for their use and, thus, possible conflict between the two countries. Illustrative of actual or potential water quality problems from transboundary surface flows are the San Pedro, Santa Cruz, and New River Studies.

2.2.1   The San Pedro River   The San Pedro River flows north from Sonora into south-eastern Arizona. There is substantial concern in Arizona over contaminated flows in the San Pedro which emanate from Sonora, upstream. The flows at times are extremely discoloured; farmers are concerned about possibly damage to their agricultural land and crops, residents are disturbed about possible health effects on themselves and their families. A likely source of this contamination is the large copper works in the Cananea area in Sonora.

2.2.2   The New River   News reports detail 'Raw sewage, dead dogs, fish, and industrial waste flowing north across the Mexican border via the New River are creating a major health hazard'.[11] Headlines declare 'New River: A Sewer From Mexico', and 'California Fights River Flow of Mexican Wastes'.[12] The New River rises in Mexico near Mexicali and flows north into California to the Salton Sea, south-east of Palm Springs, carrying highly contaminated water. The contamination is said to come from inadequately treated sewage and industrial discharges. The extent of the problem is that such American officials have had to erect signs warning that the water is contaminated, and the aforementioned newspaper articles quote one California health official as saying 'You could find a river as dirty as this, but I challenge anyone to find one dirtier', and a bacteriologist declaring 'It is disgusting. I don't know where I have seen anything like it'.

2.2.3   The Santa Cruz River   The Santa Cruz River recharges groundwater supplies for both Nogales, Sonora, and Nogales, Arizona. The river rises in Arizona, flows south into Mexico, and then turns and flows north again, back into Arizona. Therefore, both nations are upper and lower riparians on the same river. Since both cities indirectly depend upon the surface flows of the Santa Cruz for drinking water, water quality questions are a major concern to the residents on both sides of the international frontier. The problem has been met by building an international treatment plant. Both cities discharge waste water into the treatment plant. Nogales, Arizona, discharges 3400 acre-feet per year into the plant, and it has been reported that it is possible to infer a discharge from Nogales, Sonora, of about 4000 acre-feet per year. In 1975, 3 000 000 gallons per day were treated at the international plant before discharge into the Santa Cruz River.

These three examples are only illustrative of the types of water quality problems that are of current concern or may arise along the border region. The international cooperation at Nogales, through the efforts of the International Boundary and Waters Commission, is also suggestive of how these problems can be dealt with when one considers that the population of the border region is concentrated in the urban areas, particularly in the so-called 'twin cities' which grace that frontier. The informed and amicable resolution of the problems is essential to the economic development of the border region.

Conflicts over transboundary resources in the US–Mexico border region are not new, and can be expected to increase in frequency and intensity as demand for these resources increases. In summary, as population and economic development increase along the border, in view of the likely concentration of this growth in selected urban areas, this increased demand will be focused in a relatively few areas. Thus it can be anticipated that natural resources problems will increase in number and severity and will be concentrated in a very focused way in direct response to projected demographic and economic increases.

2.3   *The Rio Grande*

2.3.1   Quantity   The Rio Grande rises in the Rocky Mountains of Colorado. It then quickly descends to the arid lands of New Mexico, where it flows past the Jornado del Muerto before passing on to form the boundary between Texas and the Mexican states of Chihuahua, Coahuila, Nuevo Leon, and Tamaulipas. The area drained by the Rio Grande can be divided into the upper and lower basins. The upper basin lies between the Colorado headwaters and Fort Quitman, Texas; the lower basin extends from Fort Quitman to the Gulf of Mexico. The Rio Grande has for centuries been the giver of life to this water short region. Disputes inevitably arose as population increased along the river valley.

These disputes led to the 1906 Rio Grande Irrigation Convention, which provided an amicable solution by quantifying the Mexican share of the flow of the upper basin. Under the Treaty of 1906, the US is obligated to deliver in perpetuity to Mexico 60 000 acre-feet each year in the bed of the Rio Grande. Deliveries of this water are distributed throughout the year pursuant to an agreed schedule, without cost to Mexico. The US pays the cost of storing the water in a dam at Engle, New Mexico, now known as Elephant Butte Dam. There is an escape clause which allows the amount delivered to Mexico to be reduced in the same proportions that deliveries to the US are reduced, in the event of a serious drought or accidental failure of supply in the US.

Then, in 1944, the waters of the Lower Basin were allocated, after nearly a half century of discussions and intermittent negotiations, by the Rio Grande, Colorado, and Tijuana Treaty of 1944. Some 1200 miles of the boundary between Mexico and the US is formed by the Rio Grande. All but 100 miles of this river boundary is below Fort Quitman, and is thus in the lower Rio Grande Basin. Drainage from Mexico accounts for 70 % of the water flowing in the lower Rio Grande, and that from the US contributes approximately 30 %. The Treaty of 1944 allocates the waters of the lower Rio Grande about equally between the two countries. To the US is allocated: all of the waters contributed to the main stream by the principal US tributaries below Fort Quitman; one-half of the flow in the main channel of the Rio Grande between the lowest major international storage dam; one-third of the flow into the main stream from the principal Mexican tributaries above Salineno, Texas, which is guaranteed by Mexico to average at least 350 000 acre-feet per year over a five year period; and one-half of all other waters flowing into the main channel of the Rio Grande, except that water coming from the San Juan and any return flow coming from land irrigated by these two rivers.

Mexico is not guaranteed any of the flow of the principal US tributaries below Fort Quitman. She receives two-thirds of the flow of the principal Mexican tributaries above Salineno, Texas; all of the waters reaching the main channel from the San Juan and Alamo Rivers; and one-half of all other flows occurring in the main channel of the Rio Grande. Thus, although the larger portion of the waters of the Rio Grande below Fort Quitman comes from Mexican tributaries, the US receives about one-half of all the water of the river. These allocations and their administration by the International Boundary and Waters Commission have been a model of international cooperation.

2.3.2   Quality   Although water quality problems in the Rio Grande have
not reached the point that they did on the Colorado prior to the negotiation
of Minute 242, there certainly is potential for increasing water quality
concern as population and economic development increase along the Rio
Grande on both sides of the border. The quality of the surface flow of the
Rio Grande is of great interest both to the US and to Mexico, and it is
important that analytical studies on historical water quality records be
carried on so as to detect changes in quality before serious adverse effects
occur.

3   Demands on groundwater resources

The heaviest groundwater users in the US are the states contiguous
to Mexico and yet, paradoxically, the law and institutions of the border states
are woefully inadequate to control the exploitation of their groundwater
resources. In addition, international competence over aquifers divided by the
frontier is largely undefined; it is fair to say that the legal and institutional
situation is chaotic. None of the border states has adequate legislation or
regulations for the protection and management of diminishing supplies
within the state and along border areas. New Mexico has the only public
control system, but regulations under it do not contemplate joint controls in
the border area. Texas has virtually no controls except voluntary ones, and
the California law is beholden to similar rules of capture which do little to
discourage excessive pumping and waste. Arizona has recently enacted a
new groundwater law which is a step in the right direction.

In contrast to the legal situation on the US side of the frontier, Mexico
does have legal authority to control groundwater withdrawals. The national
government, through the Secretariat of Water Resources, can regulate
extraction and the Secretary, on his own initiative, can establish prohibited
groundwater zones if existing developments or the aquifer are in danger of
being adversely affected, or if it is otherwise in the public interest.

Coincident with the legal near-vacuum, significant population increases
are projected on both sides of the border, making it reasonable to anticipate
that there will be increasing investment in groundwater facilities and
accelerating demand placed on groundwater resources bisected by the
international boundary between the two countries. The coming together of
these two factors could be combined with a striking absence of institutions
for either resolving disputes or managing the resource; the potential for
dispute between the two countries has to be something more than imaginary.

3.1   *The legal context*

The situation of a legal near-vacuum is not unique to the US–Mexico frontier, since only recently has much attention been directed to groundwater resources. Traditionally there has been a failure to focus on the regulation and management of groundwater in most legal systems. Professor Robert Emmet Clark adds that 'Legislative attention to the physical relationship between surface and groundwater sources is scarcely older than the concern for pollution'.[13] It has been, in fact, a question of being out of sight and out of mind. The primary attention of domestic water law has been focused on surface water, and there is an almost complete lack of groundwater practice at the international level. There are some treaties, such as the agreement between Poland and the USSR, signed at Warsaw on July 17 1964, which refer to groundwaters. That treaty came into force on February 16 1965 by an exchange of the instruments of ratification at Moscow and, in a general way, includes groundwaters 'intersected by the state frontier' in frontier waters. There is also Minute 242 between the US and Mexico which limits pumping on both sides of the frontier in the Yuma area. The International Boundary and Water Commission has dealt successfully with groundwater problems on a pragmatic, *ad hoc* basis but by and large, groundwaters have not been a matter of concern at the international level. As in the case of groundwaters generally, this is less a case of mismanagement than of non-management.

Ludwik Teclaff points out that frequently groundwater has not been included in the established surface water law regime: '[i]t was thought quite adequate to treat groundwater either as part of the land . . . or as a commodity, susceptible of ownership through the act of capturing it by sinking a well'.[14] For example, under Spanish law, which has influenced the groundwater law in Latin America and the Philippines, groundwaters had traditionally belonged to the owner of the superadjacent land'. English common law also has given absolute ownership of groundwater to the superadjacent property owner. Wells Hutchins states that the English common law doctrine 'in its original form accords exclusive property rights in the water to the land owner; it gives him any quantity, for any legitimate enterprise, either on or off the overlying land; . . . but if the effect of heavy pumping by a land owner, while engaged in any legitimate enterprise . . . is to exhaust the groundwater supply of his neighbor by drawing all the groundwater from the substratum of the latter's tract, it cannot become the ground of an action'.[15] Texas follows the English common law theory and the Texas law of groundwater has been summarized as 'you can steal your neighbor's water, but you can't pollute his well'.[16] It has been suggested that, to achieve the optimum sustained yield of a nation's or a region's total water resources, integrated legal and management regimes need to be created.

3.2   *The economic context*

Under the common law doctrine, each owner's right to the water itself, or the right to use the water, is insecure because other pumpers may take possession of the mobile resource at any time. Accordingly, the individual surface owner is encouraged to exploit the groundwater resource as quickly as possible, so that the fluid and mobile water resource will not be captured by others. S. J. Ciriacy-Wantrup points out that '[T]he definite property rights belong only to those who are in possession – that is, who gets there "fastest with the mostest". Every user tries to protect himself against others by acquiring ownership through capture in the fastest possible way. Deferred use is always subject to great uncertainty; others may capture the resource in the meantime'.[17] Terrance S. Veeman adds that '[i]n the absence of effective social institutions to guide resource use, private groundwater use can be predicted eventually to generate excessive investment and extraction costs; induce a pumping rate which is greater than socially optimal, and which may lead to irreversible depletion; dissipate economic rent or producer surplus; and in general create economic waste and resource inefficiency'.[18] This situation leads to great insecurity for all existing users of water from an aquifer, although the concepts of security and flexibility are essential criteria for an adequate water rights system. Underlying the concept of physical security is the premise that holders of groundwater rights must have a reasonable degree of certainty; the supply of water must not be unreasonably uncertain. Ordinarily, the physical supply of groundwater is more secure than surface water because the aquifer frequently stores water in seasons and years of heavy rain and above average recharge that can be used in seasons or years of low rain fall and lower recharge.

In addition, however, there is the factor of 'tenure security'. Tenure security does not refer to reliability of supply, but to the effect of human actions on the reliability of supply, that is, the security of the land owner from the unreasonable use or export of groundwater by his neighbor. The common law rule of absolute ownership obviously increases tenure insecurity because it countenances the unrestrained right of one's neighbor to pump all the water he may need, without restraint or liability to other overlying owners for any adverse effects of his pumping. This has the economic effect of stimulating investment in groundwater development because of the uncertainty of one's property right over this 'fugitive resource'. There is an incentive to each landowner to protect himself against his neighbor's lawful acts by capturing as quickly as possible as much of the resource as he can. Therefore, there is an economic incentive for over-investment and for depletion, rather than for conservation of the resource.

This conceptual approach has been elaborated on by Kelso, Martin, and Mack:

> Two aspects of water rights most significant for an understanding of men's behaviour relative to water and to one another over water are: (1) that whatsoever rights they hold to water and its use will be stable and dependable over time, and (2) the flexibility permitted to them to effect changes in use and location of use of the water covered by their rights, and to acquire and transfer water rights from and to others. . . . Security and flexibility are the twin essences of socially efficient property relations.[19]

And Veeman points out: '[t]he indefiniteness of property rights associated with a fugitive resource such as groundwater leads to its rapid development and, perhaps, depletion'.[20]

Specifically, in regard to the situation along the US–Mexico border, it cannot be said that water users have security in their expectations, nor can it be said that whatever rights they hold to water and its use will be stable and dependable over time. Quite the contrary: there are (1) projections for growing population along both sides of the border; (2) a situation in which no state north of the broder, with the exception of New Mexico, has legal institutions adequate to control pumping; and (3) no international control except at Yuma under the interim arrangement of Resolution 5 of Minute 242, which can prevent either nation from 'stealing its neighbor's water'. Therefore, a situation exists which encourages each nation to outdo its neighbor by developing its groundwater resources as rapidly as possible, perhaps even to the point of depletion of the groundwater resource. The legal situation encourages over-development; over-development results in over-investment in developing the resource and, therefore, both economic waste and resource waste are likely to occur due to the insecurity arising from inadequate institutional controls.

3.3   *The physical context: three case studies*

3.3.1   Example I: San Luis   Near San Luis, Sonora, a well field was put
into operation in 1972. The field contains 63 wells with pumps and concrete
lined laterals. The water is collected in a canal, and flows westerly to San
Luis for irrigation. This pumping by Mexico from the underground
reservoir tends to deplete groundwater underlying both the US and Mexico.
The groundwater basin is straddled by the international boundary. Further,
the water being pumped on the Mexican side came originally from the
Colorado River, in that the water used to irrigate the mesa lands in the Yuma
area was diverted from the Colorado. After being placed on the fields in
Arizona, it gradually percolated down, forming a mound of groundwater.
Because Mexico was pumping water from this underground base, it really
was taking Colorado River water which was not charged against the Mexican
allocation under the Treaty of 1944, since underground flow across the
border is not considered as deliveries in satisfiaction of the Treaty.

In order to avoid a 'pumping war' between the two nations, the
governments of the US and Mexico agreed to limit to 160 000 acre-feet
annually pumping of groundwaters within five miles of the Arizona–Sonora
boundary near San Luis, and the US is proposing a protective and regulatory
groundwater pumping scheme. Well fields capable of pumping 160 000
acre-feet per year will be located on the south Yuma Mesa (Yuma Mesa
Boundary well field) and in the south-western part of Yuma Valley (Yuma
Valley Boundary well field). The Yuma Mesa Boundary well field includes
25 wells located one mile north of the international border, and spaced at
one-half mile intervals. Each would be 500 feet deep, with the lower
200 feet screened to pump water from the underlying groundwater reservoir
at the rate of 7.5 cubic feet per second. The wells will be connected by a
15 mile underground pipeline, which will carry water west to the afterbay of
the Boundary Pumping Plant where it will flow by gravity across the
international border. The Yuma Valley Boundary well field will have ten
wells in the west Yuma Valley along the east side of the Yuma Valley Levee
next to the West Main Canal. Each will be 400 feet deep, with the lower 200
feet screened to draw water from the underground reservoir at the rate of
7.5 cubic feet per second. A 5.3 mile connecting underground pipeline will
carry water south to the afterbay of the Boundary Pumping Plant. A 4 foot
earth cover over the pipeline will allow farming. The well fields will be
powered by a 35 mile, 34.5 KV transmission line from the desalting plant
switchyard, answering a peak demand of 7 megawatts and an electrical

energy requirement of 52 000 000 kilowatt hours per year. These figures are based on an 85 % plant factor.

The pumped water will be used for delivery to Mexico as part of the commitment under Minute 242, and for agricultural and other uses. In the US 35 000 acre-feet per year is scheduled for agricultural and other uses, while 15 000 acre-feet per year is to be delivered to Mexico at the border, for a total of 160 000 acre-feet of pumped water.

3.3.2 Example II: Nogales

In the Nogales region, both the city of Nogales, Sonora, and the city of Nogales, Arizona, are supplied by groundwater for their municipal and industrial uses. On the Mexican side, there are well fields along the Santa Cruz River to supply the city of Nogales, Sonora. On the Arizona side, five wells supply the city of Nogales, Arizona. The Santa Cruz River rises in Arizona, flows into Sonora, and then loops back into Arizona, so that the city of Nogales, Sonora, is in fact upstream to the city of Nogales, Arizona. The pumpage from the Nogales, Arizona wells in 1975 was 883 000 000 gallons, or 2700 acre-feet per year. The wells of the city of Nogales, Arizona, show an immediate response to river flows in the Santa Cruz, so the depth of water in that city's wells fluctuates from 30 to 80 feet. With both cities looking to the same limited water supply for their survival, one can readily see there is potential for conflict between the two countries as population continues to grow on both sides of the international boundary.

3.3.3 Example III: Juarez–El Paso

The metropolitan area of Ciudad Juarez, Chihuahua, and El Paso, Texas, has nearly one million inhabitants. Both cities depend largely on shared groundwater reservoirs for their municipal water supplies. Studies indicate that both sides are now pumping water at a rate faster than the groundwater reservoir is being recharged. Day reports that

> Between 1903 and 1976, water levels fell as much as 73 feet in the center of El Paso and 85 feet in Cd. Juarez. Based on a digital model study, Meyer predicts extensive Hueco Bolson drawdown by 1991 concentrated in the center of Juarez and northeast El Paso. Annual recharge to bolson aquifers may be as little as 5 % of the annual withdrawal.[21]

He suggests that 'Indigenous Rio Grande groundwater supplies are already overdeveloped and serious doubts exist that there is sufficient water to support expected growth in total water demand'.[22] He goes on to conclude:

> Although the imbalance in expanding water use and long-term availability does not pose an immediate problem, over the long-term water supplies for the international community, which is presently heavily dependent on the Hueco Bolson, will probably become more distant, more expensive, more scarce, and possibly of lower quality. Scientific evidence at hand does not permit an accurate estimate of the cost.[23]

4   Conclusions

In conclusion, it can be said that there has been considerable success in dealing with surface waters by amicable agreement. These are achievements of which the two countries may be proud. However, in addition to those past achievements, there are major challenges for the future. Undoubtedly, these will include the design of institutions to manage transboundary groundwaters in a cooperative fashion, and the protection of water quality in view of greatly increasing populations and economic activity.

Notes

1. Alba, Francisco (1982), 'La Frontera Norte de Mexico: Un Marco de Referencia', 22 *Natural Resources Journal* 749–63; (1977) *La Poblacion de Mexico, Evolucion y Dilemas*, El Colegio de Mexico, Mexico D.F.
2. *Id.*
3. Hedderson, John (1982), 'The Population of Texas Counties Along the Mexico Border', 22 *Natural Resources Journal* 765–95.
4. Hansen, Niles (1982), 'Economic Growth in the Texas Borderlands', 22 *Natural Resources Journal* 805–21.
5. Sepulveda, Cesar (1978), 'Instituciones Para la Solucion de Problemas de Superficie Entre Mexico y Los Estados Unidos', 18 *Natural Resources Journal* 131, 140.
6. Meyers, Charles (1967), 'The Colorado River', 19 *Stanford Law Review* 367–411.

7. Brownell & Eaton (1975), 'The Colorado River Salinity Problem with Mexico', **69** *American Journal of International Law* 255.
8. Brown, F. Lee *et al* (1977), 'Some Remarks on Energy Related Water Issues in the Upper Colorado River Basin', **17** *Natural Resources Journal* 635–48.
9. Bishop, A. Bruce (1977), 'The Impact of Energy Development on Colorado River Water Quality', **17** *Natural Resources Journal* 649–71.
10. *Id.* at 669.
11. Stein, Jane W. (1978), 'New River: A Sewer From Mexico', *The Washington Post*, Dec. 11 1978, at A3, col. 3–6.
12. Hill, Gladwin (1978), 'California Fights River's Flow of Mexican Wastes', *The New York Times*, Nov. 20 1978, at A19, col. 3–6.
13. Clark, Robert Emmet (1972), 'Western Groundwater Law', in R. E. Clark (ed.), **5** *Waters & Water Rights*, Sec. 440 at 411.
14. Teclaff, Ludwik (1972), *Abstraction and Use of Water: A Comparison of Legal Regimes*, U.N. Doc. St/ECH/152 62.
15. Hutchins, Wayne (1956), 'Reasonable Beneficial Use in the Development of Ground Water Law in the West', *Ground Water Economics and the Law* 24 (Western Ag. Econ. Res. Council Comm. on Econ. of Water Resources Dev., Rep. No. 5).
16. Tyler (1976), 'Underground Water Regulation in Texas', **39** *Texas Bar Journal* 532–3.
17. Ciriacy-Wantrup, S.J. (1968), *Resource Conservation, Economics, & Politics*, 141–5 (3d ed.).
18. Veeman, Terrence S. (1978), 'Water Policy and Water Institutions in Northern India: The Case of Groundwater Rights', **18** *Natural Resources Journal* 569–87.
19. Kelso, M., Martin, W. and Mack, L. (1973), *Water Supplies and Economic Growth in an Arid Environment: An Arizona Case Study* 52, 54.
20. Veeman, *supra* note 18.
21. Day, J. C. (1978), 'International Aquifer Management: The Hueco Bolson on the Rio Grande River', **18** *Natural Resources Journal* 163–80.
22. *Id.*

Part II

Legal and diplomatic resolutions in international environmental diplomacy

6

International commissions and implementation of international environmental law

Konrad von Moltke

Adjunct Professor, Dartmouth College, USA and and Senior Fellow, The Conservation Foundation

The last decade has seen quite extraordinary diplomatic activity in relation to environmental affairs. The number of conventions which has been negotiated and signed runs into the hundreds – even the number of multilateral conventions is in excess of 150[1]. The number of bilateral treaties, agreements and other arrangements is unknown but, at a guess, it must by now exceed 500. This body of environmental law excludes the European Community, distinguished by its own legislative mechanism, with its some 80 legal instruments. International environmental law is certainly unfinished – but it is sufficiently developed to raise questions as to its implementation. Undoubtedly many of our energies during the coming years will need to be devoted to better understanding how international environmental law is implemented, and how to make it function better.

The misfit between environmental phenomena and institutional arrangements to deal with them is a cause of much difficulty in institutions at all levels[2]. In academic institutions, this misfit produces 'interdisciplinary' approaches, much touted and ill-loved. In governmental institutions it produces endless coordinating committees and continual uncertainty about the real status of environmental authorities. To this day, the search goes on to find an appropriate solution for what the first French environments minister aptly called 'le ministère des l'impossible'[3]. At the international level, the misfit creates a proliferation of environmental institutions which, however numerous, still prove to be not numerous enough[4]. It also produces the United Nations Environment Programme (UNEP), the United Nations version of an interdisciplinary program.

There are two basic options for dealing with environmental matters at an international level: one can adapt existing institutions to deal with newly arising problems; or one can create new, special purpose institutions which then must stand more or less alone. There is an important difference between this situation and the options at national levels, even though they appear superficially alike: new institutions at a national or sub-national level inevitably become part of a complex institutional web in a unified system. Lacking an overarching international order, new international institutions will stand much more alone, with an urgent need to establish their identity in competition with other international institutions and without an accepted arbiter between them. We all know what this produces: competition rather than cooperation, duplication of effort and a fragmentation of resources.

The advantages and disadvantages of existing institutions as compared to new ones are relatively clear:

(i) Existing international institutions sometimes have power which can then be brought to bear in favor of environmental issues. Such power is of course relative, but the European Community (EC), the Organisation for Economic Cooperation and Development (OECD) and the United Nations (UN), weak as they are, must all be described as powerful institutions when compared to any other international body. This power, and the pre-existing mandate, are essentially the reason why these organizations are active in environmental affairs: a lack of power is the reason why the Council of Europe (CoE) has never played a significant role in relation to pollution of the Rhine, for example, despite the fact that all concerned parties are indeed member states of the CoE, while the EC has become a real force in this area despite the fact that two of the parties are not members of the EC. Neither the EC nor the OECD cover a region which is geographically well-defined and the UN, being global in orientation, can have great difficulty in dealing with the many regional issues which are the bread and butter of international environmental policy. Nevertheless all three have played and will continue to play a significant role in relation to international environmental policy.

(ii) New institutions are weak institutions, almost by definition – but they can be tailored to fit the environmental dimensions of an issue. Hence they are frequently more satisfying from a theoretical point of view.

The choice between these two approaches is made over and over again. While the often very substantial programs for environmental protection in the major international organizations are by now quite well-known[5] – pre-eminent among them the EC[6] – the new institutions which have been created in the environmental field have tended to go relatively unremarked although almost everyone knows one or several of these arcane bodies – the International Whaling Commission (IWC), the International Joint Commission (IJC), the Rhine or the Danube Commission, the Paris, Oslo or Helsinki Commissions. In fact, environmental protection has given rise to a quite remarkable number of small, special purpose international bodies, and while no survey exists either of environmental or of other special purpose international bodies, I would guess that by now those dealing with environmental affairs constitute the largest single group of such institutions worldwide. Two (incomplete) lists of international commissions (dealing with international river basins and multilateral agreements involving OECD countries) compiled in 1978 listed 20 river basin commissions and 40 conventions – many of which gave rise in turn to a commission[7].

The reason for the need to create institutions is really quite simple: the environment needs monitoring and management at an international level, and neither is possible without a minimum of institutional structure. This need for monitoring and management distinguishes environmental issues from most others on the international agenda, which can frequently be handled through the traditional procedural principles of international law that assumes that sovereign states are the legal individuals at an international level.

The tendency to create new institutions for environmental management is not a recent one; it is inherent in the nature of the issues. Among the oldest institutions for the management of an environmental resource are those dealing with the allocation and use of water: the Commission for the River Rhine was established at the Congress of Vienna (but did not begin to function until 1868 when the Treaty of Mannheim fleshed out the principles established in Vienna). The Danube Commission was established in 1878. In North America, the International Boundary and Water Commission of the US and Mexico was established in 1889 and the International Joint Commission of the US and Canada (IJC) 20 years later. In recent years, Commissions have been established for rivers as different as the Niger, the Senegal and the Moselle and for lakes such as Chad, Constance and Geneva, to give a random sample which indicates the scope of the phenomenon.

The most dramatic special-purpose international institution created in recent years is the Agency established by the Law of the Sea Treaty to administer the deep-sea bed, but there is great likelihood that it will become the premier example of the problems associated with lack of power in special purpose institutions[8]. Less dramatic – but perhaps more effective – have been the commissions set up to deal with relatively well-defined parts of the ocean – the Paris and Oslo Commissions for the North Sea[9], the Baltic Commission[10] as well as a whole series of conventions negotiated through UNEP and its regional seas program[11]. The fight which broke out over funding and control of the Barcelona Convention dealing with the Mediterranean is a good indication of the issues implied in the choice between new and existing international institutions[12].

Finally, a number of conventions dealing with wildlife have spawned small institutions of their own – the International Whaling Commission is arguably the most prominent among these, but the Secretariat of the Washington Convention is fast increasing in importance.

This plethora of international environmental institutions should not give rise to misunderstandings: they are all very closely controlled by the states which have set them up, and they are all very small. Typically they will have a permanent staff of one to five persons and have no discretionary budgets to speak of: in other words, the commissions are dependent upon the resources of the member states. More often than not, members of the commissions are not only nominated by the signatory states – they will tend to be high-level civil servants answerable to their country of origin. This is no revolutionary departure and there is no reason to expect dramatic initiatives from them. Nevertheless, these commissions form a vital, and poorly understood, link in the current international system for managing the environment – and their work needs to be much more closely monitored.

The fact that the commissions are poorly known is not a matter of chance

– they have not exactly sought the limelight. In fact, they have tended to avoid it, since they are the creatures of civil servants and diplomats, not a breed of person renowned for effusive public statements. It can prove exceedingly difficult to obtain information about the commissions if they do not choose to publish regular reports on their activities, as all the larger ones by now do.

The work of international water basin commissions was the subject of a seminar organized by the OECD in 1977[13]. The conclusions of the seminar covered such areas as groups of technical commissions; periodic information regarding a commission's activities; strengthening of water pollution control; harmonization of data; measurements abroad; the sending of data to a commission; measurements by joint teams; checking of data supplied by a country (not yet desirable); data relating to national tributaries; organisation of emergency aid; financing of the Commission and its bodies; bylaws of the Commission and its bodies. This long list is an indication of the number, complexity and potential significance of issues covered by the commissions. The final comments of this report are worth quoting at length.

> During the last ten years, a marked strengthening of international cooperation has been noted for solving problems of transfrontier pollution in international water basins. More Commissions had been established and yet others were now the subject of negotiations, with the result that there would soon be a Commission responsible for each frontier in OECD countries where bodies of fresh water were exposed to transfrontier pollution.
>
> Existing Commissions were increasingly active and had taken on added responsibilities. Some Commissions now had permanent secretariats. In response to the increasing demand, the public was being more fully informed.
>
> The existence of International Commissions with very different powers and aims was noted. In North America, nationally or internationally, Commissions mainly played a technical advisory role. On the Finnish–Swedish frontier the Commission acted as an administrative court substituting for national bodies. Most other Commissions in Europe had fewer powers than those mentioned above and mainly functioned on intergovernmental level as a body for cooperation, concertation, consultation and, if necessary negotiation. It would be futile to confer the same

powers or methods of action on all Commissions, since their nature is different.

One point the Commissions had in common was that groups of national technical experts were called upon to give impartial advice based on the best scientific and technical data. The effectiveness of Commissions vitally depended on the quality of the advice they received and on the independence of the experts consulted.

These conclusions still hold true, though one must add to them the need for periodic review of the progress achieved (or not achieved) in international commissions. A vital issue in this respect is how far such reviews should go: the ultimate purpose of international measures for environmental protection is the improvement of environmental practices and of environmental quality. Good practices alone do not always ensure good environmental quality. Hence any implementation review of international measures and bodies must include a review of environmental quality itself.

Over the past 15 years, environmental protection has been a field of dramatic and controversial developments. At the international level, there is much still to come as countries exhaust the national means at their disposal and discover that the problems they were grappling with remain unresolved. In fact, environmental issues are fast becoming the third major pillar of the emerging international system (together with security and economic issues). But as we continue to develop the institutional arrangements for international environmental protection, it will also be necessary to do some housekeeping: the coming years will see the emergence of major new international environmental issues. We must make sure as we proceed that we know what has been achieved, what is working and what is not: this will necessitate paying much more attention to the commissions.

Notes

1. See *International Environmental Law – Multilateral Treaties* (Beiträge zur Umweltgestaltung B 7), Berlin: Erich Schmidt Verlag: loose leaf; Bureau of National Affairs, *International Environment Reporter Reference File*, Washington, DC: Bureau of National Affairs: loose leaf.
2. See in general Lynton Keith Caldwell, *International Environmental Policy*.
3. M. Poujade, *Le ministère de l'impossible*.
4. See Konrad von Moltke, 'Needs and Action: Obstacles to International Policies', in World Resources Institute (WRI), *Journal '84*, Washington, DC: WRI, 1984 pp. 6–15.

5. See the (now no longer updated) compendium by P. de Reeder, *Environmental Policy of International Organisations*, North Holland: loose leaf; and Caldwell (note 2 above).
6. Commission of the European Communities (CEC), *Ten Years Environmental Policy of the European Community*, Brussels: CEC, 1984; Nigel Haigh, *EEC Environmental Policy and Britain. An Essay and a Handbook*, London: Environmental Data Services, 1984.
7. Organisation for Economic Co-operation and Development (OECD), *Transfrontier Pollution and the Role of States*, Paris: OECD, 1981 133–202.
8. Wolfgang Graf Vitzthum (hrsg.), *Die Plünderung der Meere. Ein gemeinsames Erbe wird zerstückelt*, (Fischer Informationen zur Zeit). Frankfurt/Main: Fischer Taschenbuch Verlag, 1981.
9. Oslo and Paris Commissions, *The Oslo and Paris Commissions: The First Decade*. London: Paris and Oslo Commissions, 1984.
10. Bertil Hägerhäll, International Cooperation to Protect the Baltic, *Ambio* 9, Nos. 3–4 (1980).
11. Peter Hulm, The Regional Seas Program: What Fate for UNEP's Crown Jewels?, *Ambio* 12, No. 1 (1983), pp. 2–13.
12. The conflicts can be perceived between the lines in: Lynton Keith Caldwell, *International Enviromental Policy. Emergence and Dimensions*. Durham, NC: Duke University Press, 1984, pp. 133–4.

7

The role of
international law in solving
certain environmental conflicts

Patricia Birnie

Department of Law, London School of Economics

1   Introduction

1.1   *An example of the problem*

When attending a recent conference on Antarctica I was interested to hear a lawyer from a Foreign Office Legal Advisers' department state 'I am a lawyer but I am, of course, also a diplomat'. It was not an aspect of the legal adviser's work that I had confronted before but the relevance of the remark to the resolution of Antarctic conflicts is becoming increasingly apparent as negotiations on a minerals regime for that continent proceed. Faced with the problems of resolving the difficulties raised by the possible exploitation of Antarctica's natural resources, the most urgent of which relate to minimising the effect on its delicate environment, law has, however, been the principal tool to which the negotiators have resorted. The drafting skills of lawyers are the main instrument for constructing the obligations and ambiguities by which the conflicts concerning such issues as sovereignty, the interests of the international community, the treaty parties' responsibilities and liabilities for environmental damage, are being resolved. Conflicting interests are accommodated and balanced in an Antarctic regime skilfully constructed by legal means. By subtle draftsmanship the destructive effects of claims to sovereignty are avoided, duties and obligations are laid down, and a series of treaties interlinked to form an integrated whole. The treaties developed contain in a solemn binding form the compromises arrived at by the negotiators amongst whom the lawyer diplomats play a particularly important role. Whether the result will be internationally acceptable is another issue but there is no doubt that past and present negotiations concerning Antarctica provide one of the most vivid illustrations of the role of law in resolving environmental conflicts. Moreover, if the results of the present legal diplomacy fail to gain sufficiently wide acceptance to form a viable regime, the negotiators will merely re-assemble and exercise their legal skills again to express in yet more subtle terms the further compromises necessitated.

The legal adviser's remark in the context of the above problem led me to wonder, however, what precisely was the role of the lawyer in the diplomatic service. The dictionary tells us that diplomacy is 'the art of negotiation, especially of treaties between states' and that 'to negotiate' is 'to traffic, bargain, to confer for purposes of mutual arrangement, to arrange for or by agreement, to cope with successfully, to manage'.[1]

1.2   *Constitutional aspects*

This chapter will, therefore, concentrate on the extent to which law has not only been used to evidence and make binding by means of treaties and other legal regimes the arrangements by which states are coping with and managing environmental problems, but also on the range of forums and techniques constituted by legal means within which and by which the continuing differences can be resolved by negotiation on a regular formal but flexible basis. International law's constitutional aspects are as important to the processes of conflict resolution as are its more familiar roles of providing ordered regimes and dispute settlement mechanisms.

1.3   *Definitions*

The title of this chapter sets a formidable challenge. Both the scope of the term 'environment' and of the role of law in resolving conflicts relating to it are very wide indeed. The European Commission, for example, defines environment as:

the combination of elements whose complex inter-relationships

> make up the settings, the surroundings, and the conditions of life of
> the individual and of society, as they are or as they are felt.[2]

The range of possible examples of the law's role in resolving environmental
conflicts is thus vast, given not only the breadth of the possible definition but
of the ways in which and the levels at which the law can act in this respect. It
has to provide definitions not only of the environment as such but of all the
terms used in developing protective regimes – 'pollution', for example.

1.4   *The drawing of lines*

As an international lawyer I shall deal only with the role played by
international, not national, law, in this field; because the issues are so broad,
I shall confine my analysis to the role of environmental law (thereafter
referred to as IEL) in preventing pollution and conserving natural resources,
and shall illustrate this with selected examples only. It was once succinctly
stated by a US judge that the purpose of the law was to draw a line;
individuals and states must keep within its bounds but as long as they do so it
does not matter how close to the line they get. Most disputes revolve round
the location of this line. If the line is clear disputes should be avoided except
by those who wilfully transgress. Unfortunately, since international law is a
decentralised system, the line, if drawn at all, is often not drawn with a very
bold pencil. Since also the system is based on consent, which may only be
obtained by negotiation of compromises or deliberate ambiguities, as in
Antarctic treaties, or may not be forthcoming at all, the line may not always
be straight or clearly visible. Conflicts are blurred rather than resolved by
these means.

Lines are seldom dictated by international law though in certain instances
the occurrence of environmental disasters, such as the grounding of the
Torrey Canyon or *Amoco Cadiz*, has dictated solutions previously resisted and
in some areas commissions have been established with specific but limited
power to lay down behavioural rules. Sometimes also, when states urgently
require that territory be clearly divided between them so that it can be used,
specific boundaries are legally identified consensual bases of international
law. The need to develop customary law by widespread or regional or even
bilateral state practice, or by identifying established principles or by
concluding treaties frequently results in such faint marking of the line – the
criteria for drawing it having been left deliberately ambiguous in order to

attract consensus (the 1982 UN Law of the Sea Convention[3] and the 1967 UN Convention on Outer Space[4] are cases in point) – that in effect more than one line can be drawn, i.e. states have a choice of lines.

1.5   Machinery for settlement of disputes

The disputes concerning delineation of the continental shelves of adjacent or opposite states that have come before international tribunals recently illustrate this in a practical way.[5] These disputes arise from the vagueness of the existing principles, treaties and customs concerning the methods to be used for drawing such boundaries, which in effect allocate access to the living and non-living resources of the shelves and thus the authority to manage and conserve them. Thus lines must be settled. The law provides means for resolving these disputes by arbitration or resort to the International Court of Justice (ICJ), as a result of which the lines were either drawn by the courts or by the parties themselves on the basis of the court's judgments. It is also noteworthy that in the Gulf of Maine Case 1984, an ICJ panel considered that in choosing the factors relevant to the location of the delimination line between the shelves and Exclusive Fisheries Zones (EFZs) of Canada and the US in this area, it should reject ecological or geological 'natural' boundaries such as the boundaries of the fish stocks or water masses of troughs both because they were too uncertain and because the judges were not competent to evaluate the scientific evidence. They preferred to rely on the effect of the geographical configuration of the coastline as offering more clarity and certainty for this purpose.

2   Traditional development and application of international environmental law: its adaptation to new values and demands

2.1   Means of international law-making

All is not lost if the law does not in the first instance clearly draw the line or does not draw one at all, since there are many other ways in which the law can act to avoid potential conflict or to control or remedy the situation if a dispute arises. International law can be developed from three long-established and well-tried sources: treaties; custom based on state practice evidencing a sense of legal obligation; and general principles of law. Decisions of national and international tribunals and the writings of publicists provide secondary sources. UN General Assembly resolutions and resolutions of other UN bodies and of UN conferences contribute greatly to these processes, though their precise significance is disputed. But the better view is that although certain important resolutions, if adopted unanimously or by consensus, can have normative effect and do establish states' views on issues, some evidence of state practice in implementing them is required, especially the practice of the states most directly affected, before such resolutions can be regarded as legally binding.[6] Such resolutions enter into customary law by the usual processes and are not a form of 'instant custom' except in certain unusual circumstances when the UN member states make this intention clear, as they did in relation to Outer Space in 1963. The negotiation of such resolutions in important global forums often gives them some normative effect and can facilitate their entry into customary law. Developing countries in particular regard such General Assembly resolutions as those on Permanent Sovereignty over Natural Resources[7] and the Declaration of Principles Governing the Exploration and Exploitation of the Deep Seabed Beyond National Jurisidiction[8] as having such effect, and some General Assembly resolutions such as that adopting the Stockholm Environment Conference's Declaration of Principles[9] or that promulgating the World Charter for Nature[10] clearly have important normative effects leading to their being acted upon in some if not all respects.

2.2   *The old legal order*

The sources of international law respect the basic principle of international law that states are sovereign and thus their consent or at least their acquiescence is required to develop the law. Their acquiescence may be assumed if they do not protest at the critical point when new customs are crystallising, however. Thus accommodation of interests by diplomacy, whether by cooperation or negotiation before or after conflict leads to development of a legal order even in a system of international law which lacks centralised legislative organs. The shared nature of the physical environment, whether through water courses, the sea, the atmosphere or outer space, necessitates increasing development at regional and global level of laws, standards, dispute settlement machinery and concomitant mechanisms for these purposes. This can be seen to be happening on a large scale, to the extent that the traditional legal order relating to the environment is rapidly being superseded. This order, as Jan Schneider pointed out, was essentially a laissez-faire system oriented towards the unfettered freedom of states.[11] Such limitations on freedom of action as did exist in the traditional order had been formulated from perspectives other than the specifically environmental. Thus such few international tribunals as ever had the opportunity to hear cases concerning the environment could refer only to narrow formulations of state responsibility and liability for damage derived from the laws of property and tort. They found, as in the *Trail Smelter* case,[12] that state responsibility was not engaged unless a legal wrong could be clearly established to have been committed, involving violation of a legal right or duty, and real and serious damage could be proved to have occurred. The concepts of property ownership and damage to property were dominant. Damage to the environment as such was not catered for.

2.3   *Demands for change: new principles and approaches*

Changing perspectives on the need to protect the environment and also to protect it as a whole, as well as changing socio-economic factors in the international system, were not responded to with the alacrity demanded by either environmentalists or the rapidly growing number of newly independent states, most of which were in a process of development. As a result they neither consumed resources nor produced or used polluting advanced technology at the rate of the developed states. Their demands for a New International Order (NIEO) spilled over into demands for a New International Environmental Order articulated at the UN Human Environment Conference (UNCHE) in Stockholm. The required formulation of environmental law henceforth had to accommodate the special needs of their development without prejudicing protection of the environment. Lawyerly skills have accommodated this by framing obligations in broad terms that allow for variety and flexibility in interpretation, application and enforcement; prime examples are the Stockholm Declaration itself, the World Charter for Nature and the environmental provisions of the 1982 UN Convention on the Law of the Sea (UNCLOS), especially its Chapter XII. The detailed legal responses to the demands for environmental protection will be dealt with later in this chapter. At this point it should be noted that 11 of the new basic principles adopted in the UNCHE Declaration of Principles, took account of the necessity for developing states to develop and to take their development needs into consideration in adopting their own environmental policies and using the best means practicable for them, whilst at the same time subjecting these states to the same legal responsibilities to protect the environment as other states.[13] This had become an explosive issue both at Stockholm in 1972 and in what became the third UNCLOS Committee III on Protection and Preservation of the Marine Environment from 1970 onwards, since the developing countries originally sought to escape the duty to protect the environment, at least during their period of development, and to apply so-called 'double standards'. The UNCHE, by providing the forum for negotiating a compromise and by laying down the compromise in the form of a basic environmental principle, avoided a serious conflict. Though the principles took the form of recommendations and were therefore not binding, they were adopted in solemn form, approved unanimously by both the UNCHE and later the UN General Assembly, and were seen to have attracted a wide degree of support. So much so that they are now generally regarded as becoming part of customary law; some have already done so, as evidenced by the fact that many of them are now the basis of international conventions such as the Convention on Trade in Endangered Species (CITES),[14] the London and Oslo Conventions on Dumping of Waste at Sea [15] and the 1982 UNCLOS.

A notable aspect of this approach to resolving disputes concerning environmental obligations that arise from the discrepancies in the levels of development of states is the evolution of flexible approaches. The trend is either to resort to non-binding Declarations of Principles, which leave time for states to adopt them gradually as the internal economic, political and administrative difficulties are overcome, or to use very general so-called 'framework' or 'umbrella' treaties, which set down obligations only in general terms, leaving states gradually to elaborate and apply them through national law processes at their own pace. These generally provide for parties eventually to expand the original treaty by adopting existing or further *ad hoc* protocols on specific aspects. This interlinking of instruments also leads to the ecological approach now demanded by environmentally-minded states and groups. It is used by UNEP in its Regional Seas Programme; the Antarctic System is also evolving in this way. The framework treaty approaches, as well as the development of non-binding principles or recommendations, are often referred to as 'soft' law, as compared to the more traditional 'hard' law methods. 'Soft' law can be adopted more speedily and easily; 'hard' law involves a longer wait to attract consensus on adoption of specific, detailed and binding obligations. Moreover, the framework treaty and linked protocol approach allows different approaches to be taken in different regions. The contrast in terms between the 'soft' UNEP Regional Seas 'umbrella' treaties and the 'hard' Oslo Convention on Ocean Dumping or Paris Convention on Land-based Pollution[16] evidence the differences of approach. Moreover, various codes and declarations promoted by such influential bodies as UNEP, International Maritime Organization (IMO) and International Union for Conservation of Nature (IUCN) now cover a very wide variety of normative instruments which, though not having the binding status of treaties, nonetheless carry sufficient weight and have sufficient effect on state practice to avoid conflicts. IMO's Dangerous Goods Code,[17] UNEP's Principles on Shared Natural Resources,[18] the Helsinki Final Act[19] (which relates to the environment as well as to security) and the 1979 Convention on Conservation of Migratory Species of Wild Animals[20] provide other examples of this species of 'soft' law. But this does not mean that the role of 'hard' law has been superseded. Many activities require it, but the size of and disparities within modern international society make it more difficult to lay down. The 'soft' approach can be a step on the way to the 'hard', as IMO's practice illustrates.

2.4   *Concepts of common spaces and common heritage*

As we have seen, the law has been able to respond to new environmental demands by developing a flexible approach based on principles and 'soft' law treaties to accommodate the interests of developing states in developing. But other conflict situations arise. Of particular concern are situations in which damage could be caused to internationally shared areas such as the high seas or the atmosphere, the so-called 'international commons'. Here the over-exploiting or polluting activities of one state could harm the international area or its resources, thus adversely affecting the interests of the inter-national community as a whole, or alternatively, an otherwise harmless use by one state might interfere with other uses of the area made by other states and prejudice their interests in using this environment. An example is the interaction of uses of the high seas such as weapons testing and military manoeuvres, fishing, waste disposal, scientific research, and navigation.

The old order based on laissez-faire had resulted in the doctrine of access to international spaces, of which the high seas is the prime example, being based on freedom of entry for all states. Their activities, however environ-mentally damaging, could thus be restricted only with their consent, generally evidenced by conclusion of *ad hoc* treaties such as those establishing fisheries commissions and those on pollution prevention. The underlying assumption of freedom from control made it difficult for fisheries bodies ever to enact regulations of the stringency advised by scientists as necessary to preserve the resources on a sustainable basis and, as is well known, over-exploitation of many stocks occurred; the whales[21] and the North-East Atlantic herring stocks[22] being amongst the most notorious examples. Developing states demanded that IEL respond to this situation as part of the NIEO, both in its economic and environmental aspects. They proposed extension of national jurisdiction over 200 mile Exclusive Economic Zones (EEZ) or Fishing Zones (FZ) and beyond that limit considered that international areas should be regarded as the 'common heritage of mankind'. Their solution, in other words, was a redrawing of jurisdictional limits, using new lines and new concepts, to re-allocate resources and the competences to manage and conserve them.

The 'common heritage' concept has been confined in the 1982 UNCLOS to the deep seabed beyond the continental shelves. That treaty is not in force, and the US and some other states have rejected the form of common heritage regime laid down in that treaty. It has also been applied in modified form, however, to the Moon and other celestial bodies in the Moon Treaty[23], and demands are now being made that Antarctica be similarly regarded.[24] Conflicts concerning the juridical content of the concept are thus spreading to other forums. As yet, so far as general international law – that enforceable by treaty or established custom – is concerned the concept, in the view of certain major developed states that have not ratified the Moon Treaty or the 1982 UNCLOS, has not advanced beyond a vague 'Soft law' principle, since neither of these treaties is in force and the Antarctic Treaty,[25] as presently written, does not establish common heritage status for this area. Until a legal regime is developed which accommodates the interests of all states in these areas, it cannot be said that the law has sufficiently evolved to meet the demand for common heritage status for these areas, though it does now offer a framework for resolution of the dispute concerning the deep seabeds. It remains for lawyers, following further negotiations, to express whatever compromise emerges, in juridical terms acceptable to all states.

Meanwhile, the common heritage principle has been laid down in 'soft law' form in the UN's 15 point Declaration of Principles Governing the Exploration of the Seabed Beyond National Jurisdiction. This calls upon states only to exploit the area under an international regime to be established for the benefit of mankind as a whole, taking into particular consideration the interests of developing states and includes a reference to prevention of pollution. Though this was approved unanimously by the General Assembly in 1970, several leading states abstained on the vote and made it clear that their approval of the principle was conditional on institution of a regime acceptable to them.

Although the common heritage debate arose at the outset of UNCLOS III in relation to access to seabed resources in international areas, the concept also has other important connotations which eventually will have to be dealt with by international environmental law. It is increasingly being related to the idea that there are Laws of Nature which must be observed by human laws. As expressed by one Third World expert recently in a paper entitled 'Le Droit de l'Humanité à une Maison-Terre Habitable', there is also dissatisfaction with IEL's exclusive concern to protect the physical environment and demands for it to move 'vers un nouvel ordre socio-ecologique' drawing on that 'reservoir inépuisable du droit . . . la moral'.[26] In his view international environmental law has also focused too closely on the 'voisinage' and should take a more global perspective. The adoption by the UN, in the form of a General Assembly Resolution, of the World Charter for Nature in 1980 encourages this global and natural law approach. It points, as Professor Kiss has phrased it, to 'l'intérêt commun de l'humanité'[27] in the environment which necessitates the safeguarding of its essential elements to maintain a global ecological equilibrium. The common heritage approach has been developed yet further into the theory that present generations hold the environment in trust for future generations to whom they are under an equitable obligation to conserve it, keeping open various options for the future.[28] Thus they must not eliminate any species or diminish the quality of the environment and must leave the planet as they found it. Sovereignty, in the view of such theorists, is obsolete and should be replaced by a concept of planetary citizenship. The law is far from recognizing such concepts, however; sovereignty, for example, still seems to be a concept highly valued by all states and though they are increasingly perceiving the need to protect the environment and the utility of new legal approaches to this end, they are proceeding cautiously and pragmatically, relegating the holistic comprehensive approach to the most general of general declarations of principles, such as the World Charter for Nature.

3   New uses of old means of law-making

If the impression has been created so far that law has been used mainly as a vehicle for enunciating principles, this is because in relation to the most recent, most progressive, and therefore, most controversial demands for environmental action this is so. But there are many other ways, at the more specific and functional level, that law has been used to resolve or avoid disputes concerning protection of commonly used or held spaces and to control activities affecting the environment that traverse frontiers. These include transfrontier pollution and the movements of such animals, fish, birds and plants as regularly cross boundaries or have their habitats in, or are traded in, countries other than those which they presently frequent and thus require protection to survive.

International law has many important roles to fulfil in avoiding or resolving conflicts concerning such issues. These include its most obvious regulatory role by which a common legal order can be established to protect and conserve the environment and its resources; the provision of forums for resolution of conflicts by negotiation of regulations or other solutions; and the establishment of jurisdictional boundaries or allocation of jurisdictional competences so that states can identify both the nature and source of authority of behavioural codes for particular areas or particular activities. Such boundaries are also the means of legally allocating natural resources either exclusively or inclusively. The law can also deter transgressors by providing for enforcement and punitive sanctions against violations; it can compensate victims and lay down the principles of state responsibility and liability for this purpose, avoiding attempts to redress wrongs or secure compensation by violent means. It can provide disputes settlement machinery, through which these processes can be peacefully adjusted. In its regulatory role it can require (i.e. lay down binding obligations) states to cooperate; to both collect and widely disseminate the data and information – scientific, economic, technical, general – necessary to arrive at sound environmental policies and acceptable codes for their implementation; to monitor the environment and to analyse the data. Finally, it can also require that the states party to international conventions undertake the responsibility of educating and training their populations concerning the purposes of environmental protection and the need to exercise restraint in carrying out certain activities, together with the underlying reasons for this. This leads to self-enforcement of required standards and avoids the adversarial situations which all too often occur when the imperatives of environmental law require restriction of existing activities that are beneficial in purely economic terms. Informed citizens can insist that governments fulfil such legal obligations as they have undertaken and lobby them to do so.

Let us now look at some examples of these roles, though the need for brevity requires that they be few.

3.1   *The comprehensive role; definition and regulation*

Treaties are the main vehicle for this. Obligations can be expressed in solemn, binding, written form. The ratification process ensures that states cannot become bound without their consent (unless the treaty in whole or in part is codifying existing custom or results in growth of new customs). The certainty provided emanates from one of the oldest, best-established and widely-accepted principles of international law; *pacta sunt servanda* (treaties are made to be kept) or, as a US Supreme Court judge once put it, 'great nations like great men should keep their word'.[29] UNEP's Register of International Treaties and Other Agreements in the Field of the Environment[30] lists 108 important conventions concluded from 1933 to 1982; there are many more at the bilateral level. The list includes numerous fisheries conventions, creating bodies with powers to lay down the Total Allowance Catch (TAC) of fish, quotas for species and states, and conservatory measures such as gear regulations, restrictions of vessel type, open and closed areas and seasons. The International Convention on Regulation of Whaling 1946 (ICRW)[31] and the Convention on Conservation of Antarctic Marine Living Resources 1979 (CCAMLR)[32] are cases in point; the latter defines its area on an ecological basis and takes account of interdependence of species. Increasingly such conventions also take account of their relation to, or are affected by, in form or practice, other relevant conventions, such as those on Trade in Endangered Species (CITES); on Conservation of Migratory Species of Wild Animals (Bonn Convention); on the World Cultural and Natural Heritage;[33] on Wetlands of International Importance;[34] on Conservation of European Wildlife and Natural Habitat (Berne Convention)[35] and the 1982 UNCLOS. All these tackle the same problems of possible over-exploitation or ecological disturbance from different perspectives. The newer conventions sometimes admit as parties entities other than states, for example the European Community, which then enact the regulations on a regional basis.[36] In the case of fisheries, of course, the EC now formulates its own policies and regulations, which can become binding

through the processes laid down in the Treaty of Rome. IUCN's consti-
tution provides for membership by states, inter-governmental and now
governmental organisations. Other important treaties include the 1968
African Convention on the Conservation of Nature and Natural
Resources;[37] the 1976 Convention on Protection of the Rhine Against
Chemical Pollution,[38] the 1977 Convention on the Prohibition of Military or
Any Other Hostile Use of Environmental Modification Techniques;[39] the
UNEP Regional Seas Conventions;[40] the 1972 London and Oslo Dumping
Conventions; the 1979 Convention on Long-range Transboundary Air
Pollution;[41] the numerous IMO conventions on prevention of pollution from
ships and safety standards on ships and ILO conventions on the standards of
crew, conditions, training and certification.[42]

Many of these treaties (e.g. the fishery conventions, including ICRW and
CCAMLR; the dumping conventions; CITES; the Bonn and Berne
Conventions) establish important devices for conflict resolution in addition
to regulation *per se*. They establish either permanent commissions, which
meet at least annually (the fishery conventions, including ICRW and
CCAMLR; Oslo Dumping Convention) or regular meetings of parties
(Bonn, CITES; London Dumping, Berne conventions). The UNCLOS
established a Preparatory Commission (PrepCom) in its Final Act to draft
the regulations applicable by the International Seabed Authority (ISA)
established by the 1982 UNCLOS once it starts operations following entry
into force of that treaty. PrepCom is also working out the details of the ISA
itself and of the International Tribunal for the Law of the Sea (ITLOS), also
instituted by the UNCLOS. Non-signatory states have expressed the hope
that PrepCom will be able to draft all these provisions in a moderate manner
that will sufficiently accommodate their interests and concerns and thus
enable them eventually to accede to the convention. These provide diplomatic forums for negotiation of disputes concerning interpretation and
application of the convention; they establish annexes to which the species
protected by the convention or the pollutants to be controlled are allocated
by the Commission or meeting. This is a flexible mechanism, allowing
dynamic growth in environmental regulation but at a pace which meets to
some extent the economic, technical and resultant internal political problems
experienced by the parties. As the forum is international it allows those states
which wish to proceed more quickly to exert pressure on those which resist
regulation and facilitates negotiation of acceptable compromises.

Some conventions (e.g. ICRW, CITES, London Dumping) permit

non-governmental observers (NGOs) as well as inter-governmental observers (NGOs) to attend. These add to the environmental pressures and
enable NGOs, to some extent, to participate in the negotiating process. In
some bodies, such as the International Whaling Commission (IWC) they
have had a considerable impact, having, by experience, learnt how to
influence the legal processes to their advantage. Numbers of NGOs at the
IWC rose from 5 to 50 over a period of about 10 years. Not only did they
circulate to official delegations factual information on infractions (otherwise
not available) and scientific assessment and questions of legal interpretation,
but they actively and successfully encouraged more non-whaling states to
join in order to increase the votes for the moratorium on all commercial
whaling, as a result it was legitimately adopted in 1982. The so-called
'like-minded' conservationist states took advantage of the legal procedures
available under the ICRW, as applied and interpreted by the IWC itself, to
set zero quotas on all commercially exploited stock. US NGOs have since
successfully brought an action against the relevant US Secretary of State to
force him to certify Japan, which had legitimately objected to this moratorium,
as undermining the ICRW, thus making mandatory certain US economic
sanctions against Japan. The US District Court of Appeals recently
supported the NGOs view.[43] NGOs are now using similar techniques in the
London Dumping Convention, strenuously lobbying states in order to
augment the vote in favour of an indefinite moratorium on the dumping of
low-level radioactive waste in the oceans despite the inconclusive evidence
from scientific studies commissioned under that convention concerning the
need for such a moratorium. NGOs and like-minded states are not merely
protesting but are legitimately using the legal processes to secure their ends.
These methods, however, themselves produce protests from states and
industrial interests affected, and may make such states reluctant to enter into
further international agreements. For example, doubts are being cast on the
continuance of the ICRW in its present form.

As well as allocating species and pollutants to annexes, the relevant
commissions have to decide on definitions of key words in the convention,
which have often deliberately been left undefined because they are controversial. Examples are such terms in the Oslo Dumping and Paris Land-
based Pollution Conventions as 'pollution', 'likely to result in harm', 'liable
to harm', 'interference with other legitimate uses of the sea', 'toxic',
'noxious', 'persistent'.[45] The same problems arise concerning EC directives
implementing the latter. The dispute extends to the means to be used for

achieving the control or elimination of pollution, however defined. Some states favour the setting of uniform emission standards (UES). Others prefer to take advantage of the ability of some receiving waters to dispose of pollutants more quickly and effectively than others; they support the setting of environmental quality objectives (EQOs), so that measures need not be taken unless and until the quality aimed at is likely to be impaired. In both the Paris Commission and the EC, member states have arrived at the legitimate compromise of leaving for the time being the choice of option to states. Definition is a political issue because of its economic implications; the law records and embodies whatever compromise results from the annual negotiations. States seek definitions and resultant controls that ensure parity of economic sacrifice. This, as well as desire to protect the environment, is the main motive for entering into such agreements.

Similar problems occur in other conventions – CITES, CCAMLR, etc. The Transboundary Air Pollution Convention's terminology is deliberately ambiguous to avoid, *inter alia*, the controversy surrounding the alleged harmful effects of acid rain. The forum for negotiation of this convention was the UN's ECE. Its parties undertake only to 'endeavour to limit, and as far as possible, gradually to reduce and prevent air pollution', using 'the best available technology economically feasible'. Conflict arises concerning the measures actually required. As one commentator has remarked 'The Convention is the perfect solution to the victim countries' need for international recognition of the acid rain problem and the polluting countries' need to continue to pollute'.[45] Nonetheless the Convention is contributing to resolution of this conflict: meetings of its parties have provided a forum for a majority of its states to resolve that they will reduce sulphur dioxide emission by 30 %, though the major offenders did not join in this commitment, as explained elsewhere in this book.[46]

Frequently, as stated earlier, conventions or organisations prefer to adopt non-binding resolutions or recommendations which set standards which influence the development of customary law at a slower pace, rather than attempting to negotiate immediately binding rules. Such an approach is apt when technology is advancing, but slowly, as in the case of control of carriage of hazardous and noxious cargoes at sea, nuclear ships and materials and air pollution. Here the IMO, ILO and IAEA find codes of practice a less contentious method of proceeding.

3.2   *Forums and secretariats*

As indicated above conventions can have a constitutional role in establishing commissions to administer the convention, or establishing or identifying bodies to convene regular meetings. For CITES the Secretariat does this; for the London Dumping Convention, the IMO; for the Bonn Convention, the UNEP; for the Berne Convention, the Council of Europe; for the Transboundary Air Pollution Convention, the ECE. For all bodies the law lays down the conditions of membership; terms of withdrawal or suspension; provides for finance; equips them with appropriate organs; details their powers and voting systems; and establishes dispute settlement procedures, if any.

Many standing bodies also provide the forum for negotiation of *ad hoc* conventions to regulate particular problems. The 1982 UNCLOS, Part XII makes frequent reference to the use of both *ad hoc* diplomatic conferences and existing international organisations at the global, regional and sub-regional level to develop laws and standards to prevent pollution from all sources and protect living resources. It calls on occasion for such bodies to be established when they do not exist, for example for highly migratory species and urges cooperation with and through such bodies. It was the UNCLOS, not the Convention, however, that established PrepCom, which is not a permanent body or UN organisation.

The UN itself provides such a forum as do virtually the whole range of UN Specialised Agencies and Regional Commissions and other regional bodies: the Organisation of African Unity (OAU), which provides the secretariat for the African Convention; the Organisation of African States (OAS); the EEC; the European Parliament; NATO, which has an environmental Committee on the Challenges of Modern Society; the Council of Europe, which has promoted a number of environmental conventions and conferences; and the IUCN. As yet there is no overall environmental forum for negotiation. The Brundlandt Commission is, however, drawing up proposals for the world environment and resource problems in the context of development and security for the world community. Its report on a Common Future is expected in 1987 and may advocate a World Commission on Environment and Development. If so the law will be employed to provide its constitution.

3.3   *Responsibility, liability compensation*

Law has an obvious role to play in this aspect of environmental disputes, but it is one in which it has not yet developed its full potential. It is an area which gives rise to serious disputes, especially following transfrontier disasters, but as there are sensitive issues involved pertaining to their sovereignty, states are reluctant to establish principles of strict or absolute liability, preferring generally to rely on the need to prove both that a wrong has been committed and that damage has occurred. The problem is exacerbated by lack of compulsory dispute settlement procedures (see below). It is particularly difficult when dealing with states to establish that fault has occurred and, in the case of the environment, that damage to it as such has occurred (e.g. from low-level radioactive waste dumping or discharge; acid rain or moderate discharges of oil or chemicals). Yet this is what international law requires in most instances, unless a treaty provides otherwise, as established in the *Trail Smelter* case.

Some progress has been made in the oil pollution field – the 1969 IMO Convention on Civil Liability for Oil Pollution Damage[47] established the strict but limited liability of tanker owners for oil pollution damage (defined in limited terms which excludes environmental damage); it has been backed by a Fund Convention.[48] Limits of compensation under both were raised in 1984 by protocols[49] which also extended the scope of compensable damage to cover environmental damage, but the protocols are not likely to enter into force for some time. An attempt to conclude a similar convention for Hazardous and Noxious Substances failed;[50] the 1976 Convention on Civil Liability for Pollution from Offshore Operations,[51] which imposes strict liability on North-West Europe's offshore operators, has not been ratified by any of its 12 signatories. A Convention on Civil Liability in the Field of Nuclear Energy[52] is not in force; one on Civil Liability in the Field of Maritime Carriage of Nuclear Materials is in force[53] but for 11 states only, excluding the US, UK and USSR; an OECD Convention on Third Party Liability in the Field of Nuclear Energy is in force but though the UK is a party the US is not.[54] The 1969 Treaty on Principles Governing the Activities of States in the Exploration and Use of Outer Space established the responsibility of states for their activities in outer space and is backed by a subsequent treaty establishing the liability of the launching state for damages caused by objects in space.[55] 'Soft law' is not much help in this field; only 'hard law' provides the certainty required.

There are, however, no treaties covering transboundary damage generally or damage resulting from atmospheric pollution or chemical pollution. Here the law's role is left to provision of general principles, as in the *Trail Smelter* and *Corfu Channel*[56] cases. In the former a tribunal decided that

> Under the principles of international law . . . no state has the right to use or permit the use of its territory by another or the properties or persons therein, when the case is of serious consequence and injury is established by clear and convincing evidence.

In the latter case the ICJ decided that every state is under an obligation 'not to allow knowingly its territory to be used for acts contrary to the rights of other states', but left these rights unspecified. The questions of liability and responsibility raised by Australia and New Zealand in the 1974 *Nuclear Test* case[57] were never decided by the ICJ before which they were brought. Australia alleged *inter alia* that it had a right to be free from atmospheric weapons tests, that depositing of radioactive fall-out in its territory violated its sovereignty, whereas France argued (diplomatically) that in the absence of ascertained damage attributable to France's nuclear experiments they did not violate any norm of international law. The court granted Interim Orders to restrain the tests causing fall-out in Australia pending a decision on the case; even so one judge dissented, taking the view that national security and defence considerations over-rode environmental ones, as long as the offending state compensates the injured parties for any damage caused (assuming, of course, that they can prove damage). No doubt, however, if the case had not been withdrawn by the ICJ following France's declaration that henceforth it would only test underground, the judges would have succeeded in identifying a legal principle on which to base a decision, as they did in the *Corfu Channel* and *North Sea Continental Shelf* cases.[58] In the latter they relied on 'equitable principles' in the absence of any binding custom or convention on continental shelf delimitation.

3.4   *Enforcement, penalties; sanctions*

Much of international law is left to states to enforce: relevant treaties require that states take the measures necessary to prevent violations, etc. As appropriate, states can arrest and fine offenders, for example under fisheries conventions, though the 1982 UNCLOS prohibits states from imprisoning offenders. Under some fisheries conventions, especially those established before much of the oceans was reduced to 200 mile EEZs or FZs, joint enforcement schemes operated on the high seas.[59] States, through the treaty mechanism, surrendered some of their rights to jurisdiction over their ships on the high seas as flag states and permitted boarding, inspection and report (but not arrest) by other states of ships flying their flag which were reasonably suspected of violations. Under the ICRW an Observer Scheme operates whereby participating states exchange observers on the basis of bilateral arrangements, but the observers are appointed by the IWC and report infractions both to the flag state and to the IWC. The EC has established a small inspectorate of 13 which sails on certain vessels fishing in 'EC waters'. But, these examples apart, international inspection is rare and enforcement and penalties are generally left to national states. However, the 1982 UNCLOS Part XII, when it enters into force, will introduce a new concept of port state jurisdiction for some oil pollution offences; the system allows the state whose port has been entered voluntarily by a vessel that has illegally discharged on the high seas or in another state's EEZ (at that state's request) to prosecute the offending vessel. The UNCLOS provides that the vessel can leave if it deposits a bond, and that the port state can prosecute only if the flag state does not do so on being presented with the evidence.

Generally, as states are jealous of their rights to freedom of the high seas and to jurisdiction over their flag ships, foreign states are reluctant to provoke diplomatic controversy by exercising their jurisdiction over ships that pollute or over-fish on the high seas or in other state's jurisdiction unless some treaty specifically approves this. Thus in Europe, despite strong demands for them to proceed against sub-standard vessels, the most that European states felt they could do was to allow their administrations to conclude a Memorandum of Understanding[60] under which they agreed to inspect a set target of vessels entering their ports to check their observance of the standards laid down in certain widely-ratified conventions and codes, and to report their flag state vessels falling below these standards.

States are even more reluctant to resort to sanctions for fear of reciprocal hostile action. The US action in certifying states that undermine international conservatory conventions to which the US is party and then either cutting their access to fisheries in the US EEZ or banning the fish and fish product imports into the US of the certified state[61] is not likely to be repeated by less powerful states. Thus CITES remains the only example of an internationally organised system of economic sanctions in which a large number of states participate; under it states agree to ban or to control the import and export of species or specimens thereof, which are listed in its

Annex according to the degree of threat to their survival trade in them represents. To this end states party to it operate a system of import and export licences and must establish both a Management Authority to operate it and a Scientific Authority to give the appropriate advice.

3.5   *Dispute settlement*

Those not familiar with international law may be surprised that this role has been addressed last in this paper, not first, since resolving conflicts suggests that they be brought before some tribunal with powers to determine a final and binding solution. Unfortunately, states are unwilling to surrender to third parties the control over the outcome of disputes that the doctrine of state sovereignty allows them. Only a few treaties provide for binding settlement of disputes and the Statute of the ICJ does not confer compulsory jurisdiction upon it. Even the new UNCLOS, which provides in Part XV for a fine array of dispute settlement procedures, ranging from the ICJ, Arbitration, Special Arbitral panels for specific disputes (on fisheries, navigation, scientific research, and pollution), a Seabed Disputes Chamber, and a Conciliation Commission, does not, for the issues most likely to give rise to conflict (i.e. those concerning access to fisheries, determination of quotas, consent for research and delimitation of maritime boundaries), provide for a final and binding decision. For such disputes compulsory conciliation is required, but the outcome of this procedure is left ambiguous, without delivery of a clearcut mandatory judgment. Nonetheless many disputes covered by the 1982 UNCLOS will be subject to the compulsory settlement procedures provided, at least for states party to it, since on signing or ratifying states are required to state which method of compulsory settlement they accept: the ICJ, ITLOS, or arbitration. If they do not, or if both parties to a dispute have not chosen the same method, arbitration will generally prevail.

Under the 1982 UNCLOS, however, as well as under most treaties, including the UN Charter, states are left free to resort to settlement to any peaceful means of their choice. These include negotiation, inquiry, good offices, mediation and conciliation, in addition to judicial settlement or arbitration. These means relate to diplomacy rather than to legal processes, though formal bodies can be established by agreement for some purposes (e.g. fact finding inquiries, conciliation commissions). Some conventions, such as CCAMLR (Article XXV), provide that failure to agree to binding settlement procedures does not absolve the parties from the responsibility of continuing to seek to resolve the dispute by the other peaceful means. The diplomatic ball is thus kept peacefully rolling. Many treaties establish arbitral procedures or provide for reference to the ICJ but do not *require* parties to resort to either; examples are the Bonn Convention (Article XVIII); CCAMLR (Article XXV); CITES (Article XVIII); Transboundary Air Pollution (Article XIII); African Convention (Article XVIII). The last provides only for submission of disputes not settled by negotiation to the Commission of Mediation, Conciliation and Arbitration of the OAU. The power to reject resort to binding dispute settlement procedures is one of the attributes of sovereignty most strongly supported by states, as evidenced by the recent US announcement of its termination of its acceptance of the ICJ jurisdiction under its optional clause. The growing awareness of interdependence in environmental matters has not persuaded states to give up their right to reject third-party decisions. However, the Berne Convention on Habitats provides for reference to arbitration at the request of either disputing party if resolution of the dispute by friendly settlement under the auspices of a Standing Committee fails (Article XVIII).

4   The response to the new approaches

Clearly, in resolution of environmental disputes the law can proceed only at the pace of states' political willingness to adopt so comprehensive an approach. There seems little enthusiasm to establish any new over-arching environmental agency. It seems likely that, using UNEP's Action Plan for the Global Environment the UN's World Charter for Nature and the future report of the Brundtland Commission on Environment and Development as 'soft law' standard setters, the international community will continue as it has done in the past to proceed on the *ad hoc* basis of allotting priority to either the issues most current for political reasons, such as oil pollution and acid rain, or the protection of species of animals and plants most threatened, as under the Convention on Trade in Endangered Species (CITES); the African Convention on Conservation of Nature; the Convention on Conservation of Migratory Species; the Convention on Wetlands of International Importance; the World Heritage Convention; the Polar Bears Convention;[62] the European Convention on Protection of Habitats, and others of this kind. The law provides the ideal mechanism for allocation of such priorities on an ongoing basis. The trend in modern treaties for

prevention of pollution, protection of endangered species, etc., and in EC
Directives and Regulations implementing some of these, is to establish
commissions with powers to add species or pollutants for protective
purposes to annexes on a regular basis, following internationally laid down
criteria.

Global Conventions or Declarations of Principles are also often used to
provide the framework, the powers to develop detailed rules, to apply,
administer and enforce them being delegated to national or regional
authorities. The law provides the diplomatic forums in which disputes can
be resolved peacefully on a continuing basis, much as in a continuing
multilateral conference or bilateral inter-state negotiations. The international framework provides as yet only an imperfect answer to the
ecological approach demanded by many within which states would fulfil the
role of trustees of the environment not owners of its resources, and would
establish and observe an integrated framework of international environmental law covering all its aspects. Difficulties are thus likely to continue to
surface within existing commissions; unilateral actions by governments (such
as Canada's 1970 Arctic Waters (Pollution Prevention) Act[63] and by
non-governmental organisations (NGOs) such as a Greenpeace (e.g. its
intervention in areas where whaling and nuclear tests take place) are likely to
continue. Unilateral actions can bring about changes in the law in the long
run but are not *per se* a source of law, except in the state taking the action.
They do not become part of international law until they are accepted into
custom or incorporated in a treaty. Peaceful settlement of disputes involving
such NGOs is being encouraged by their increasing admission as observers
at international commissions and organisations, such as the IWC and IMO.
Rules of Procedure of such conventions can be expanded, on terms and
conditions, to accommodate a wider range of such observers in an orderly
way, as in the examples cited above. Exposure to the economic and political
difficulties of negotiation in international forums arguably will both enhance
their perception of the problems and enable them to form contacts which
facilitate the bringing to bear of their views and influence. It can also assist
government delegations to solve difficulties by making first hand information
available to them and providing unseen assistants, especially to small
delegations, in negotiation. Some disputes in the IWC, for example that
concerning 'pirate' whaling, have been solved through such activities,
inter-relationships and information.

Conclusion

It will be seen that the law can play many roles in the resolution of environmental disputes and other problems. Not so much by offering the means for the final and decisive resolution of disputes but by providing compromise formulae seeking to avoid them or to transfer them to forums where debate and negotiation can take place in a peaceful and formal manner. Its main role in the environmental field is avoiding or minimising disputes by establishing the framework for the building of a legal order within which activities that might adversely affect the environment take place only within a regulated, monitored regime. This does not mean that every activity has to be closely subjected to strict legally binding rules. Rather, the law, as it is developing, provides the means for establishing priorities and for grading activities according to their harmful effects; pollutants according to the harm they might cause; species according to the degree of threat to their survival and consequent need for protection. Some activities the law may then prohibit, some pollutants it may ban from discharge, some species it may protect from all taking. Others, however, it will merely control, subject to internationally laid down criteria, or will allocate to national jurisdiction on a similar basis. Yet others it may subject to recommendations or non-binding codes of practice. The approaches are flexible in method, often annexes to conventions which are amendable by relevant commissions on an annual or biennial basis are used.

The choice of level of operation is also flexible. The EC in its series of Action Programmes on the Environment has particularly stressed the importance of acting at the appropriate level: national, global, regional, sub-regional.[64]

It is important to states, if they are to accept restrictions of their military, economic or other activities for purposes of enviromnental protection, that other states should simultaneously accept the same restrictions, in view of the economic or security considerations. Development of common laws through Treaties or customs provide the sure means of accommodating state interests in this respect. Sometimes, however, treaties will merely evidence the state's willingness to disagree or to allow different standards to operate concurrently by accepting various interpretations of terms.

Innovative legal concepts such as common heritage or inter-generational trusts are having some effect on international environmental diplomacy but their role in the legal process remains disputed and uncertain. No doubt the role of law in dispute resolution could be enhanced if states were more willing to establish and use binding dispute settlement procedures but at present they are not. We can conclude, however, that the law does now provide many tools; it remains for states to get on with the job.[65]

Notes

1. *Chamber's Twentieth Century Dictionary*, revised edition.
2. *European Community's Environmental Policy*, Periodical 1/1984 (2nd ed.).
3. *United Nations Convention on the Law of the Sea*, A/CONF. 62/122, 7 October 1982.
4. Treaty on Principles Governing the Activities of States in the Exploration and Use of Outer Space, Including the Moon and Other Celestial Bodies 1967; **10** *U.K.T.S.* (1968).
5. See the arguments of the rival parties in, for example, cases concerning: the continental shelf: *Tunisia–Libyan Arab Jamahiriya, ICJ Rep.* 1982, 143; *Delimitation of the Maritime Boundary in the Gulf of Maine Area*; *ICJ Rep.* 1984, 246; the continental shelf: *Libya–Arab Jamahiriya/Malta, ICJ Rep.* 1985, 13.
6. The basis of this dispute is well illustrated in two contrasting chapters in B. Cheng (Ed.) *International Law: Teaching and Practice*, Stevens & Son, London 1982; *viz.* Ch. 2; I. MacGibbon, 'Means for the Identification of International Law: General Assembly Resolutions: Custom, Practice and Mistaken Identity' at 10–26, and Ch. 3, R. Higgins, 'The Identity of International Law', at 27–44.
7. *GAR* 1803 (**XVIII**) 14 December 1962, reproduced in I. Brownlie, *Basic Documents in International Law* (Clarendon Press 1983); hereafter referred to as 'Basic Documents', at 230.
8. *GAR* 2749 (**XXV**) 17 December 1970, in *Basic Documents*, n. 7 *supra*, at 122.
9. *Report on the U.N. Conference on the Human Environment*, U.N. Doc. A/CONF. 48/14; **XI** *International Legal Materials*, hereafter referred to as *ILM*, (1972) 1416; pub. UN, New York, 1983.
10. World Charter for Nature, *UN GAR* 35/7 of October 30, 1980.
11. Jan Schneider, *World Public Order of the Environment: Towards an Ecological Law and Organization*, Stevens, 1979.
12. *Trail Smelter Arbitration, US* v. *Canada* (1938, 1941); **3** *R.I.A.A.*, 1905.
13. See *op.cit.*, n.11.
14. Convention on International Trade in Endangered Species of Wild Fauna and Flora 1973, **993** *U.N.T.S.*, 246.
15. The Convention on the Prevention of Marine Pollution by Dumping of Wastes and Other Matter, **XI** *ILM* 1972, p. 302; Convention for the Prevention of Marine Pollution by Dumping from Ships and Aircraft, 1972, **XI** *ILM* 1972, 263.

16. Paris Convention for the Prevention of Marine Pollution from Land Based Sources 1974, **XIII** *ILM* (1974) 546.

17. *International Maritime Dangerous Goods Code*, pub. IMO, London (as amended from time to time); for other IMO Codes see IMO: *What it is etc.*, IMO pub., 10–11.

18. Principles of Conduct in the Field of the Environment for the Guidance of States in the Conservation and Harmonious Utilization of Natural Resources Shared by Two or More States, *UNEP/IG* 12/2 and *UNEP/GC* 6/17; for other examples see *Environmental Law in the UNEP*, UNEP, Nairobi, 1985, 9–11.

19. Final Act of the Conference on Security and Co-operation in Europe, Helsinki, 30 July 1975; Section 5: Environment.

20. **XIX** *ILM* (1980) 15.

21. See P. Birnie, *International Regulation of Whaling*, Oceana (1985).

22. A. Koers, 'The Freedom of Fishing in Decline: the Case of the North East Atlantic; in Churchill, Simmonds, Welch, *New Directions in the Law of the Sea*, Vol. III, Oceana, 1973, 19–35.

23. Agreement Governing the Activities of States on the Moon and Other Celestial Bodies 1979, **XVIII** *ILM* (1979) 1434.

24. See statement by D. S. Dr. Bin Mohamed, 37th Session of the UN General Assembly, 29 September 1982, reproduced in B. J. Theutenberg, *The Evolution of the Law of the Sea*, Tycooly Int., 1984, 259.

25. The Antarctic Treaty, 1959, **402** *UNTS*, 5778.

26. H. Sanson, 'Le Droit de l'Humanité – a une Maison-Terre Habitable', paper given at *Symposium of the Hague Academy of International Law and the United Nations University on the Future of the International Law of the Human Environment*, 12–13 November 1984, hereafter referred to as Hague Symposium.

27. A. C. Kiss, 'Le Droit International de l'Environnement: Un Aspect du Droit International de l'Avenir?', paper given at Hague Symposium, *supra*.

28. E. Brown-Weiss, 'Conservation and Equity Between Generations': paper given at Hague Symposium, see n. 26.

29. See the concluding paragraph of chapter 12 of this book.

30. Register of International Treaties and Other Agreements in the Field of the Environment, *UNEP/GC/Information II Rev. 1 and Corr. 1*, UNEP, Nairobi (1985); see also W. Burhenne (ed.), *International Environmental Law: Multilateral Treaties* (IEL) and *ibid.*, *Environmental Law of the European Communities*, Erich Schmidt Verlag (looseleaf); B. Ruster, B. Simma, M. Boch (eds.) *International Protection of the Environment: Treaties and Related Documents*, Oceana 1973 (30 vols).

31. International Convention on Regulation of Whaling 1946; pub. International Whaling Commission 1964; the text of this and many other wildlife conventions is given in S. Lyster, *International Wildlife Law*, Grotius Publications Ltd, 1985, with analysis.

32. Convention of the Conservation of Antarctic Marine Living Resources, 1979, **XIX** *ILM* (1980), 841.

33. Convention Converning the Protection of the World Cultural and Natural Heritage 1972, **XI** *ILM* (1973), 1358.

34. The Convention on Wetlands of International Importance Especially as Waterfowl Habitat (RAMSAR) 1971, **XI** *ILM* (1972), 963.

35. Convention on the Conservation of European Wildlife and Wetlands of International Importance 1979, European Treaty Series No. 104, Council of Europe, **5** *Environmental Policy and Law*, (1979), 52.

36. The UNCLOS and the Paris Convention on Land-Based Pollution. The UNCLOS also provide for entities such as the UN Council for Namibia and the Cook Island Territory to become parties.

37. African Convention on the Conservation of Nature and Natural Resources 1968; *IEL*, 968 68/2, *op.cit.*, n. 30.

38. Convention for the Protection of the Rhine Against Chemical Pollution 1976, **XVI** *ILM* (1977), 242; Convention on Protection of the Rhine Against Pollution by Chlorides 1976, *ibid.*, 265.

39. Convention on the Prohibition of Military or Any Other Hostile Use of Environmental Modification Techniques 1977, **XVI** *ILM* (1977) 88.

40. For a brief summary see *Environmental Law in the United Nations Environment Programme*, UNEP, Nairobi, 1985, 4–6; Siren, *UNEP Regional Seas bulletin*, *passim*; D. W. Abecassis, *Oil Pollution from Ships*, Stevens 1985, Pt. II, Sec. 7.

41. Convention on Long-Range Transboundary Air Pollution 1979; **XIX** *ILM* (1979), 1442; see also Vienna Convention for the Protection of the Ozone Layer 1985, **14** *Environmental Policy and Law*, 72.

42. For a detailed analysis of all conventions relevant to prevention of pollution from ships see Abecassis, *op.cit.*, n. 41.

43. *American Cetacean Society et al.* v. *Malcolm Baldridge et al.*, 1985, **604** *F.Supp.*; *CA (App 1a–55a)* **768** F.2d 426; *Japan Whaling Association and Japan Fisheries Association* v. *American Cetacean Society et al.*, No. 865, *US CA*, D.C. (1985); the US Supreme Court in June 1986 reversed these decisions; report not available at time of writing.

44. For discussion of these problems see M. Tomczak, 'The Definitions of Marine Pollution: A Comparison of definitions used by international conventions', **8** *Marine Policy* (1984) 311–22; A. L. Springer, 'Towards a Meaningful Concept of Pollution in International Law', **26** *Int. and Comp. Law Quarterly* (1977), 531.

45. A. Rosencranz, 'The ECE Convention of 1979 on Long-Range Transboundary Air Pollution', **75** *AJIL* (1981) 975.

46. see p.174ff, this volume.

47. Brussels International Convention on Civil Liability for Oil Pollution Damage 1969, **IX** *ILM* (1969), 45.

48. International Convention for the Establishment of an International Fund for Compensation for Oil Pollution Damage 1971, **XI** *ILM* (1972), 284.

49. Protocols to Conventions referred to in notes 50 and 51, **XVI** *ILM* (1977), 617.

50. See **1** *IMO News* 1984, 1 for outline.

51. London Convention on Civil Liability for Oil Pollution Damage Resulting from Exploration for and Exploitation of Seabed Mineral Resources 1976, **XVI** *ILM* (1977), 1450.
52. Vienna Convention on Civil Liability for Nuclear Damage 1963, **II** *ILM* (1962), 727.
53. Convention Relating to Civil Liability in the Field of Carriage of Nuclear Material 1971, IMO pub. Note also the Brussels Convention on the Liability of Operators of Nuclear Ships 1962, 57 *AJIL* (1963) 268, which is not in force.
54. Paris Convention on Third Party Liability in the Field of Nuclear Energy 1960 (amended), 55 *AJIL* (1961), 1083.
55. Convention on International Liability for Damage Caused by Space Objects 1972, **XI** *ILM* (1972), 965.
56. ICJ Rep. 1949, 4; 66 *AJIL* (1972), 702.
57. See also Treaty Banning Nuclear Weapons Tests in the Atmosphere in Outer Space and Under Water 196 , **480** *U.N.T.S.* 45.
58. *ICJ Rep.* 1969, 1.
59. See P. Birnie, Legal Measures for Conservation of Marine Mammals, *IUCN Environmental Policy and Law Paper No. 19*, IUCN, Geneva, 1982.
60. Paris Memorandum of Understanding on Port States Control, 1982.
61. See Birnie, *op.cit.*, n. 59, 99–105 (Packwood–Magnuson amendments to Fishery Conservation and Management Act 1976; Pelly Amendment to Fishermen's Protective Act 1967).
62. Agreement on the Conservation of Polar Bears, 1973; **XIII** *ILM* (1975), 13.
63. Arctic Waters Pollution Prevention Act 1970, *New Directions in the Law of the Sea*, Vol. I, 199–210.
64. For a succinct analysis of the EC Environmental programmes, EC implementing measures, and the actions taken to implement them in the UK, see N. Haigh, *EEC Environmental Policy and Britain*, Environmental Data Services Ltd. 1984; See also *Ten Years of Community Environment Policy*, Commission of the European Communities, March 1984.
65. For future development prospects see Report of the Ad Hoc Meeting of Senior Government Officials Expert in Environmental Law, held in Montevideo 1981, *UNEP/GC.10/1/Add.2*, Annex Ch. II (1981). It recommended a long-term Programme for the Development and Periodic Review of Environmental Law, which was adopted by UNEP's Governing Council in 1982, endorsed by the UN General Assembly in Resolution 37/217, 1982, and integrated into the UN's System-Wide Medium Term Environment Programme for 1984–1989 *UNEP/GC/* 10/7 (1982). For further details see *Environmental Law in the United Nations Environmental Programme*, UNEP, Nairobi, 1985.

8

Resolution of environmental problems: the use of diplomacy

Lars Björkbom
Swedish Ministry for Foreign Affairs

1   Introduction

The scope of the subject matter – the use of diplomacy for the resolution of environmental problems – is virtually as wide as the environmental problems themselves. The basis for this statement is, of course, that most serious environmental problems are of a transboundary nature. Thus they do affect international relations. And diplomacy – in a wide definition – is the tool of governments to see to it that those international relations are kept under control so as to avoid the use of always more expensive and less effective methods of problem solving, such as reverting to military force.

Although environmental problems have a very long history – overuse of the natural resource base has in many cases caused empires and civilizations to crumble – the concept of environmental diplomacy is rather new. It is, in fact, a concept that is so new, it has up to now gained acceptance only in very few, if any, ministries for foreign affairs round the world.

It is, however, my opinion that the concept eventually must be accepted as an important aspect of modern diplomacy. The reason for this is, of course, that, in our world of heavy and growing international inter-dependence, almost no realistic national decision related to the well-being or functioning of modern societies can be taken today by government without considering its international dimension. This reality puts serious demands on diplomatic services in a large number of areas outside the scope of traditional diplomacy. It is a development which most foreign services have great difficulty in coming to grips with.

This is especially relevant in the case of handling environmental issues. The handling of such issues, nationally as well as internationally, entails very special difficulties. This depends to a large extent on the fact that environmental problems are dimensions of human activities in most sectors and do not therefore constitute a sector of their own. Most, if not all, national governments have, however, organized themselves in sectoral structures. The same pattern is, consequently, also the rule in the international, multilateral organizations within or outside the UN system, which constitute fora for resolution of problems related to our interdependence. I shall later revert to this special problem. By way of introduction, I just wish to state that this specific character of environmental problems is a very serious obstacle to the resolution of transboundary environmental problems and it makes environmental diplomacy a particularly difficult task.

2   Institutional framework for multilateral environmental diplomacy

Given the novelty of the concept 'environmental diplomacy' and the collateral newness of the activity itself, it is only natural that much of the efforts so far have been devoted to the creation of special instruments, through which diplomacy can act in its search for solutions or at least containment of international environmental problems. Such instruments are *inter alia* international fora, with supporting governing boards and secretariats and international legal conventions.

If one takes into consideration that governments started to perceive the need for such instruments less than two decades ago, the results of environmental diplomacy in this special respect have up to now been impressive indeed. This is not the place to list all the international organizations now established and the great number of international conventions now signed and in force, through which diplomacy can act – should governments be prepared to do so – to help solve transboundary environmental issues. A very short general listing of these institutional creations could, however, be described as follows.

Much of this institutional building is the child of the UN Conference on the Human Environment held in Stockholm in 1972, although there are some instances of international environmental committees and conventions before that date. The most conspicuous of the multilateral fora established is, of course, the United Nations Environment Programme (UNEP). UNEP is *inter alia* the coordinating and catalytic instrument for drawing attention to the environmental aspects of the operational activities of the UN Secretariat and the Specialized Agencies within the UN system as well as of the activities of the member governments of the UN. It is the only instrument for handling environmental issues of a global character. In all UN Regional Economic Commissions there are today subsidiary bodies, with the task of coming to grips with those environmental problems which are considered to be of a regional scope. Other bodies outside the UN system, such as the OECD, the EEC or the Nordic Council of Ministers, have also during the 1970s created institutions to take care of those environmental issues that member governments have considered necessary to approach in common.

Mainly as a result of the work of these various international bodies an impressive base of international agreements has been negotiated and adopted to regulate multilateral cooperation for the resolution of environmental problems common to the respective parties to the conventions, be it in the medium of the sea, inland waters, the air or soils.

Most of these conventions have established secretariats of their own to take care of the work and the servicing of the Parties to the respective convention. A full list of the multilateral agreements already in force or pending, is published annually by UNEP in its *Register of International treaties and other agreements in the field of the environment* (latest issue, May 1985). The international institutional framework now in existence, however impressive in size and diversity it might seem to be, is yet by no means perfect as a tool for environmental diplomacy. We can therefore probably foresee further efforts of organizational and legal ingenuity on the part of diplomacy to sharpen the instruments.

3   Governmental readiness to act in international cooperation

But the hub of the matter is, of course, the use you make of this framework. Here it is much more difficult to recapitulate a success story, although there are exceptions. This is especially the case if you look for concrete problems which have to be addressed. I do not think it is fair to hold environmental diplomats responsible for this relative failure, although more skilful diplomatic capability might be in the hands of those governments that take a cautious or even negative attitude towards concrete international cooperation in the field of the environment than in the hands of those governments which actively promote such cooperation.

So, not surprisingly, behind it all is the will and power of national governments to use diplomay for constructive, concerted action.

It is quite evident that most governments hitherto have seen the large numbers of resolutions, decisions, recommendations and agreements which have come out of the diplomatic process inside the institutional framework, as end products. Their will, readiness and capacity to implement what they therein have consented to do is, indeed, less evident.

There are numerous examples of lack of will and preparedness among governments to address concretely environmental issues in international cooperation. Many regard such cooperation as an infringement on the sovereign rights of the nations they are respectively trying to govern. In theory and words they may subscribe to the famous Principle 21 of the 1972 Stockholm Declaration, which reads:

> States have, in accordance with the Charter of the United Nations and the principles of international law, the sovereign right to exploit their own resources pursuant to their own environmental policies, *and the responsibility to ensure that activities within their jurisdiction or control do not cause damage to the environment of other States or of areas beyond the limits of national jurisdiction.* (My italics.)

When it comes to practice and deeds, however, the second part of the principle is far too often disregarded. And, of course, it is precisely this part that constitutes the basic prerequisite for diplomatic action and international environmental law.

It is by no means surprising that national governments tend to be more or less reluctant to take responsibility for what might be environmental effects beyond their borders and outside their jurisdiction which results from activities inside those borders. After all, their political responsibilities, as they see them, are foremost towards their own citizens. National governments tend mainly to react internationally when it is clear that sources of pollutants that affect the environment or the health of citizens inside the borders of their own jurisdiction stem from abroad. A precondition for joint international action is, therefore, in most cases, met when it becomes clear to governments involved that they are exporters *as well as* importers of pollutants.

4 Diplomacy and the problem of transboundary air pollution: a case study of SO_2

A very good case in point is the development of international cooperation in the field of transboundary air pollution in the ECE region. When, in the course of the last few years, it was established beyond doubt via EMEP statistics that all countries in the region were both – more or less – 'victims' and 'aggressors' in the non-intended chemical warfare waged with SO_2, parties to the framework Geneva Convention on Long-range Trans-boundary Air Pollution (below referred to as LRTAP Convention) were ready to seriously negotiate reductions of emissions of this chemical compound. Those parties to the Convention which are preponderantly 'aggressors' and only to a marginal or lesser extent 'victims', owing to their geographical position in relation to heavy industrial areas and predominant wind patterns, have been the ones to drag their feet in these negotiations.

Consequently the governments of those countries which are down-wind and are getting much or most of their acid depositions imported from SO_2 emission sources abroad have been in the vanguard for promoting international concerted action with the purpose of alleviating the pressure on the environment in their own countries.

The intensive diplomatic activities employed by the ECE governments (which are all, but for a few exceptions, Parties to the LRTAP Convention) to reach the signing of the Protocol on SO_2 emission reductions, afford a good example of the subject matter of this paper. The history of these activities has been dealt with from various angles (see for example *Pollution across Borders: Acid Rain – Acid Diplomacy*, Proceedings of a Conference, Ed. John E. Carroll, University of New Hampshire, 1984). There can be no 'final' history until 1993, when it should be possible to assess the real effects of these diplomatic efforts. By 1993 (at the latest) the Contracting Parties shall, namely, according to the obligation in the Protocol (article 2), have reduced their national annual emissions of SO_2 by at least 30 %, based on the emission levels of 1980.

I shall not here endeavour to write a 'mid-term' evaluation of a history, which started at the end of the 1960s and went on to the signing of the SO_2 Protocol in 1985. The function of the chronological table below, which is by no means complete and only gives the crucial developments, is only to give a background to a discussion on how diplomacy has been used to promote the resolution of a specific environmental problem, i.e. that of acid rain.

Late   Swedish scientist Svante Odén demonstrated the inter-relationship
1960s   between SO_2 emissions outside Swedish borders and the acidification of lakes within Sweden.

1972   Sweden's case study for the UN Conference on the Human Environment in Stockholm dealt with 'Air pollution across national boundaries. The impact on the environment of sulphur in air and precipitation'. The immediate interest for this issue from other participant governments was nil or neglible.

1972–7 The OECD study of the long-range transport of sulphur pollution (under Norwegian leadership) established that long-range transport of pollution takes place and also that international concerted actions are required to combat transboundary air pollution.

1976–9 The Soviet Union proposed within the framework of the CSCE process a number of high-level meetings among ECE members, *inter alia* on environmental problems. After two years of negotiations a high-level meeting was held in Geneva in 1979 on *inter alia* the subject of transboundary air pollution, when the LRTAP Convention was also signed by 34 ECE governments.

1977– Establishment of an international (European) program for measuring movements of air pollution, in the first instance sulphur compounds across international borders (EMEP). The program produces annual accounts of the quantities of sulphur pollution deposited in each country and its countries of origin.

1977–8 OECD study of the costs and benefits of SO_2 control, indicating that costs of reductions of this compound are offset by benefits up to quite a high level of control.

1982   International conference in Stockholm on Acidification of the Environment, where broad agreement among the 20 participant governments was reached on the effects of long-range transport of sulphur compounds and on the need for strengthened and internationally-coordinated action to reduce emissions.

1983   The LRTAP Convention came into force. As of September 1985, 32 Parties have ratified.

1983   Proposal by Finland, Norway, Sweden (and Denmark, with reservation for possible EC position) at the first meeting of the Executive Body (EB) of the LRTAP Convention for at least a 30 % reduction of SO_2 emissions before 1993, using the 1980 emission levels as a basis.

1983   EEC recommendations concerning SO_2 (and NO_x) emission reductions.

1984   In Ottawa 10 countries met in March at a ministerial level and committed themselves *inter alia* to reduce their SO_2 emissions along the lines proposed by the Nordic countries in 1983.

1984   At a multilateral Conference with ECE members at a ministerial level in Munich in June, 18 countries both from East and West committed themselves to the 30 % reduction target and the Conference agreed that these commitments should be defined in a specific agreement.

1984–5 Such a specific agreement was negotiated by a working group under the EB and was adopted by the EB at its third meeting in Helsinki in July 1985 as a Protocol within the framework of the LRTAP Convention. 21 Parties to the Convention have so far (September 1985) signed the Protocol, which will enter into force when 16 signatories have ratified the instrument.

This skeleton history, covering roughly 15 years, of the efforts of some 30 governments to come to grips with *one* chemical compound which is active in the process of the acidification of the environment in the ECE region, gives us a good opportunity to analyse the role and methods of work of environmental diplomacy.

The foremost observation one can make is that many venues and paths have to be used to bring a problem to the attention of the national decision-makers and the international community supposedly involved. As Sweden and (somewhat later) Norway were the countries in Europe which first observed that they were 'victims' of air pollution from sources abroad, they tried initially to bring this problem to the attention of the world community via the UN Conference on the Human Environment. That venue was evidently premature. Then they tried to involve in their cause the technical and scientific expertise of the Western industrialized countries via the *OECD* and gained some positive and usable results. Then, new efforts were made to anchor the problem in political quarters both in the West and the East. The opportunity arose in the aftermath of the 1975 Helsinki

Agreement on Security and Cooperation in Europe (CSCE). The East European socialist countries wished to set off Western pressure on basket-three issues (human rights, freedom of information, culture, etc.) *inter alia* by promoting basket-two issues (trade, scientific exchange, environment, etc.). This brought the ECE into the focus of negotiations, and after some years the process ended in a general acceptance among ECE governments of the existence of a problem. This acceptance became codified in the LRTAP Convention. For the East European side, to which the substance was not a priority matter, this was a clear foreign political gain, demonstrating the viability of the CSCE process. For the West European and North American side, where a majority of governments were lukewarm or downright negative at that time to do anything which could entail costly investments, the Convention, with its watered down demands for action, was a cheap price for showing good international will. For the, at that time, still very few governments which took the issue seriously, such as Scandinavia, the Netherlands, Canada and also the US, the Convention constituted a major breakthrough in their search for widened political visibility of the transboundary acid rain issue.

The growing evidence of the negative effects of acidification on forests in Central Europe, combined with changing political patterns in the Federal Republic of Germany through the first years of the 1980s, very quickly changed the forces for and against taking concrete international action towards combating air pollution. The political temperature for action rose and was used *inter alia* first by Sweden at the 1982 Stockholm Conference on Acidification of the Environment, by West Germany, the Netherlands and Denmark *within the EC framework* and by Canada (perhaps, mainly, to put pressure on the US, which by then had joined the doubters about the transboundary nature and negative effects of sulphur pollution) to convene like-minded countries to the Ottawa Conference. The East–West breakthrough came soon after. In the wake of the missile deployment crises the government of West Germany, responding to signals from the Soviet Union for retaining some forum for East–West talks, invited ECE member governments to a Multilateral Conference on the Causes and Prevention of Damage to Forests and Waters by Air Pollution in Europe, which was held in Munich in June 1984. At that conference the Soviet Union and its allies saw the opportunity to gain growing political influence in Western Europe by playing on the negative positions of the US and the UK on concerted actions to reduce emissions of sulphur compounds. The price that the socialist countries in search for such influence had to pay was to commit themselves to the 30 % SO_2 reduction target (thereby, of course, also having in mind the relief of their own heavily-acidified environments). This commitment was successfully played upon by the Ottawa group of governments in the ensuing negotiations *within the framework of the EB of the LRTAP Convention*, which ended with the signing of the Protocol in Helsinki.

To these many venues should also be added a great number of international *seminars and symposia on various scientific, technical and economic aspects of the acid rain issue*, arranged by various interested governments. Furthermore, the multilateral venues here referred to have, of course, been supported by an *active bilateral diplomacy* by many governments involved over the period. Seen in a Swedish context, the bilateral environmental agreements, which Sweden has signed with the Soviet Union and some of the East European countries, have to a growing extent focused on acidification problems. The sometimes acid diplomatic exchanges between Canada and the US on this issue are also well known, to mention a few of many instances.

Another point, however trite, I wish to make from this example is that environmental diplomacy in its basic character is no special branch of diplomacy, if you consider its modes and methods of work. The substance might no doubt be unusual stuff, perhaps even *terra incognita*, to traditional diplomacy. The sensitive spots from a foreign political point of view are often, for most traditionally schooled diplomats, hidden in difficult technical/scientific documentation. But when these spots are detected and brought into the light, diplomacy again is on its old, usual ground. Diplomacy again comes into play in the service of national interests – however perceived – always looking for common bottom lines of opposing or like-minded interests of other nations concerned, as spelled out by respective governments, to establish or keep an acceptable *modus vivendi* in the international community.

A further obvious point to make is that it takes a long time to reach agreements in cases where concrete, often expensive, actions are presupposed to be taken by the parties to an agreement. One may reflect on the risks that the slow pace of the work of multilateral diplomacy in the field of the environment might delay action until a time when the problems involved are already beyond control. Again, one has to accept that there are no constructive alternatives to diplomacy when many governments are involved and that the pace of the diplomatic process is wholly dependent on the insights, will and capacities of the national governments concerned.

Then, as a Swede, I might also be permitted to make a final, however parochial, observation on this special case history. Our initial quest for concerted international action to address this very important issue for Sweden and, as it later turned out, for many other European countries, has on the whole been very successful. I do not pretend that this is solely the outcome of very good Swedish diplomacy. The changing political contexts over time, the growing evidence of the damaging effects of sulphur emissions on soils, waters, historical monuments and also on human health, have successively helped us out of our earlier diplomatic isolation in this specific field. Still, the example shows that pertinacity and readiness to grab and use up-coming political opportunities may yield good results, not only for the initial plaintiff but also for other countries and the general ambience of international cooperation.

5   The coordination problem

The case study on SO_2 as described in the foregoing section, however, does not properly lend itself to formulating a general observation, which should be common to most diplomats who have their main experience from the work in the governing council of UNEP, the results of which observation are then supposed to be spread through the UN system at large.

In the introductory section of this paper I briefly mentioned the fact that environmental problems are related to human activities in most sectors of life, that they do not constitute a sector of their own, and that this poses special difficulties for diplomacy in the management of international cooperation in the field of the environment.

Most governments would surely admit the difficulties they meet in handling national environmental issues through their own administrative systems, which are as a rule organized on a sectorial basis. Ministers for environmental affairs have to bring to the attention of their colleagues responsible for industry, physical planning, agriculture, energy and even finance, to mention but a few relevant sectors of government, the environmental dimensions and consequences of policies and actions in these sectors. This often entails a complicated coordinating process for environmental legislation and management.

In the international field the same sectoral structure prevails and the same coordinating problems arise. The matter is, however, complicated further by the lack of *one* unifying government. In the UN sphere, environmental diplomacy is mainly concentrated on the work of the governing council of UNEP in Nairobi. But the UN Systemwide Environmental Programme (SWMTEP), which the governing council proposes for adoption by the UN General Assembly, has then to be implemented and to a varying degree financed by a great number of operative agencies within the UN system, such as the FAO, UNDP, WMO, IMO, UNESCO, just to mention a few of the more important agencies cooperating in the program. Of course, UNEP has had numerous inter-secretariat contacts with these agencies before presenting the program to its governing council. But in order to secure implementation by the operative agencies it is important and at times necessary that their governing boards are also prepared to support and adopt the environmental elements proposed in the respective programs of these agencies.

This complicated system can only function properly if the governments taking part in the work of the governing council of UNEP are prepared to support the environmental programs there agreed upon, not only in the General Assembly, but also in the various governing boards of the relevant operative agencies. This means that governments have to coordinate at home their conduct in all concerned fora, or, as the saying goes in UNEP headquarters in Nairobi: 'Coordination begins at home'.

This necessary coordinating work in capitals rarely works as it should, if it even takes place at all. That this should be so is by no means surprising, considering the number of different ministries and interests and hence representatives of those participating in the international work. Perhaps an efficient multilateral international cooperation on such a scale and of such complexity is beyond the capacity of any administrative management system?

For my purpose here it may suffice to point out that the complexities described do severely hamper the work of environmental diplomacy at large in multilateral fora and particularly those in the UN system. Preparatory work and feedback processing for coordination put a heavy extra burden on environmental diplomacy, which competes with the attention to the proper function of this diplomacy, i.e. negotiations between governments with the purpose of addressing and hopefully solving international environmental problems.

Somehow, these difficulties have to be overcome. The UN and the UN system has become increasingly important during the past decade and it is perhaps the only possible instrument for joint efforts by member states to cope with the large-scale environmental problems, such as soil erosion, protection of genetic diversity and the build up of CO_2 in the atmosphere. And these problems are closely connected with the long-term survival of mankind.

6 Environment and international security

I mentioned in the introductory section that the concept of 'environmental diplomacy' – partly because of its novelty – has yet to be established and accepted as a household word in the ministries for foreign affairs.

One may wonder why the evident threats to humanity, which the ongoing large-scale destruction of the global environment might imply, have not evoked more anxiety and reaction in foreign policy quarters. Threats of similar magnitude, such as the risks of nuclear war or the imbalance between developed and developing countries, have led to impressive responses in ministries for foreign affairs all over the world. For these purposes they have established large departments, staffed with highly competent people and with large resources allocated to them, which have the full and day-to-day attention of foreign ministers, prime ministers and presidents. These threats are also the dominant themes in the general debates of the UN General Assembly and in other lofty fora, where statesmen of the world and their colleagues of lesser status meet in efforts to prevent our mutual destruction and bring about a safer world to live in.

I do not deny the importance of these threats, nor do I question the need for this massive response on behalf of national and world diplomacy. The foreign political attention given and the diplomatic capacity allotted to meet the comparable environmental threats to mankind, are, however, beyond all comparison. Having had the privilege of participating actively in the field of environmental diplomacy over the last five years, I well know how very limited are the resources in personnel and other capacities allocated for this branch of foreign policy in most if not all governmental chanceries. Offices for international environmental affairs are not only small and understaffed but often organizationally hidden as subdivisions of departments, which have their main attention elsewhere. One writer, Philip W. Quigg, described in his book *A Pole Apart* the US State Department Bureau of Oceans and Environmental and Scientific Affairs as a 'grab bag of left over missions that have not found a place elsewhere'. I can assure you that this is a realistic description of the situation in many or most of the ministries for foreign affairs around the globe. Further, if you read through the speeches delivered by ministers for foreign affairs or heads of government in the general debates of the UN General Assembly over the last decade, you will find very few references to the environmental situation and still more rarely will you find these references given a prominent place.

I think it is proper when dealing with the subject matter of this paper to dwell briefly on why this is so.

One obvious partial explanation is the relatively recent awareness of the existence of a problem of regional or even global magnitude. Rachel Carson with her book *Silent Spring* was certainly not the first to present a message on the environmental issue to us, but she was no doubt one of the first to reach a wide audience and hence help to bring about visibility of the issue in political quarters. But that was only 25 years ago, which is not a very long time to get new perceptions of the world we live in firmly rooted.

Another explanation is the magnitude of the problems combined with a feeling that international environmental issues somehow are very long-term issues, which will not have to be attended to immediately or at least not before the next election. Both these elements strongly provoke ostrich behaviour among decision-makers.

Further, it is quite evident that the scientific explanations of what is really happening to the biosphere under constant pressure from man's activities often differ and that scientific schools of thought are at loggerheads on many issues. There are also many competing views on what you could and should do to redress the imbalance in nature. This also, naturally and understandably, promotes a wait-and-see attitude among governments.

Furthermore, these are politically very sensitive issues. Economic growth and employment are often considered to be in jeopardy, at least in the short run, if we give too much attention and resources to environmental protection. In many developing countries the options are often much more brutal. Who is there to decide on the deaths of perhaps millions of people as the cost of safeguarding a sustainable natural resource base for future generations?

This may suffice for an understanding of why governments tend to be less prone to crisis consciousness about the large environmental issues and do not act as they try to do in other areas threatening international security and human survival.

Is there no way to bring the looming environmental issues to the close attention of the power centres of the world? Attracting such attention seems to be necessary if we are to see serious efforts and resources set aside to solve or at least contain the major international environmental problems, using or not using diplomacy as part of such efforts.

A number of influential writers and reports from prestigious international committees and commissions have pointed out the risks to international security from the ongoing environmental degradation and the non-sustainable use of living natural resources. They have stressed that security is a wider concept than that of military security alone, that the growing imbalance between man and nature threatens the well-being and thus the security of all nations. They have pointed out that the resource scarcities and ecological stresses constitute real and imminent challenges to peace, that those challenges are fundamentally non-military, and that it is imperative that they should be addressed accordingly.

This widened security concept, although it seems to be reasonably clear and relevant to the problems facing mankind, evidently still lacks something in quality to make it accepted by experts on international security issues or to function as a basic concept for international crisis management. It might be that the economic, social and political inter-relationships with the funda-mental imbalances developing in the interaction between man and his environment are so complicated that only the symptoms and effects of this imbalance and not the underlying causes become visible.

So far, the literature on these inter-relationships seems to me to be mainly of a descriptive character, covering areas such as the ongoing African drought crisis, its roots and consequences, the motives behind and impacts of the rapid devastation of tropical rain forests and the projected conse-quences of the build-up of CO_2 in the atmosphere, or historical studies on the long-term fate of ancient empires and civilizations which based their economies and cultures on large-scale irrigation systems that salted their soils to deserts.

Such studies often are fascinating and at times terrifying to read, but serve mainly as background documentation. What is needed seems to be better analytical work which lays bare the crucial links between environmental degradation and social, economic and political destabilization. Major con-certed research efforts involving ecologists, economists, sociologists, political scientists, conflict researchers and representatives of other relevant disci-plines need to be directed towards such analytical work and the results must be presented in terms familiar to politicians and experts on international security issues. Such joint research might help governments to perceive

more clearly the role that forceful efforts to redress the ongoing environmental destruction could play in preventing build-up of international crises,
which because of their fundamental causes could be difficult to control and
contain.

7 Summing up

This paper has briefly touched upon some of the aspects relevant to
the use of diplomacy for the resolution of environmental problems. My
purpose has not been to give an exhaustive description of how and in which
circumstances diplomacy could make a valuable contribution. I have felt that
it might be more useful to concentrate on factors which tend to constrain
national governments' use of diplomacy for this purpose. These constraints,
it seems to me, have to be seriously considered and overcome if constructive
international joint actions in this very important field of international affairs
is to have a chance of becoming more successful than has hitherto been the
case.

Part III

The case of acid rain

9

The acid rain issue in Canadian–American relations: a commentary

John E. Carroll

Department of Forest Resources, University of New Hampshire

Awareness of an acid rain problem began to arise in Canada in the late 1970s and in portions of the US in the early 1980s. Careful study of the geological, geographical and geopolitical context of the acidic pollution in Canada relative to that of the US gives clear evidence as to why there is and indeed logically should be a decided difference in both awareness of and attitude toward acid rain between these two nations and their peoples.

Canada is the complainant on the North American acid rain scene for a number of very good reasons:

1. Canada is one of the most vulnerable nations on earth when it comes to damage from acid deposition, in both aquatic and terrestrial environments. Like Sweden and Finland in Europe, Canada's geology is composed largely of granitic shield bedrock as old as the Precambrian period; it is thus already largely acidic in nature and has very little buffering protection from further acidic deposition. It further supports a vast territory of highly acid-vulnerable spruce-fir forest. Canada's few well-buffered or well-protected areas are the exception rather than the rule, and include only the prairies of the interior, desert valleys in British Columbia, the agricultural districts of south-western Ontario, the island of Montreal, Prince Edward Island, and a

few other places. The vast portion of Canada, peopled and unpeopled, is very vulnerable to damage from acidity, a fact well known to Canadians.

The US is quite the opposite, or at least thus far perceives itself to be (which is the same thing in diplomacy and politics). The only US regions which perceive themselves to be vulnerable are the New England states, New York, Wisconsin and Minnesota. Much of the rest of the nation has buffering protection or believes itself to have such protection (although unpopulated high-elevation forest areas such as the Great Smoky Mountains of North Carolina and Tennessee, the Cascades of Oregon and Washington, and areas of the Rockies clearly are vulnerable to damage).

For these reasons of geological differences, the people of the US are significantly less aware of and less interested in acid rain and its possible effects than are their Canadian neighbors. Given that many Americans across a vast portion of the country are also dependent on the problem-causing gaseous emissions for the sustenance of their economies, there is additionally a lack of openness to learning about the problem in these regions.

2. A second factor underlying Canada's complaint is the imbalance of pollutants moving back and forth across the border. While both nations contribute to each other's acidity, the US is responsible for at least 50 % of Canada's total acid deposition, spread over a vast area. Canada is responsible for less than 20 % of US acidic deposition, and this is largely restricted to northern New York and New England. Thus, Canadians know that regardless of how much sacrifice they may make to curb their own emissions, they will still suffer over 50 % of their damage. The imbalance is indeed so great that in common discussion Canadians always associate acid rain with the US and the problems in Canadian–US relations, even in spite of their awareness of their own considerable pollution sources. This imbalance in pollution flux (movement) across the border is not a point of disagreement between the two countries, as it has been admitted from the beginning by the US Environmental Protection Agency. However, it contributes to the resentment of the Canadian people as the complainants in the dispute.

3. As a result of their down-wind position and vulnerable environment, the Canadian people have been far more aware of the problem, its causes, its likely effects, and its involvement in bilateral relations than have the American people. Media saturation and wide public discussion and debate over acid rain in Canada starting in 1978 led to an awareness differential as high as 85 % awareness among the Canadian population to only 15 % by

the American population by about 1980. Today's differential is perhaps 90 % Canadian – 50 % US. The only area of the US which has an awareness level approaching that of Canada is New England, an area with strong Canadian identification. The feeling of the Canadian people of being 'dumped upon' by uncaring American neighbors significantly exacerbates the problem.

4. Canada is more dependent on forest products and forest exports than virtually any nation in the world. Forest products (pulp and paper, newsprint, lumber, etc.) is critical to the economic well-being of all Canadians. Canada already has significant disadvantages in its forest industries (old and outdated infrastructure, cold climate, short growing season, very high labor costs in the woods, etc.). To the extent that acid rain either retards the growth of commercially valuable forests or kills the trees outright, Canadian society needs to have deep concern over the future welfare of the forest in that it relates to the future welfare of the nation. North American forests are today suffering (both in growth rate declines and dieback). While narrow cause and effect linkage with acid rain has not been proven, it is likely that acid rain, ozone, drought and other stress, much of it from air pollution, is now taking its toll. Scientists in general and foresters in particular are worried, and it is a forest-dependent nation like Canada which is first to respond to that worry, since in Canada it affects all echelons of society. Although the US has considerable forest industry and commercially valuable forests, concerns in the US are significantly diluted and forest products constitutes a much smaller proportion of the national economy.

5. A factor not well understood by Americans but close to the hearts of Canadians is the acid pollution impact and particularly the aquatic damage discovered in the Muskoka Lakes – Haliburton Highlands Region of Ontario, an area which is perhaps as close as any one area could be to a culture hearth for the Canadian people. Here, Canada's best painters (including the Group of Seven), novelists, storytellers, poets and others practised their art. The very lakes and forests which form the setting for that art are now at stake, and much of the arriving acidic pollution comes from the US. The generations-old ownership of summer cottages on these lakes by the most prominent of Canadians also contributes a degree of personal concern in high places. While this famous and beautiful lakes region and its potential loss may not have quite the same effect as the loss of the Black Forest to the Germans, there is perhaps some analogy which Europeans and others can well understand. The people of the US do not now feel such a

threat to anything which could be considered to be such a universally beloved resource.

Thus, for these reasons and because of the cost of significantly reducing emissions, there has been an insufficient constituency in the US to take action to reduce emissions, although there has been a sufficient constituency to insure further publically funded research into acid rain effects, and perhaps a constituency to support some research and development into low-polluting coal-burning technologies. Canada's considerable grass-roots constituency for action has led to Canada's steady international leadership on this question, and to its strong linkages in this matter to Sweden, Norway and other like-minded nations. In contrast, although the US position might be likened to that of the UK, the US administration has paid relatively little attention to the issue and has helped to overcome the consistent demand from New England, New York and a few other areas that action be taken.

Canada under the Trudeau Government had been a very outspoken and visible leader on the acid rain question, demanding, in bilateral diplomatic fora, in multilateral diplomatic fora and through its encouragement of citizen diplomacy, that very tangible action be taken to reduce emissions. The Mulroney Government now in power, though representing the same grass-roots constituency of acid rain concern, is significantly less vocal on the question, since it has other priorities, including a bilateral free trade agreement, that could be threatened by acid rain and other irritants in the relationship. Leadership on acid rain in Canada has now shifted to the scientific community and citizens organizations, while the Ottawa government seeks quietly to maintain all former commitments and positions, such as 50 % reduction in SO_2 emission over ten years and Canada's membership in Europe's '30 % Club'.

The US position opposing emissions reduction is gradually softening (though very gradually) and a long-term consensus to eventually reduce emissions may be obtained soon. The Reagan Administration in the Spring of 1986 for the first time admitted to the existence of the problem (in contrast to a consistent five-year stand that it might be a problem but that more research was needed). Further, the Reagan Administration pledged to the Mulroney Government a commitment to underwrite the cost of research into new low-polluting coal-burning technologies over the next several years. In the meantime, various US downwind states are taking their own actions to curb emissions within their borders, in the hope this sacrifice will ultimately lead to support for broader measures in the up-wind high pollution-emitting states.

Most discussions in North America about resolution of the problem revolve around wet sulfur scrubbers, a high capital-intensive and expensive technology with its own set of environmental costs, and fuel-switching, which in North America means increasing dependency on low-sulfur coal, largely from the West. The latter technique would be economically disastrous for the Mid-western industrial heartland with its great reserves of high sulfur coal, and environmentally disastrous for the water-scarce West where most of the low-sulfur coal is found.

Some discussion has taken place around coal pre-washing before burning, a utility operational technique known as least-emissions dispatching (which means placing base-load electricity generating capacity on newer, less-polluting but more costly to operate plants, and placing peak-load generating capacity on older, more-polluting, but less expensive to operate plants; it is the opposite of today's practice, which is known as least-cost dispatching). These two techniques, especially together with energy conservation, can lead to some pollution reductions (30 % or so) but not of the order of magnitude (50 %) called for by Canada, Sweden, New England, or American environmentalists.

The North American debate continues to rage around proof of cause and effect, the uncertain role of acid rain in conjunction with other pollutants and natural sources, who is doing what to whom, what will the cost be, who should pay the cost, and what is the best remedy. Remedies are being addressed almost exclusively in terms of a 'technological fix'. There has been virtually no suggestion in North America, not even in Canada, a most endangered complainant, that the problem, its consequences, and therefore its remedies, may be much bigger and broader than has been assumed. That there may indeed be a linkage between acid rain, nuclear waste storage issues, toxic air pollution, toxic water and groundwater aquifer contamination, water pollution derived from air pollution, and even air pollution toxics in some instances being derived from water pollution, in the Great Lakes and elsewhere in North America. That acid rain and these other problems may only be symptomatic of the heavy pressure now being exerted by both Americans and Canadians on their environment. And that acid rain or similar alternative problems and their consequences may have to be accepted if that pressure continues.

Be that as it may, North American lakes, forests, agricultural crops, buildings and statuary, human health and ecosystems in general are being impacted. Because that impact is unbalanced between two countries, Canada and the US, and because one has considerable capacity to damage the other, we have in North America a very considerable transboundary environmental problem and a challenge for those who practise the art of environmental diplomacy.

10

Balancing the interests:
an essay on the Canadian–American
acid rain debate

Michael S. McMahon

Benesch, Friedlander, Coplan & Aronoff, Cleveland, Ohio.

1 Introduction

The acid rain issue has developed into one of the most intractable issues of this decade. The issue has been identified by Canada's minister of the environment as the 'single most important irritant in US–Canadian relations'. In the US, the acid rain debate has raised some of the most divisive and irreconcilable regional differences since the American Civil War. The debate has risen to a level of such intensity, both in the US and internationally, that the participants in the debate frequently focus their attention on attacking and defending relatively insignificant points in the hope and out of fear that the entire issue will be settled once and for all. Participants have resorted to emotional appeals, intellectual obfuscation, half-truths and every other imaginable rhetorical technique, which demonstrates how high the stakes are perceived to be.

The purpose of this essay is to provide an analysis of arguments in the Canadian–American acid rain debate from the perspective of those parties confronted by demands that they make costly reductions in their sulfur dioxide (SO_2) emissions. In the context of the Canadian–American debate, this refers to the US. In the context of the debate within the US, this refers to (1) the electric utility industry, which accounts for roughly two-thirds of the American SO_2 emissions and (2) the mid-western states, principally Ohio, Indiana, Illinois, Kentucky and West Virginia, which have been targeted by proposed legislation for the bulk of the emission reductions. One of the principal failures of these groups has been their inability to impress upon the course of the acid rain debate the magnitude and significance of the accomplishments they have already made in SO_2 control. This paper provides a description of what the American electric utilities and the American Mid-west have accomplished and why they resist current proposals for acid rain control.

This essay analyzes the positions of three groups. The first position is the one held by the parties, identified above, who must respond to demands for further emission reductions. To understand their position, one must have an understanding of the US Clean Air Act. This Act provides detailed mechanisms for SO_2 control in the US. A review of the framework of the Act and its implementation is necessary to understand where SO_2 control in the US has been, where it is now, and where it will be in the future. The second position is the one taken by Canada, which has repeatedly professed a strong interest in this debate. The third position is the interest of the environment, i.e. the scientific imperative for acid rain legislation.

It is important to distinguish between the interests of those who purport to represent the environment and the interests of the environment itself. The environmentalist is an advocate. The environmentalist's role is to advance the abstract interest of the environment, and to do so without regard to the impact on other public interests, in the same way that an attorney zealously promotes the interests of a client. The interest of the environment itself, however, must be determined as a matter of overall public policy, competing against the welter of other public interests. Phrased in another manner, there is no absolute interest in environmental protection. Environmental protection is undoubtedly a strong interest of which society must remain ever cognizant, but it is by no means an absolute interest.

This is a necessary concept because it may determine the outcome of the acid rain debate or, at the very least, provide a reassessment of the arguments used in the debate. Carried to its logical conclusion, an absolutist position on environmental protection would force human activities to cease. This very issue arose in the US, in another context, during the 1960s and 1970s when the interest of environmental protection began to challenge the previously near-absolute public interest in economic growth. Just as the interest of economic growth ultimately was determined to have its limits, the swing of the pendulum now provides an opportunity for the US to determine the limits of society's interest in environmental protection. The happy medium is, no doubt, robust economic growth within the confines of environmental protection. Where ascendency of either interest threatens the vitality of the other, this balance must be redressed.

The American electric utility industry provides a good case study to examine the balancing of these interests. It is the public policy of the US, set into law in many states decades ago, that electric utility companies must provide electricity to consumers upon demand. State regulatory boards scrutinize pricing and distribution to ensure that electricity is not so expensive as to be unavailable to any segment of the population. Commencing, in a significant way, with enactment of the Clean Air Act in 1970, electric utility companies must now meet the mandate of universal production and distribution within the confines of environmental protection.

2   The Clean Air Act of the US

The Clean Air Act is the comprehensive vehicle for the control of air pollution in the US. This Act, with its implementing regulations, is probably the strongest and most detailed piece of air pollution control legislation in the world. The structure of the Act, as it now exists, was adopted in 1970. Significant amendments were made to the Act in 1977 to deal with issues which arose during the first years of implementation.

The structure of the Clean Air Act reflects the desire of Congress to set national standards within the context of statewide control. The need for national standards was indicated by the manner in which previous attempts at local or even statewide control of air pollution had failed. Local entities were unable to accept the possibility that new, or even existing, businesses would locate elsewhere, thereby depriving local citizens of their employment. Out of the fear that 'pollution havens' would develop to attract industry away from states with tough air control programs, the need for uniform national standards was accepted.

The rationale for allowing the states to administer the national standards developed out of several considerations. First, some states desired to impose air quality standards more stringent than the national standards, irrespective of the loss of jobs. This discretion was left to the states. Second, Congress realized that requiring the states to implement the program lessened federal expenditures. Third, state government is viewed as having a better understanding of local concerns than the federal government. The concept of a completely national program was too great a departure from the American federal system of government for Congress to accept. Therefore, the states were permitted to administer the national standards, or more stringent state standards, subject to the supervision of the federal government.

2.1   Requirements on existing sources

Section 108 of the Clean Air Act requires the Administrator of the Environmental Protection Agency (EPA) to list those air pollutants which the Administrator determines may reasonably endanger public health or welfare. The Administrator must collect scientific studies on the identifiable effects of the listed pollutants on public health and welfare and determine the cost of various pollution control techniques. The Administrator must issue a criteria document containing this information within 12 months after a pollutant is listed.

Section 109 of the Act requires the Administrator to set national ambient air quality standards (NAAQS) for each criteria pollutant. There are two types of NAAQS. A primary NAAQS must be set at the level of ambient air quality which, based on the criteria documents and allowing an adequate margin of safety, will protect the public health. A secondary NAAQS must be set at that level of ambient air quality which, based on the criteria document, will protect the public welfare from any known or anticipated adverse effects associated with the presence of the pollutant in the ambient air. The Administrator is required to complete a thorough review every five years of the criteria documents and the NAAQS to reflect the latest scientific knowledge. The Administrator has issued primary and secondary NAAQS for the following pollutants: sulfur oxides (including SO_2), particulate matter, CO, ozone, NO_2, and lead.

The NAAQS establish ceilings which are not to be exceeded anywhere in the US. The primary NAAQS for SO_2 are: (1) an annual arithmetic mean of 80 micrograms per cubic meter (0.03 parts per million); and (2) a maximum 24-hour concentration of 365 micrograms per cubic meter (0.14 parts per million) not to be exceeded more than once per year. The secondary

NAAQS for SO_2 is a maximum three-hour concentration of 1300 micrograms per cubic meter (0.5 parts per million) not to be exceeded more than once per year. The Administrator will eventually consider whether a one-hour primary NAAQS is necessary.

The NAAQS are not enforced directly against specific polluters; rather, the NAAQS are used to determine appropriate emission limitations for individual sources of pollutants. These limitations are the core of the state implementation plans (SIP). The SIP is the key tool for the control of air pollution and the major vehicle for state involvement in air pollution control. Section 110 of the Act places primary responsibility on the states for the control of air pollution from specific sources and development of the SIP. The Administrator of EPA reviews each SIP, and each SIP revision, to determine that certain basic elements are included. For example, the SIP must provide for the attainment of the primary NAAQS within three years of the date of approval of the SIP, and provide for the attainment of the secondary NAAQS within a reasonable time. The SIP must contain emission limitations for pollutant sources and schedules of compliance for the sources to meet those limitations. The SIP must contain monitoring programs, enforcement procedures and a demonstration that the state will commit adequate personnel, funding and legal authority to carry out the SIP. Should the state fail to prepare a SIP within the statutory deadline, or fail to include all the required elements, the Administrator has the authority, which he has exercised on several occasions, to issue a SIP or a portion of a SIP that does meet the requirements.

Each state has wide discretion to devise the control strategy used in the SIP and to allocate emission reductions among sources, if necessary, so long as each SIP contains the required elements. The states may use the SIP to protect certain industries considered as important to the state at the expense of other industries deemed to be less important by placing more lenient controls on the valued industries. The controls must still be sufficient to attain the NAAQS. Even if a state imposes an emission limitation that is technologically or economically infeasible, the source has no recourse with the federal government. The US Supreme Court has held that the Administrator has no authority to examine the feasibility of the technology or economics of a particular control strategy selected by a state, so long as the strategy will attain the NAAQS. Although federal requirements remain the driving force behind the SIP, important decisions still remain in the hands of the state.

The specific emission limitations for sources are the elemental units of the SIP. Emission limitations are usually expressed in terms of the sulfur content of the fuel or in terms of the allowable pollutant output, such as pounds per MBtu actual heat input (or nanograms per joule heat input). Emission limitations must be adequate to ensure that the ambient air around the source will meet the NAAQS. This is done through computer modeling of atmospheric conditions, not through monitoring of actual conditions surrounding the facility. The computer models apply typical pollutant dispersion patterns under the worst case meteorological conditions to project an emission limitation that will attain the NAAQS even under the worst case meteorological conditions. Obviously, much depends on the type of model chosen and the biases inherent in the model. The models used are those approved by the Administrator or specially developed site-specific models which meet the modeling guidelines issued by the Administrator.

There are several modeling issues, some as yet undecided and others just recently decided, that could have the effect of making emission limitations more stringent. First, the number of years of atmospheric data used is important. Many sources were originally modeled with one or two years of data. Five years of data is now required. Additional years of data may reveal worse 'worst case' meteorological conditions, thereby allowing the formula to project a lower emissions limit.

Second, it has not been determined whether the modeling must be done in rolling averages of 24 hour periods for the primary SO_2 NAAQS (such as midnight to midnight, 1 am to 1 am, 2 am to 2 am, etc.) rather than the block averages (calendar day). The rolling averages technique, if it has any impact, can only reduce the emission limit by identifying additional 'violations' in time periods that are not examined when the model is run under block averages. There are other modeling issues in dispute but these give the flavor that any remodeling of a source's emissions will probably result in a lower emission limitation.

The Act, and its regulations, affect emission limitations in other ways. The stack height rules issued under Section 123 prevent an emission source from receiving credit in the modeling circulation for the height of the stack in excess of that determined by good engineering practice to be necessary to avoid the downwash of pollutants into the local ambient air. This requirement was imposed with the 1977 Amendments to prohibit the reliance upon dispersion techniques such as tall stacks rather than emission limits. Another dispersion technique prohibited by Section 123 is the use of intermittent control systems to vary emission rates with changes in atmospheric conditions so as to increase pollutant output where possible. In June 1985, the Administrator issued revised regulations to implement the Section 123 prohibition against the use of tall stacks and dispersion techniques. These new regulations and the accompanying remodeling are projected to reduce SO_2 emissions by 1.7 million tons (1.9 million metric tons) per year from current levels.

Section 126 of the Act prohibits a source from emitting a pollutant in amounts that will prevent the attainment or maintenance of a NAAQS in another state, even though the emissions do not violate a NAAQS in the source's state. In December, 1984, the Administrator denied a Section 126 petition from several New England states on the grounds that they were unable to demonstrate that SO_2 emissions from mid-western states prevented the attainment of any NAAQS in their states. This decision is currently being appealed in the courts.

The 1977 amendments to the Clean Air Act included several new requirements designed to bring certain areas that had not achieved the NAAQS into attainment. These so-called 'non-attainment plans' require states to impose reasonably available control measures on existing sources in a non-attainment area as expeditiously as possible and to provide for reasonable annual progress toward attainment of the NAAQS. These plans also require a new source capable of emitting specified amounts of a pollutant to demonstrate, among other things, that the source will achieve the lowest achievable emission rate before it can receive a permit to commence construction in the non-attainment area. These requirements have been effective in improving air quality since the non-attainment area designations were made in 1978.

The provisions of the Act discussed so far relate to the regulation of emissions from existing sources. The emphasis on these regulations is principally on the protection of local air quality. These provisions are what Congress deemed was necessary to protect the health and welfare of the US public. There are additional provisions of the Clean Air Act which, in the context of the acid rain debate, can only be described as the world's first comprehensive acid rain control program. The basic elements of this program are the new source performance standards (NSPS).

2.2 *Requirements on new sources: the acid rain program of the US*

Section 111 directs the Administrator to establish allowable emission

limitations for categories of fossil fuel fired stationary sources which reflect
the 'degree of emission reduction achievable through application of the best
system of continuous emission reduction which . . . the Administrator determines has been adequately demonstrated'. Any new source and any source
modified to change its method of operation must meet the NSPS emission
limitations. Needless to say, the NSPS limits are significantly more stringent
than emission limits designed only to meet the NAAQS.

The purpose of Congress in setting up this bifurcated system of control
was simple. The costs of retrofitting new pollution control technology on
existing sources which were not designed for such controls was, and is,
prohibitively expensive. Since existing sources should not endanger public
health, the NAAQS and other requirements became the environmental
parameters of their operations. New and modified sources, on the other
hand, have notice of the new, more stringent NSPS requirements and can
design their facilities with the new pollution equipment in mind, thereby
achieving a significant savings over the cost of retrofitting those devices onto
older facilities. Moreover, the Administrator must review the NSPS periodically and tighten the NSPS emission limitations if newer technology is
adequately demonstrated.

The current NSPS SO_2 emission limit for electric utility steam generating
units is 1.2 lbs/MBtu (520 nanograms per joule heat input). This should be
compared to average emission limits roughly three to six times higher at
many existing facilities. New sources must install scrubbers (flue gas
desulfurization units) as part of their pollution control and achieve a
70–90 % reduction in SO_2 emissions even if they can meet the 1.2 lbs/
MBtu limit without a scrubber.

It is obvious that the NSPS program is an acid rain control program in that
it mandates the minimization of SO_2 emissions over time. As older,
costly-to-operate facilities are retired in favor of newer, more efficient
facilities, total SO_2 emissions will decrease to the lowest levels technologically feasible. The NSPS system mandates the reduction of SO_2 emissions,
but it is flexible enough to accommodate new technologies of pollution
control that may emerge.

The NSPS system is not the only type of control faced by new sources.
The 1977 amendments imposed a program to prevent the significant
deterioration (PSD) of air quality in areas that happened to be cleaner than
the NAAQS. Congress deemed this to be necessary in order to prevent new
sources from locating in previously pristine areas and then polluting, at the

NSPS rate, up to the NAAQS. Section 165 of the Act requires a new source with the potential to emit more than 100 tons of a pollutant to undergo a new source review. A source can avoid new source review if it obtains, from existing sources, sufficient emission reduction to offset the expected emissions from the new facility.

New source review requires the potential source to demonstrate, prior to construction, that it will not violate any NAAQS, or any PSD increment. A PSD increment is the statutorily limited amount of emissions permitted above current air quality, as defined according to type of area. The restrictions imposed by the limited availability of the PSD increments control allowable growth in areas subject to PSD requirements. A new source must also apply best available control technology (BACT) which is defined in a case-by-case determination of the maximum emission reduction achievable by the facility, after accounting for cost, energy, and other factors. The BACT standard can be more stringent, and more expensive, than the NSPS standard. The PSD program has conclusively determined that air resources in the US are scarce resources.

2.3   *Significance of the Clean Air Act*

The foregoing review of the US Clean Air Act is useful because it demonstrates several factors. First, the US has implemented a comprehensive program designed to protect the public health and welfare from the adverse effects of SO_2 emissions. The continuing administrative development of that program will likely reduce SO_2 emissions from existing sources. Second, the US has developed and is implementing a program with the long-term goal of minimizing SO_2 emissions. This point is critical because it refutes the assertion that the air pollution program of the US is concerned solely with local effects. The US government has not taken, and needs not take, further legislative measures such as those recently adopted by Canada or West Germany to reduce SO_2 emissions. US industry will make those reductions as it upgrades its physical plant. Such piecemeal reductions are not the sort of grist for governmental pronouncements on new acid rain programs, but the 'invisible hand' of a market economy works just as well and perhaps more efficiently than the whims of politics in this area.

Third, this review of the Clean Air Act raises several questions concerning the credibility of claims about massive acid rain damage heard so often. This issue will be dealt with directly later on, but it deserves analysis in the context of the Clean Air Act. If there is scientific proof that SO_2 emissions, at current levels, adversely affect public health, then why not present that proof to the Administrator as part of his periodic review of the SO_2 criteria document? Credible scientific evidence of SO_2-related health effects would force a change in the primary NAAQS and then require revisions in the SIPs to ensure that the new NAAQS for SO_2 would be met.

This argument extends to the other effects attributed to acid rain, such as aquatic effects, forest damage, and building deterioration, which are properly termed welfare effects. If the evidence is so conclusive about the SO_2-related nature of these effects, then why not make a scientifically-based demand for revision of the secondary NAAQS for SO_2? Instead of presenting their evidence in a scientific forum, advocates of acid rain controls focus their attention on attempts to enact new legislation through Congress, which is much less likely to base its judgment on the scientific evidence than on an emotional public outcry over alleged effects. On the other hand, if the primary and secondary NAAQS do indeed protect the public health and welfare, then there is no need to make dramatic changes in the Clean Air Act.

2.4 *The environmental impact of the Clean Air Act*

The Clean Air Act has already had a remarkable effect in reducing SO_2 emissions. The US should be recognized as a 'precursor member' of the so-called "30 % Club" of nations that have promised to reduce their SO_2 emissions 30 % by 1990 from 1980 allowable emission levels. In 1970, the year that the Clean Air Act was adopted, SO_2 emissions in the US totalled 28.4 million metric tons. By 1982, the year before the 30 % Club was formed, US emissions had been reduced to 21.4 million metric tons. It has been projected that, without the Clean Air Act, US SO_2 emissions in 1982 would have totalled approximately 35.0 million metric tons. Instead of a 25 % increase in emissions, the Clean Air Act achieved a 25 % decrease – a significant turnaround. These reductions are all the more dramatic in light of the fact that the American electric utility industry increased its consumption of coal from 291 million metric tons in 1970 to 539 million metric tons in 1982 – an increase of 85 %. Obviously, both total SO_2 loadings and SO_2 removal efficiency have been dramatically improved in the US.

The minimization of SO_2 emission levels through retirement of existing plants and application of the current NSPS is projected by the Electric

Power Research Institute to yield an annual total SO_2 emissions level of under 10 million tons in the US around the years 2005–10. This is well over a 50 % reduction from current levels. This projection is not fanciful. The Clean Air Act is working to minimize SO_2 emissions. The effectiveness of the NSPS is reflected, in part, by the fact that in December 1984 there were 119 scrubbers in operation in the US, 38 more under construction, and 63 additional scrubbers planned. Existing sources cannot be operated indefinitely and economic reality dictates that they must be replaced or modified to such an extent that the NSPS will apply. Moreover, the development of new, efficient and cleaner generating technologies offers the potential to reduce annual SO_2 emissions in the US to levels under 5 million tons.

American electric utilities have learned to live within the confines of the Clean Air Act. The Act imposed new restrictions that were difficult to implement, but the US $25000 per day per violation civil penalties authorized by the Clean Air Act did much to encourage US utilities to accept the expensive requirements of the Act. According to the EPA, American utilities spent US $41 billion from 1970–81 in capital, operation and maintenance costs, and premium fuels to comply with the Clean Air Act. EPA further estimates that these utilities will spend an additional US $96 billion during the current decade for air pollution control. These costs have been passed on to US consumers and businesses in the form of higher electricity rates.

3   **The meaning of the acid rain debate in the US**

The acid rain debate in the US differs from the manner in which that debate is structured in other countries. It is not a debate over whether there should be pollution controls or no controls. That issue was settled with the adoption of the Clean Air Act requiring all sources to control their emissions to meet the NAAQS. The debate is not over whether there should be a long-term reduction of SO_2 emissions. That issue was settled in favor of cost-effective SO_2 emission minimization by the issuance of the NSPS. The debate is not over whether industry or government should pay for pollution control. The figures provided above on the air pollution control expenditures by the US electric utility industry alone conclusively indicate who won that issue. The main issue of the acid rain debate in the US is whether a significant reduction of SO_2 emissions, which will be achieved in any event, should be achieved approximately one decade earlier. In other terms, the question is whether a 50 % reduction in SO_2 emissions should be achieved by 1995–97 by government fiat or whether the same reduction should be achieved around 2005–10 under the status quo. There are several subparts to this question.

The first subpart questions whether the fundamental framework of the Clean Air Act is inadequate. Obviously, the majority of emissions to be reduced by acid rain legislation will be squeezed out of existing sources, not sources subject to the NSPS. This will require a policy choice to impose costly pollution control retrofits on sources that will be retired in due course. The Congress that adopted the Clean Air Act deliberately refused to make that choice and relied on the public health and welfare protections offered by the Clean Air Act. Congress relied on the cost effective approach of the market to decide which plants should be retired in favor of the new plants which would achieve SO_2 emission minimization. Proponents of acid rain legislation must demonstrate that these protections are inadequate and that the government can decide better where emissions should be reduced.

The second subpart questions whether US society can, or should pay, for a new acid rain program. It is altogether accurate to identify US society as the eventual payer of any new program because the costs paid for the pollution controls are eventually passed on to society in the form of higher prices, just as the billions spent to date have been passed on. In the event that a facility cannot afford new pollution equipment and should close as a result of the new program, the most obvious victims are those employed at the facility and at its supplier, such as a coal mine. US society must decide whether, out of all the public policy choices and demands for its resources, it should spend over US $100 billion to accelerate its pollution control program.

The third subpart is a matter of regional politics. Since most of the members of Congress in favor of acid rain legislation represent New England, all of the legislative proposals that they have proposed have targeted other regions for the bulk of the emissions reductions. For example, even though New York and Kentucky emit approximately the same total tonnage of SO_2, a bill that has been approved by the Senate Committee on Public Works and the Environment would require New York to reduce its emissions by 21 % while Kentucky would be required to reduce its emissions by 63 %. A brief lesson in geography is in order. Northern New York is the location of the Adirondack Mountains, a site of alleged acid rain damage. Kentucky is located hundreds of miles to the south-west. The only scientific justification for this anomaly is the fact that Kentucky's representatives were not in the same room with New York's representatives when the proposed legislation was drafted.

The unmistakable purpose of the acid rain legislation currently proposed in the US is that the mid-western states bear the brunt of any emission reduction. This area is an old industrial region currently attempting to re-industrialize and attract new businesses. The last recession caused the loss of approximately 500 000 jobs in Ohio alone. These jobs have not and, due to structural economic adjustment, may not return. One acid rain control proposal seriously considered by Congress in 1984 would have increased average industrial electricity rates in Ohio in 1981 by an average of 28 % and driven additional jobs from the state.

The blatant inequity of the current proposals in the US is an issue which exacerbates the regional tensions inherent in this debate. At most, the scientific evidence upon which an American control strategy might be based (such as the 1982 study by the National Academy of Sciences) supports a 50 % emission reduction *from all sources* in eastern North America. No proponent of acid rain legislation has dared to propose such a seemingly equitable plan. There is no scientific evidence to suggest that reductions in SO_2 emissions in the Mid-west will produce appreciable benefits hundreds of miles down-wind.

The fourth subpart of the general question involves the foundation of the nation's decision to accelerate its SO_2 control program by a decade. This subpart is perhaps the most interesting because it deals with the nature of the evidence in the acid rain debate.

As proponents of acid rain legislation are fond of pointing out, the acid rain issue differs from prior air pollution issues because of the difficulty in establishing a source–receptor relationship. When a steel mill belched forth smoke that caused smog in the area of the steel mill, the remedy was clear because the causal link between the smoke and the smog was clear. Where the alleged damages and the putative causal agents are hundreds of miles apart, the legal framework for identifying a remedy is much more difficult. Proponents of acid rain legislation use this argument to call for new legislation or new treaties, but they frequently gloss over the fact that they have asserted a substantial change in the nature of the proof of the causal link.

The nature of the proof of the source–receptor relationship has changed from demonstrative, in the case of local air pollution, to speculative, in the case of the long-range transport of air pollutants. Another way of describing the change in offered proof is that it has gone from probable, or even certain, causation in the case of local air pollution, to possible, or even plausible, causation in the case of acid rain. The methodological tools and data base which are necessary to produce a higher level of proof simply are not yet available. It is poor public policy to spend significant amounts of money when it is only plausible that the program will succeed. Such a public policy is simply throwing money at a perceived problem whether or not the problem is real.

The fact that the proof of acid rain damage caused by mid-western SO_2 emissions in the US requires a 'leap of faith' from demonstrative to speculative causation can be seen in the reliance upon 'worst-case' scenario analysis by proponents of acid rain legislation. Such analysis assumes that negative trends will continue and probably accelerate while positive trends will either cease or never materialize. Worst-case analysis is regularly used when the goal is to avoid all risks, including those which are only possible or merely plausible. Worst-case analysis often contributes to enormous cost overruns in US governmental programs.

The best examples of worst-case analysis run amuck usually come from the US Department of Defense. In its attempt to eliminate all the risks of military reversal, including the risks which are only plausible, the Department of Defense sometimes proposes extremely costly solutions to problems which may never materialize. The difficulty with using this analysis as the basis for legislative proposals is that the public treasury is not inexhaustible and other public programs, which are demonstrably successful, require funding.

This analogy to the Department of Defense is useful because environmental advocates play something of the same role. The duty of the Department of Defense is to protect US society from foreign military threats. The self-appointed duty of environmental advocates is to protect the world from environmental threats. Both defenders fear possible and plausible risks, and propose solutions to those risks. However, just as war is too important to be left to the military, environmental protection is too important to be left to the environmental advocates. Worst-case analysis may be useful to define the range of potential problems, but it is not a sound basis for making public policy choices because no interest can claim to be an absolute interest. Public policy decisions must be made by weighing the proof of the perceived risks, the competing interests, and the costs involved in each course of action.

4   Balancing the interests in the acid rain debate

4.1   *Re-examination of the early claims about acid rain and the scientific imperative for legislation*

The fact that the US is implementing a system of SO_2 emissions minimization is not sufficient to dismiss the calls for acid rain legislation. No environmental program should be so etched in stone that it cannot be changed upon the discovery of new and compelling evidence.

In the early years of this decade, the claims made by Canadians and others about acid rain in North America did have the appearance of being new and compelling evidence. The scientific imperative for new legislation, as articulated at that time, was as follows. The pH of rainfall was becoming more acidic; a significant number of lakes and streams were in danger of losing, or had lost, their fish populations; there were large sources of SO_2 emissions in the American Mid-west; these sources of SO_2 were up-wind of the areas of alleged damage, and it was expected that the Reagan administration would relax the SIPs of these mid-western states, thereby allowing even larger amounts of SO_2 to float downwind. The little environmental damage which could be related to acidification was viewed as a harbinger of the ecological disaster to come. The cost of controlling SO_2 emissions sufficiently to prevent further damage was estimated to be a 2 % increase in electricity rates.

This scenario had all the attributes of a reasonable claim. The risks were high, the probability of success was high, and the costs were low. The claim was so reasonable that Congress immediately enacted the Acid Precipitation Act of 1980, which committed the federal government to a coordinated ten-year plan of study into the causes, effects and possible solutions to acid rain so that legislation would be based on sound scientific ground. Ironically, the scientific evidence which emerged since early 1980, in part by this federal research, has demonstrated that the early allegations about acid rain in North America were inaccurate. The pH of rainfall was not becoming worse. Several studies by the US Geological Survey demonstrated that the pH levels of rainfall in the north-eastern US were improving, not worsening. Moreover, much of the research which purported to demonstrate the rapid drop in pH levels did not survive peer review. Even enviromentalists warned against comparing recent pH tests with older pH sampling because of the differing biases of the testing techniques.

The number of lakes and streams that had become, or were in danger of becoming, fishless turned out to be much smaller than anticipated. Many, including the Governor of the State of New York, stated bluntly that 220 lakes in the Adirondacks were fishless because of acid rain. When the New York Department of Environmental Conservation conducted a thorough survey of these lakes, it discovered that only 65 were fishless. The survey revealed that only 8 % of all Adirondack lakes were fishless.

Another survey by the New York State Department of Environmental Conservation revealed that the number of lakes listed as critical (pH below 5.0) decreased significantly from a 1975–8 sampling period to a second sampling period in 1980–1. Similar surveys throughout New England and Canada failed to reveal the growing damage that had been projected.

A broader survey released by EPA in August 1985 revealed that the small number of lakes which are acidic could have been acidified by natural means and not by acid rain. Even the number of acidic lakes identified by this survey is smaller than expected. Based on EPA's random survey of 1600 lakes in the eastern half of the US, researchers estimated that 261 of the 7206 lakes (3.6 %) in the North-east had a pH level of 5.0 or lower. In the Mid-west, where SO_2 emissions are greatest in total tonnage, only 143 of the 8512 (1.6 %) lakes were estimated to have a pH below 5.0. This certainly does not indicate a crisis of such proportions that immediate action is required.

There are indeed large sources of SO_2 in the Mid-west. On a total tonnage basis, these sources are larger than those in Canada or New England. Further comparison, however, revealed that the Canadian province of Ontario emitted more SO_2 than did all but one US state. That state, Ohio, has a population that is larger than Ontario's by two million. The Canadian province of Quebec emits more SO_2 than 44 of the 50 US states. Yet neither Ontario nor Quebec were targeted for the 70 % SO_2 cutbacks reserved for the mid-western states, such as Ohio.

The importance of the up-wind location of the mid-western sources was challenged when damage caused by acid rain was alleged to exist in the south-eastern US and in California on the west coast. Since the prevailing winds do not send mid-western emissions to these disparate parts of the country, other explanations for this alleged damage needed to be found. The existence of the alternative theories, which concentrated mainly on local emissions or on nitrogen oxides and other pollutants, reduced the possibility that a significant reduction in mid-western SO_2 emissions would have a significant beneficial impact on the pH of rainfall in the north-eastern US and Canada. The logical principle of Ockham's Razor requires scientists to search for consistent explanations, not case-by-case guesswork.

The scare about massive increases in SO_2 emissions under the Reagan Administration proved to be equally as false. Mid-western SO_2 emissions continued the decline commenced in the late 1970s under the Carter Administration. This point is demonstrated by examining the change in electric utility SO_2 emissions from 1976–82 shown in Table 1.

Table 1

State	% reduction
Illinois	27.4
Indiana	10.5
Kentucky	38.2
Michigan	33.4
Ohio	22.9
West Virgina	12.4

The studies which projected minimal cost increases for an acid rain program were re-examined and found to contain unwarranted economic and political assumptions. Numerous economic studies were completed using what are recognized now to be more realistic assumptions. The cost of the acid rain legislation preferred by Canada and enviromental groups was projected at US $3 billion to US $7 billion per year for at least 25 years. The cumulative cost is projected to be at least US $100 billion. Electricity increases in the mid-western states targeted for large emission reductions would range from 8 % to 20 %. Increases for individual electric utilities would range significantly higher.

Even the recent speculation about the causes of forest damage identified to date has centered on nitrogen oxides and other pollutants, not SO_2. The proponents of acid rain legislation have been required to propose new causation theories as their older theories are refuted by new evidence. One of these new theories is that, even though the pH of rainfall is not decreasing, damage is still occurring because of the 'subtle cumulative' effects of acid rain. Cutting through to the essence of this argument, one finds an assertion that the situation is getting worse. The quantitative evidence cited above demonstrates just the opposite.

What has emerged after five years of research and analysis into the North American acid rain situation is a scenario far different from the one articulated by the Canadian government in 1980. The pH of rainfall is improving; there is no massive acid rain related damage; the sources of SO_2

in the Mid-west are decreasing their emissions and, in any event, they are not as important as local sources of SO_2 and other pollutants; the effectiveness of the proposed remedy has become highly doubtful; and it is apparent that the cost of the program would be over US $100 billion. In summary, the risks of acid rain in North America are not as high as perceived before; certainly, the immediate risks of maintaining the status quo are low; the possibility of success of the proposed measures is low and the costs would be high. In light of the emerging scientific evidence, the proposed legislation has lost its aura of reasonableness.

4.2   *The promise of acid rain research*

Although acid rain has lost its scientific imperative as a justification for immediate reduction of SO_2 emissions, at least in the form of the legislation proposed to date, the speculative risk of a long-term acidification process deserves continued study. This is necessary whether or not the potential acidification is caused by mid-western SO_2 or not. I mention this point specifically because it has been stated that the purpose of acid rain research should be to uncover dramatic effects that will spur public opinion into demanding acid rain legislation. One might call this the propaganda use of acid rain research. By whatever name, this use of research is intellectually dishonest because it closes the researcher's mind to potential solutions beyond the one already selected for political, not scientific, reasons.

There is currently a great deal of research underway in the US which is attempting to verify the speculative claims made about acid rain. The ten-year research commitment by the federal government of the US has been accelerated and the funding increased. The US government's acid deposition research budget for fiscal year 1985 is US $65 million. The research budget for fiscal year 1986 is US $85.5 million.

Private research budgets in the US are also growing. For example, the Electric Power Research Institute spent US $13 million on the study of atmospheric processes through 1984, and plans to spend an additional US $32.5 million through 1989. The Institute spent US $17.5 million on ecological studies through 1984 and will spend US $33.5 million more through 1989 on these studies. In addition, the Institute has spent US $2.4 million on environmental assessments relating to acid rain through 1984 and will spend an additional US $11.5 through 1989.

Researchers are also looking into methods of burning the Mid-west's high sulfur coal cleanly and more cheaply. The federal government has budgeted US $67 million for technology research for fiscal year 1985. The purpose of this research is to develop new technologies that could reduce the cost of emission reductions to a level that the reductions might be commercially affordable and reasonable even on the basis of a speculative risk. It is very unlikely that any of the technologies under consideration (such as lime injection multi-stage burners, coal gasification, or fluidized bed combustion) will be commercially available before the mid-1990s, so that any acid rain legislation that requires the reductions to be achieved before 1995 must rely on the costly scrubber technology. In light of the fact that the risk is not immediate, deferring a decision until these technologies are developed further appears to be in the best interest. In light of the fact that the causal agents for the alleged acid rain damage have not been identified, deferring a decision while research continues prevents the possibility of controlling the wrong pollutant. The consequences of such action could be the loss of public support for the further measures which would be necessary. It is too early to fashion an additional control strategy in the US, if one is ultimately deemed to be necessary.

5   Canada's interest in acid rain legislation

There is a growing perception in the US that Canada's demands for acid rain legislation in the US should not be given as much attention as they were accorded previously. This is due, in part, to the recognition that the scientific imperative for acid rain legislation in North America is not as strong as previously believed. It is also due, in part, to the recognition that Canada's acid rain program is grounded more in symbolism than substance.

Anyone familiar with the Canadian–US acid rain debate is aware that the Canadian government has been very active in that debate. In the late 1970s and early 1980s, the Canadian government undertook a high-profile campaign of lobbying, speechmaking, and legal activity designed to encourage or embarrass the US into reducing emissions of SO_2.

This campaign was not a sinister, secretly orchestrated scheme but it defintely was a political campaign. After the the thrust of the Canadian efforts had been underway for some months, the Canadian Parliamentary Subcommittee on Acid Rain made in October 1981 the following recommendation in its public report *Still Waters: The Chilling Reality of Acid Rain*:

The Subcommittee recommends that a major public awareness

campaign is necessary to generate public concern in the United States about the acid rain problems and the threat it poses to the Canadian and American environments. The present program should be continued and expanded and consideration should be given to inviting influential American media representatives to Canada so they can be appraised of the transboundary effects of US-sourced air pollution.

In its 1984 report, *Time Lost: A Demand For Action on Acid Rain*, the same Subcommittee on Acid Rain provided this evaluation of Canada's efforts to implement the above recommendation:

Since 1981, the public awareness program of Environment Canada and other government agencies have increased greatly. For example, in 1981 Environment Canada had a budget of about $450 000 for public awareness-related activites; in 1983 this figure had increased to about $925 000. Public awareness of the acid rain issue in both Canada and the United States has increased significantly since 1981.

Over the years, Canadian lobbying efforts have succeeded in instilling in some the belief that Canada was far ahead of the US in terms of progress on acid rain. Despite widespread evidence to the contrary, this belief persisted until early in 1985 when two public events began to bring public perception in line with reality. On 1 February 1985 Canadian Prime Minister Brian Mulroney announced that Canada must 'clean up its own act first' before demanding additional environmental control measures from the US. Mulroney officially questioned his government's criticism of the US and admitted that Canada's own pollution control program trailed the US program.

A more important statement in domestic American politics was made in March 1985 by New Hampshire Governor John Sununu at the Conference of Eastern Canadian Premiers and New England Governors. Governor Sununu has supported efforts to enact acid rain legislation in the US. Yet Governor Sununu blasted Canada's pollution control efforts because he felt that it was important to dispel the 'legend that has been propagated' that Canada is far ahead of the US pollution control program. Governor Sununu noted that, on a per capita basis, Canada emits two times as much SO_2 as does the US. On the basis of units of industrial output, Canada emits three times as much as does the US. In light of the strides taken by the US under its Clean Air Act, Canada's calls for further SO_2 reductions in the US, on equal terms as those in Canada, do not have the ring of fairness.

Over the past several years, Canada has announced several plans which purport to reduce SO_2 emissions in Canada. These measures have appeared to be progressively more stringent, but none of these plans have resulted in the reduction of one pound of SO_2 emitted in Canada.

These plans are as follows.

1   **The 25 % unilateral offer**   On 15 February 1982, Environment Minister John Roberts announced Canada's intention to make a unilateral 25 % reduction in allowable SO_2 emissions east of the Saskatchewan/ Manitoba border. Roberts proposed to make an additional 25 % reduction if the US promised to reduce US SO_2 emissions by 50 %. These reductions were to be made by 1990. No specifics were announced.

A devastating analysis of this proposal was made by Canada's Parliamentary Subcommittee on Acid Rain in 1984:

> Canada's stated intention to reduce domestic SO_2 emissions unilaterally by 25 % appeared to have little positive effect. This initiative, announced on the 15th of February, 1982, was not immediately accompanied by any information on where the emissions would be reduced. The Subcommittee believes that a proposal of this type, utterly lacking in specifics on where and how reduction will be made or how they will be financed, did not impress our critics in the United States or, indeed, in Canada . . . Even if this goal were to be achieved by 1990 – and that is not a certainty – there is the suspicion that the Federal Government is not really effecting a 25 % reduction in acid rain-causing emissions, but is manipulating statistics to give the appearance of action.

2   **The first 50 % unilateral plan**   On 6 March 1984, the Minister of the Environment, Charles Caccia, announced a decision by the federal and provincial environmental ministers to achieve a unilateral 50 % reduction in Canadian SO_2 emissions by 1994. This proposal did not contain any specifics on where the emission reductions would be made. The 50 % reduction was to be made from 1980 allowable emission levels.

3   The second 50 % unilateral plan   In February and March 1985, the government of Prime Minister Brian Mulroney announced the elements of another plan to reduce Canada's SO_2 emissions 50 % by 1994. This plan was similar to the March 1984 plan because it included no specifics as to which sources would be required to reduce their concessions and by how much. The plan did include an allocation among the provinces of emission reductions, but these allocations totalled less than 50 %. The plan simply set a target of a 50 % SO_2 emission reduction east of Saskatchewan by 1994. The sources eventually targeted for reduction will receive part of a Can $300 million subsidy from the federal government. This plan did require that new passenger cars must meet US standards for NO_2 and ozone emissions by 1 September 1987.

Each of Canada's SO_2 reduction plans employ the same technique of using 'phantom emission reductions'. All of the plans call for a reduction from 1980 *allowable* emission levels rather than a reduction in *actual* emissions. This difference is critical because the Canadian allowable emissions limit in 1980 was 4.6 million metric tons, while the actual emissions in 1980 were only 4.0 million metric tons. Since the Canadians count the 600 000 tons of allowable but unused emissions toward their 50 % reduction, approximately 20–25 % of the so-called reduction will occur only on paper.

The 50 % reduction plans cast a new light on the unilateral offer by John Roberts to reduce Canada's SO_2 emissions 25 % by 1990. It is now clear that this was not a good-faith offer because those reductions would have been purely 'phantom emission reductions'. Roberts also offered to reduce Canada's emissions by an additional 25 % by 1990, if the US would implement a 50 % reduction. Given the 1994 deadline of the new 50 % reduction plan, one can only assume that the Canadians are delaying until 1994 the reductions that they announced in 1982, or that Roberts' 1982 offer was less than forthright.

An examination of one much-touted control plan gives reason to doubt the promises of Canada's government. In January 1981, the Province of Ontario announced that Ontario Hydro, a government-owned utility, would reduce its SO_2 emissions 43 % by 1990 with an interim target to be met in 1985. This plan included the retrofitting of two scrubbers and, according to Walter Giles, deputy minister of Environment Ontario, NO_2 controls that would make Ontario the 'clear leader in the forefront of nitrogen oxides pollution control'. Many Canadians pointed to Ontario Hydro's 'success' in an effort to chide the US into adopting acid rain legislation. At a speech in Ohio in January 1981, Mr. Giles declared that:

> Hydro will be retrofitting these scrubbers onto existing plants in order to help reduce acid rain, an action which – if I may be blunt – the United States Federal and State govenment have, so far, taken steps to avoid.

In February 1982, the Ontario cabinet relaxed the NO_2 controls significantly. In July 1982, the plans to retrofit the two scrubbers were cancelled in order to save money. Today, there are no scrubbers in operation or under construction in Canada. As of December, 1984 there were at least 200 scrubbers in operation, under construction, or planned in the US, according to the Edison Electric Institute.

If Ontario Hydro had reduced its NO_2 and SO_2 emissions without scrubbers or extra controls, then the failure to install the promised scrubbers would have been inconsequential. However, Ontario Hydro's SO_2 emissions have actually increased since the 'reduction' announcement was made. In 1980, Hydro emitted a total of 460 000 metric tons of SO_2 and NO_2. Thereafter, the total increased to 530 000 metric tons in 1982, 513 000 metric tons in 1983, and 519 000 metric tons in 1984. In 1981, Hydro had projected a mere 388 000–413 000 metric tons of NO_2 and SO_2 emissions for 1984. It is doubtful that Ontario Hydro will meet its interim SO_2 emissions target of 390 000 metric tons this year.

Two specific examples illustrate the differences in SO_2 control between the performance of Ontario Hydro and US utilities. In 1973, the Cleveland Electric Illuminating Company in north-east Ohio emitted 580 000 metric tons of SO_2. By 1984, as a result of the Clean Air Act, those emissions had been reduced by over 44 % to 323 000 metric tons. In 1973, Commonwealth Edison of Illinois emitted 1.05 million metric tons of SO_2. In 1984, those emissions were down to 291 000 metric tons, a decrease of 70 %. In contrast, Ontario Hydro's SO_2 emissions have *increased* by 55 % from 1973 to 1984, despite the Canadian air pollution laws. The Canadian reduction target will simply reduce Ontario Hydro's emissions to the levels it emitted at in the early 1970s and no further. It is at least noteworthy that Ontario Hydro's SO_2 emissions increased at the same time that Canada was discovering alleged acid rain damage, which was the same time that the US Mid-west was reducing its SO_2 emissions.

According to a document released by Ontario Hydro in May 1985,

(*Strategies for Control of Acid Rain at Ontario Hydro*), Hydro will install no new pollution control equipment to meet its 1985 and 1990 targets because it plans to shift production to new nuclear units that are under construction. This scenario should be considered highly risky, particularly in light of Hydro's frequent shutdowns of its nuclear facilities and its difficulty in obtaining regulatory approval for necessary transmission lines to connect the new nuclear facilities to its distribution system. As the Subcommittee on Acid Rain stated in *Time Lost*:

> In fact, the Subcommittee has very little confidence in the stated projections and acid rain strategies of Ontario Hydro. . . . The Subcommittee feels that Ontario Hydro's stated acid rain control strategy is imprecise and undependable . . . [Hydro] has forfeited its leadership role, is at best unworthy and, at worst, irresponsible.

Since the proposed 43 % emission reduction from Hydro is counted toward Canada's overall 50 % reduction by 1994, confidence in the overall plan should be reduced proportionately.

The Canadian government's manipulation of SO_2 statistics, the multiplicity of 'plans' without details, and the harsh criticism of those plans from Canada's own Parliamentary Subcommittee on Acid Rain should raise doubts as to Canada's ability or willingness to make such emission reductions. These plans are essentially symbolic gestures designed to provide grist for Canada's propaganda campaign in the US and to satisfy domestic Canadian calls for action. For these reasons, Canada's demands for action by the United States are today viewed with less attentiveness. These facts have shifted the balance of credibility away from Canada in the Canadian–US acid rain debate.

6   Conclusion

The acid rain debate may well remain the most intractable issue of the decade. Despite the apparent weakening of their positions, Canadian and US advocates of acid rain legislation remain a powerful political force. Significant misconceptions concerning acid rain are still accepted as truth by broad segments of the public. The US utilities and the mid-western states still face the consequences of not being able to demonstrate, to a broad audience, the efforts that have been taken to date and that will be taken in the future to control SO_2 emissions. Nevertheless, the legislative proposals issued to date are wholly unattractive to the mid-western states, particularly since they offer the certainty of high costs with little guarantee in resulting benefits anywhere. The credibility of Canadian acid rain requests must be questioned in light of Canada's regulatory actions.

The Canadian–American acid rain debate may be resolved in several ways. First, in the long term, SO_2 emissions will be reduced gradually under the NSPS of the Clean Air Act. The issue may simply go away of its own accord. If the issue does not go away, it will be because different pollutants have become the focus of acid rain controls. Second, in the mid-term, the development of new coal-burning technologies offer the promise of reducing emissions more cheaply from existing sources than is possible with current technology. These technologies could accelerate reductions at a cost which might not devastate a regional economy, even though such reductions might not be justified from a scientific viewpoint.

Finally, the Canadian–American acid rain debate may be resolved the way most seemingly intractable issues are resolved, such as the one about how many angels can sit on the head of a pin. The issue may die for want to interest because much more important and more pressing issues will arise.

11

The acid rain controversy in Europe and North America: a political analysis

Armin Rosencranz

*President, Pacific Energy and Resources Center,
Sausalito, California*

Nations do not act internationally to benefit other nations, unless such action also benefits themselves. Seven years ago, 32 European nations, plus Canada, the US and the European Economic Community (EEC), signed in Geneva a Convention on Long Range Transboundary Air Pollution (hereinafter termed the 'Acid Rain Convention'). That Convention had no teeth – no numerical standards, timetables, or enforcement provisions – because several of the signatory nations were not convinced that the costs of preventing acid rain *by controlling pollution at the source* would be justified by the benefits.

Officials of the two nations most responsible for initiating the Acid Rain Convention, Norway and Sweden, have spent much of the last seven years trying to persuade their fellow signatories that the benefits of control do indeed outweigh the costs. For the last five years, the Norwegians and Swedes have been supported by environmental officials from West Germany and Canada.

West Germany originally opposed the Acid Rain Convention, even in its toothless form. They were brought to the signing table in Geneva by a combination of pressures and appeals from Sweden, Norway and fellow members of the EEC.[1] But by 1982, when a multilateral conference on Acidification of the Environment was held in Stockholm, West German officials had become convinced by their scientists and foresters that massive forest death ('Waldsterben') was resulting in Germany and elsewhere in Central Europe from air pollutants, including the sulphur and nitrogen pollutants that are the principal components of acid rain.

At about the same time, Canadian officials became alarmed by the increasing acidification of eastern Canada's lakes and the expected harsh impact that this would have for tourism. More than half of the pollution thought to be responsible for acidifying Canada's lakes originates in the mid-western industrial region of the US, whose power stations have generally been held to less stringent emissions standards than have other US power stations.

Since 1982, Canadians and West Germans have joined, and to some extent have replaced, their Scandinavian colleagues, who may have begun to grow weary of their long and lonely struggle. Moreover, Norway and Sweden import much of their acid rain from other countries, and are therefore classic *victim* countries. By contrast, a significant portion of the acid rain falling on Germany and Canada originates in those countries. West Germany and Canada are both polluters *and* victims. They import and export the stuff to and from their neighbors, and are therefore especially deeply concerned with balancing the costs and benefits of abatement.

It has never been a question of whether abatement technologies exist. The question has been whether a nation's economic resources should be applied to environmental control measures with a consequent loss, at least in the short term, for economic development.

An increasing number of the Acid Rain Convention's original signatories have become convinced that the benefits of abatement do, indeed, outweigh the costs. By July 1985, when the Acid Rain Convention's Executive Body held its third meeting in Helsinki, 21 of the Convention's signatories had become members of the '30 % Club' – i.e. they had pledged, as soon as possible, and at the latest by 1993, to reduce their sulphur emissions at the source by at least 30 % over their 1980 levels.[3] The 30 % commitment gives some teeth, or at least numerical goals, to the Convention.

Currently, the three most polluting 'holdout' nations which have refused to join the 30% Club are Poland, the UK and the US. Political leaders and economic planners in these three countries have apparently not yet become convinced that the benefits of abatement outweigh the costs. I shall now focus on what these 'holdout' nations have been doing (or not doing) to abate acid rain, and what may be developing, both domestically and internationally, to build a consensus in favor of serious abatement measures.

Poland

Let me begin with Poland, which I know least well, and end with the US, which I know best.

In Poland, an estimated 1500 square miles of forest has been damaged. Spruce trees are dead around the industrial cities of Rivnic and Czestochowa. Fir trees are dead all around Katowice, the industrial center up-wind of Cracow. This is all very recent: a generation ago, the same hillsides were covered with green and apparently healthy trees.

As long ago as 1890, scientists demonstrated that a forest near Katowice, in the center of the Upper Silesian industrial region, had been damaged by SO_2 emissions.[4] Today, every coniferous forest in Upper Silesia is deteriorating. Moreover, dispersion of Silesian air pollution through tall stacks has led to unprecedented levels of forest death all through the southern and south-western parts of Poland.

In eastern Europe, unlike North America, many cities are very old, and these cities are crumbling.[4] Cracow is the best case in point. I talked some time ago to a member of the Polish National Academy of Science, who lives in Cracow. He reported that when he walks in the streets of the city, he sees building surfaces disintegrating before his very eyes. He and his colleagues believe that the crumbling of Cracow is a direct result of acidification.

In Upper Silesia, gaseous emissions grew from 2 million tons in 1975 to over 4.4 million tons in 1980. During the same five-year period, SO_2 emissions increased from 1.1 to 1.7 million tons annually. Emissions in Upper Silesia are five times higher, per square kilometre, than in Germany's Ruhr Valley.[5]

Besides its high domestic emissions, Poland imports at least 1.8 million tons of SO_2 from foreign sources, mainly East Germany and Czechoslovakia. Almost two-thirds of Poland's acid deposition originates outside the country. Correspondingly, Poland manages to export almost half of its own SO_2 emissions to its down-wind neighbors – mainly to Sweden, Finland, Czechoslovakia and the Soviet Union – by dispersing its emissions through tall stacks.[6]

On the basis of gathered information, it seems clear that aggregate SO_2 emissions in Poland are extremely high. This is not surprising in view of the concentration of uncontrolled industrial facilities and the high sulphur content of the brown coal burned there. Ambient pollution levels seem high enough to pose very serious *health* risks as well as damage to forests, lakes, and buildings.

Poland is in a paradoxical position: it wants to be exempt from control measures, claiming that its weak economy makes abatement technologies unaffordable, and yet it also wants to save its crumbling cities and dying forests. The situation is further complicated by Poland's economic planners, who talk of increased reliance on pollution-free nuclear power plants to supply Poland's future electricity needs. Nuclear plants may cause no air pollution, but they are very expensive to build and maintain, and they have significantly more breakdowns than coal-fired power plants. Whereas the most efficient American co-generation[7] thermal power plants offer an electricity output at $500 per kilowatt, the typical nuclear plant costs about four times as much.[8]

Poland has a strong environmental movement which is not controlled by the government. The main environmental group is the Polish Ecological Club, which was founded in Cracow in September 1980. The group survived under martial law and today has working groups in all major Polish cities. It has succeeded in closing several polluting factories, most notably the large Skawine aluminium smelter, whose toxic wastes were evidently impairing the health of surrounding residents. The Club's proposals for production modifications and new equipment at Cracow's huge Lenin steel plant, aimed at reducing sulphur emissions, have now been included in official plans.[9]

Polish Ecological Club members believe in decentralization and limits to growth. Consequently, they are likely to keep the pressure up about air pollution control and are unlikely to support nuclear power generation. Time will tell whether any or all of these factors will be enough to propel Poland into the 30% Club – especially since the Polish government apparently regards water pollution as its highest environmental priority.

The United Kingdom

UK emits 3.5 million tons of SO_2 per year, of which about one million tons is exported to down-wind countries, especially Norway and

Sweden. Geographically situated as the most upwind country of Europe (except for Ireland), the UK's import of air pollutants from other countries is negligible.

Four years ago, virtually no one in the UK talked about acid rain. Even within the British environmental community, few knew much about it. But British awareness has increased very rapidly.

First, political pressure began to build at the first ECE Executive Body Meeting in June 1983.[10] Norway, Sweden and Finland called for a 30 % reduction in national SO_2 emissions by 1993. They were quickly joined by West Germany, Canada, Austria, Switzerland and Denmark, and these eight countries were the charter members of the '30 % Club'. France, with its steadily increasing reliance on nuclear power and reduced reliance on coal and oil to generate electric power, indicated its willingness to consider a reduction program. The UK was clearly in an exposed position as the only major polluting country of western Europe to resist the 30 % pledge.

Shortly afterward, limnologists began to report that acid deposition was killing lakes in Scotland and Wales. Brown trout were not reproducing and salmon streams were losing their spawning populations. Acid rain became an interesting though not particularly pressing domestic issue at that point.

In 1984, it was reported that acid rain had been damaging certain birds. A sharp decline was reported in the osprey population, and the decline was attributed, in part, to acid deposition: The fish upon which the osprey feed had been failing to reproduce at usual levels in numerous acidified Scottish and Welsh lakes.

Diplomatic pressures were also building. On 1 February 1984, one month before the Ottawa Ministerial Conference on Acid Rain, France made the unexpected announcement that it would reduce its SO_2 emissions by 50 % by 1990. Up to that point, the French had claimed that they had done all the cutting back they could by shifting from fossil fuels to nuclear power to produce their electricity. Suddenly they were now saying 'We are going to reduce SO_2 markedly and we want to go to Ottawa'. At the Ottawa Conference, with France in attendance, the UK was conspicuously absent.

At about the same time, six different British environmental organizations formed an acid rain coalition. Spokespersons for the coalition pointed out, at every opportunity, that the UK is the biggest polluter in western Europe and the Central Electricity Generating Board is the biggest polluter in Britain.[11] In mid 1982, the Environment Minister rose in the House of Commons and said 'The acid rain problem is not nearly as severe as the media make out'.

But, in February 1984, the same minister declared, 'I vigorously refute any charge of complacency. We are, in fact, stepping up our research markedly.'

During this whole 1983–4 period, the House of Commons Environment Committee, consisting of seven Conservatives, three Labour members, and a Liberal, had been examining the acid rain issue. They visited Scandinavia and Germany, and held discussions with British and European scientists. As their evidence mounted, they began to express dismay at certain representatives of the CEGB. In their eventual report,[12] they suggested that the CEGB may have deliberately attempted to mislead the committee.

The CEGB, with a total SO_2 output of 2.2 million tons per year, began to recognize that its credibility was eroding. The acid rain issue seemed to contribute to growing doubts about CEGB competence.

The CEGB also has to contend with a troubled domestic coal industry, beset by unemployment and a recent bitter and prolonged strike by miners. The CEGB has proposed to step up its nuclear power program with two pressurized water reactors. Journalists have pointed out that such a move could displace jobs in the coal industry. Desulphurization of coal, by contrast, would generate jobs and provide useful opportunities for foreign currency earnings. The UK could, for example, establish a desulphurization industry whose products could then be introduced into the export market.

In the face of contrary experience elsewhere, the CEGB has insisted, until very recently, that there is no scientific consensus that sulphur and nitrogen emissions cause acidification of the environment; that even if there were such a consensus, it would be prohibitively expensive to install emissions reduction; and that reduction of emissions at power stations may not appreciably reduce acidification damage. These assertions are contradicted strongly by the 1984 report of the House of Commons Environmental Committee[13] as well as by the 1983 report of the US National Academy of Sciences.[14]

In 1985, the CEGB saw that it could no longer 'stonewall' the acid rain issue. It produced and distributed a slick documentary film entitled 'Acid Rain'. One of the film's principal interviewees, Swedish scientist Hans Hultberg, has repudiated the film and has asked the CEGB to delete those portions of its film featuring him.

The CEGB film contains a number of subtle distortions. It talks about forest damage entirely in the context of central Europe, conveying the impression that the British Isles are not susceptible to such damage. It talks about acid rain as primarily an *ozone* problem, obscuring the fact, stated earlier in the film in another context, that ozone is formed when sunlight causes hydrocarbons to react with *nitrogen oxides*. (Current acid rain abatement efforts increasingly comprehend and address the need for NO_x controls.) Finally, the CEGB film ends with a pledge to take any abatement action that is shown to be 'cost-effective', although CEGB representatives implied earlier in the film that no abatement action can possibly be cost effective.

The CEGB further contends that is has already reduced its sulphur oxide emissions by 20% in the last 13 years. They claim that no other country in Europe has reduced its output to pre-second World War levels as has the UK. These levels *have* been reduced, but the reduction seems to have resulted primarily from economic recession and secondarily from increased efficiency of power stations and the introduction of nuclear power.

To summarize acid rain damage in the UK, some 60 British lakes are reportedly badly affected by acidification, with resulting losses of fish and bird populations.[15] Several cathedrals, notably Lincoln and St. Paul's, are slowly deteriorating, perhaps due to very high levels of SO_2 in the past. Environmental organizations elsewhere in western Europe are now attempting to organize a tourist boycott of Britain.

As if this were not enough, there is now reason to fear that the 'forest death' plaguing Germany and Central Europe may soon spread to British forests. Bengt Nihlgard, a forest ecologist at Sweden's Lund University, recently found damage to Britain's deciduous beech trees similar to that in Central Europe, and much greater than that in Sweden.[16] Similarly, a German forester recently examined 46 sites in Scotland, and has found the same air pollution mix – high ozone and hydrocarbon levels – which have been associated with SO_2, NO_x and other air pollutant damage to German forests.

Official bodies have now called for the reduction of sulphur and nitrogen emissions at the source by retrofitting flue gas desulphurization (fgd) equipment to existing thermal power plants.[17] The CEGB has apparently revised its cost estimates downward. Whereas CEGB officials had earlier talked of fgd equipment necessitating an unaffordable increase in electricity rates, they have more recently estimated an annual rate increase of about 5%.[18]

How long can UK officials withstand the pressure of mounting evidence of *domestic* damage, and the wide publicizing of this damage in reports by

government, parliamentary and environmental organs? The UK stands alone
among the populous western European countries in resisting the commitment to a 30 % reduction. The Royal Commission on Environmental
Pollution specifically recommended that the CEGB introduce fgd equipment on a pilot basis – to gain technical experience and to encourage
relevant innovations in British industry. Otherwise, said the Commissioners,
international pressures may eventually dictate reductions, necessitating 'the
adoption of expensive "crash programmes" against a background of technical inexperience' and of a need to import equipment from other countries
that have already embarked on an abatement program.[19]

The European Economic Community

The main international pressure on the UK comes from its sister
states in the EEC. Of the ten nations in the Community in 1985, only
Ireland and Greece, both with small industrial bases, stood with the UK in
staying out of the 30% Club.

Within the Community, most of the impetus for further air pollution
controls comes from West Germany. West Germany has already instituted a
control program for large stationary sources, and a draft directive modelled
on the German program has been circulated by the EEC Commission.

More important, perhaps, is the Commission's proposed directive on
control of air pollutants from mobile sources. For the first time in the
Community's history, action may soon be taken to cope with motor vehicle
emissions.[20] Most prominent among these emissions are nitrogen oxides
(NO_x), precursors of the nitric acid that constitutes at least a third of the acid
in acid rain. Moreover, while SO_2 emissions are decreasing in most
countries, mainly because of the use of low sulphur fuels, NO_x emissions are
now stable or increasing. Some scientists believe that nitrogen oxides will be
the main precursors of acid rain by the year 2000. Aside from the 'low-NO_x'
boiler which has been developed for stationary sources. NO_x control
technologies are not as advanced as those for SO_2.

The main technology for controlling NO_x and other pollutant emissions
from motor vehicles is the catalytic converter, which is mandatory on all
newer vehicles in the US. West Germany favors this approach, and will
require the installation of converters in all domestic cars (and the introduction of unleaded petrol) beginning in 1989. A proposed directive mandating

Community-wide use of catalytic converters has been circulated by the EEC Commission.

But France, Italy and the UK are resisting the use of converters. French officials have counter-proposed a Community-wide speed limit, which they contend will reduce emissions almost as effectively as converters, and with absolutely no additional cost. This, however, runs counter to every West German's God-given right to drive as fast as possible. Also, West German automobiles are more expensive than other European cars. They justify the expense by pointing to high performance at high speeds. At *lower* speeds, smaller and cheaper French and Italian cars would have a competitive edge.

British officials have counter-porposed with engine modifications, notably a lean-burning engine, which *they* contend will also achieve the same result as converters at little cost.

At the moment, the three competing approaches seem to be neutralizing one another.

One other area of possible EEC action is the proposed setting of air quality standards and/or emissions ceilings for nitrogen oxides, comparable to those set for SO_2 and particulates in the Commmunity's 1980 'SO_2 Directive'.[21]

Progress in the Community is bound to be slow, not least because EEC directives require unanimity, and the UK has thus far dragged its feet on air pollution measures. Indeed, on 21 March 1985 the EEC Council of Ministers decided to allow countries to adopt optional methods to meet a staggered series of targets for vehicle emissions. The emission standards are well below those applicable in the US, where NO_x emissions are *not* declining in spite of more rigorous controls. Motor vehicles obviously proliferate faster than abatement programs, and this is especially true of the UK and continental Europe.

The United States

The US, like the UK, has thus far refused to commit to a 30 % reduction of SO_2 emissions. But unlike the UK, the US imports considerable air pollution from its neighbors, namely Canada and Mexico. While the US sends about three times as much SO_2 and NO_x to Canada as it receives from Canada, the amount received is hardly small. Canada has no fgd systems, and its main control strategies for sulphur pollutants are the burning of low sulphur fuels and dispersion of emissions through tall stacks. The world's single largest pollution source is a smelter at Sudbury, Ontario, not far from the American border.

Recently, Mexico aired its plans to construct a massive smelter, emitting more than 500 000 tons of SO_2 annually, 60 miles south of the border in Nacozari, Mexico. This has raised concerns in US border states about air quality generally, and transboundary air pollution and acid rain in particular. This Mexican plan has undoubtedly generated diplomatic pressures from Washington on Mexico City. The contradictions and ironies in the US's double standard toward Canada and Mexico are abundantly clear.

Environmental organizations such as the World Resources Institute, the Sierra Club, the Environmental Defense Fund and the Natural Resources Defense Council have been assiduous in drawing public attention to the spread of the acid rain phenomenon to the western and southern states, and the vulnerability of the states bordering on Mexico to transboundary pollution.

In the meantime, new evidence has been accumulating that a steadily increasing number of lakes all over the country are becoming acidified and fishless. These new data have symbolic significance more than anything else: the loss of fresh-water fishing is an amenity loss that can be readily sustained.

Of far greater significance, however, are the results of various government-sponsored studies showing that economic losses from materials[22] damage *alone* may justify the costs of control.[23] In an acidic environment, materials deteriorate – and must be repaired or replaced – far more rapidly than in a non-acidic environment. Also, US foresters, timber companies and forest products manufacturers cannot look at the widespread European 'Waldsterben' without wondering whether, when, and to what extent forest deterioration will occur in the US. Recapturing losses from materials and forest damage involve major economic interests and billions of dollars, and these powerful new elements may ultimately succeed in neutralizing the power of the electricity and automobile industries, which have thus far effectively thwarted acid rain abatement efforts by resisting more stringent SO_2 and NO_x emission controls at the source.

Ironically, as acid rain has been shown to damage other areas of the country besides the north-eastern states, the pressure on the mid-western states to abate seems to have slackened.[24] The Mid-west might be responsible for acidification damage in the north-east and eastern Canada, but no one can argue that the south and west are down-wind of the Ohio

River Valley. Accordingly, the suit by six north-eastern states to compel the US Environmental Protection Agency to impose stricter emissions controls and stack height regulations on mid-western power plants has languished and no action is expected in the foreseeable future. Here, the state or regional interest in externalizing the costs of pollution seems to have thwarted the national interest in getting the polluters to *internalize* those same costs.

The current posture of the Reagan Administration coincides with that of the Thatcher government in the UK: more study and more research are needed before expensive abatement measures are undertaken. There is also a 'resting on our laurels' theme: the US has reduced sulphur emissions by 36 % over the last 15 years. Its air pollution control regulations far exceed those applicable in either western Europe or Canada, and have cost well over $200 billion. With regard to acid rain $250 million was spent on research into the causes and effects of acid rain during Reagan's first term and this represented a 100% increase over the Carter Administration's acid rain research budget. (Of course, the threat of acid rain damage was but dimly perceived during the Carter years.)

None of this augurs well for acid rain abatement. The US walked away from US/Canadian acid rain negotiations five years ago, and there are no indications that those negotiations will be resumed. Nevertheless, there are some encouraging signs. When President Reagan met in March 1985 with Canada's Prime Minister Mulroney, the Canadians made acid rain a salient issue. Reagan and Mulroney each designated a special envoy on acid rain, to study all aspects of the problem and to report back within a year. The US envoy was former Transportation Secretary Drew Lewis, who had earned a reputation as a man of action. On 13 September 1985 Lewis addressed a meeting of New England governors and observed, 'Saying that sulphates do not cause acid rain is the same as saying that smoking does not cause lung cancer'.[25] This was the first unequivocal statement on the acid rain problem by any senior official of the Reagan team.

In the face of the US National Academy of Science's (NAS) 1983 report urging that acidifying emissions be cut in half, Lewis talked of a $1 billion control program to reduce SO_2 emissions by 1 to 2 million tons. Estimates vary, but it could clearly cost many billions of dollars to achieve the 50 % reductions recommended by NAS (amounting to about 12 to 14 million tons).

Lewis also talked about accelerated research to develop clean coal technologies, and this prefigured the 'agreement' that was eventually reached when Reagan and Mulroney held their second annual meeting in March 1986. The 'agreement' called for the US utility industry to contribute $2.5 billion for research on clean coal technologies. In March 1987, Reagan renewed his pledge to match that amount with federal monies over a five year period. This agreement has not begun to be implemented, and it is hard to see how $500 million in a new annual federal appropriation would meet the stringent spending guidelines of the Gramm-Rudman Act of 1985 (since designated unconstitutional in part by the US Supreme Court, but likely to be carried out in practice in some form).

On other fronts, Senator Stafford of Vermont held hearings early in 1986 on the revised Clean Air Act. The hearings placed increased emphasis on nitrogen oxides. (Earlier testimony before Stafford's committee indicated that in the spring thaw, the nitric acid and the sulfuric acid surges are about equal. Moreover, SO_2 emissions are going down while NO_x emissions are holding steady or rising.) Senator Stafford was unable to get the Clean Air Bill out of committee in 1986.

Americans in general strongly favor environmental protection and pollution control, according to all opinion polls. The Reagan people may have thought it politically important to appease environmentalists with a high-visibility, low-cost acid rain abatement effort, along the lines agreed to by Reagan and Mulroney in March 1986.

It is probable that pure domestic political considerations, rather than Canadian or European diplomatic pressures, or cost-benefit analyses, or materials losses, or prospective forest damage, will finally bring about a small measure of acid rain abatement in the US in the foreseeable future.

Conclusion

Most industrial countries, following the lead of Sweden, Norway, West Germany and Canada, now deem it in their own interest collectively to adopt significant acid rain abatement measures. But in their own supposed interest, Poland, the UK and the US have not joined in the effort at concerted international abatement action known as 'the 30 % Club'. Poland's weak economy apparently cannot sustain the costs of abatement, and pressures from industry and electric utilities, coupled with the laissez-faire attitudes of the Thatcher and Reagan governments have thus far thwarted abatement pressures in the UK and the US.

The precedent established in the international response to today's comparatively straightforward acid rain issue will set the tone for crucial efforts to head off other international environmental problems in coming years. If major industrial countries like Poland, the UK and the US which are clear victims of acid pollution damage, continue to hold out against concerted international action, one can only suppose that environmental degradation will increase yet more rapidly in those countries than among their more internationally responsible neighbors.

Notes

A somewhat different version of this paper appeared in *Ambio*, **15**, No. 1, 1986.

1. A full description of these maneuvers can be found in Wetstone and Rosencranz, *Acid Rain in Europe and North America*, 1983, pp. 140–4. See also Rosencranz, 'The ECE Convention of 1979 on Long Range Transboundary Air Pollution', 75 *Amer. Jnl. Int'l. Law* 975 (October, 1981) and *Zeitschrift für Umweltpolitik* 511 (December, 1981).

2. The Convention on Long-Range Transboundary Air Pollution was adopted at the High-level Meeting within the Framework of the ECE on the Protection of the Environment. Held at Geneva from 13–15 November 1979, the Meeting was attended by representatives from 33 of the 34 member states of the Economic Commission for Europe. The Convention elaborates fundamental principles for protecting people and the environment against air pollution. It has detailed provisions on such matters as the exchange of information, consultations, research and monitoring. Under the Convention, the Contracting Parties undertake to develop, without undue delay, policies and strategies for combating the discharge of air pollutants, using the best available technology. It emphasizes the implementation and further development of the Co-operative Programme for the Monitoring and Evaluation of the Long-range Transmission of Air Pollutants in Europe (EMEP). The Convention entered into force on March 16, 1983.

Signatory	Date of ratification	Date of accession to the 30 % Club	Promised reductions of SO_2 from 1980
Austria	Dec 1982	June 1983	50 % by 1995
Belgium	July 1982	June 1984	50 % by 1995
Bulgaria	June 1981	June 1984	30 % by 1993
Byelorussian SSR	June 1980	June 1984	30 % by 1993
Canada	Dec 1981	June 1983	50 % by 1994
Czechoslovakia	Dec 1983	Sept 1984	30 % by 1993
Denmark	June 1982	June 1983	50 % by 1995
Fed. Rep. Germany	July 1982	June 1983	60 % by 1993
Finland	April 1981	June 1983	50 % by 1995
France	Nov 1981	March 1984	50 % by 1990
German Dem. Rep.	June 1982	June 1984	30 % by 1993
Greece	Aug 1983		
Holy See			
Hungary	Sept 1980	April 1985	30 % by 1993
Iceland	May 1983		
Ireland	July 1982		
Italy	July 1982	Sept 1984	30 % by 1993
Liechstenstein	Nov 1983	June 1984	30 % by 1993
Luxembourg	July 1982	June 1984	30 % by 1993
Netherlands	July 1982	March 1984	40 % by 1995
Norway	Feb 1981	June 1983	50 % by 1994
Poland	March 1985		
Portugal	Sept 1980		
Romania			
San Marino			
Spain	June 1982		
Sweden	Feb 1981	June 1983	65 % by 1995
Switzerland	May 1983	June 1983	30 % by 1995
Turkey	April 1983		
Ukrainian SSR	June 1980	June 1984	30 % by 1993
USSR	May 1980	June 1984	30 % by 1993
UK	July 1982		
US	Nov 1981		
Yugoslavia			
EEC	July 1982		

3. Monitoring of pollutants is carried out in each ECE country in coordination with the European Monitoring and Evaluation Programme (EMEP), a UN-supported operation.

4. 'Dry' SO_2 can continually combine with dew or other moisture on the surfaces of buildings to form a weak sulphuric acid. Over time, the acid gradually erodes the faces of these buildings.

5. This section draws on a report by Helmut Schreiber in *Acid News*, June, 1985, p. 9. (*Acid News* is published by the Swedish NGO Secretariat on Acid Rain.)

6. *Id.*

7. 'Cogeneration' plants use ordinarily-wasted steam heat as a power source.

8. Interview with John Bryson, Executive Vice President, Southern California Edison Company, 25 October 1985.

9. This is reported by Dr. Zygmunt Fura of the Polish Ecological Club, in *Acid News*, Summer 1985, p. 14.

10. The Executive Body was established by the terms of the Acid Rain Convention to coordinate abatement activities among contracting states.

11. The CEGB is responsible for more than 60 % of all UK SO_2 emissions.

12. House of Commons 4th Report, Environment Committee, Session 83–4, *Acid Rain*, Vol. I (London: HMSO, 1984).

13. *Id.*

14. President Reagan's advisors, anticipating that they would not like the findings of the National Academy of Sciences, got the president to appoint his own task force chaired by his Science Advisor, to study the causes and effects of acid rain. Unfortunately for the White House, the President's task force came up with virtually the same conclusions as the National Academy of Sciences.

15. See Report, Royal Commissions on Environmental Pollution, no. 10, p. 142 (1984).

16. *Id.* at 145.

17. See Report, 'United Kingdom: Tree Dieback,' in *Acid News*, October, 1985, p. 8.

18. Report, Royal Commission on Environmental Pollution, no. 10, p. 145 (1984).

19. *Id.* at 147.

20. To date, the main EEC directive on mobile source emissions regulates the amount of lead in gasoline (petrol). Other directives limit somewhat the sulphur content of vehicle fuels, e.g. 'gas oil' (diesel fuel).

21. For a full discussion of the SO_2 Directive, see Wetstone and Rosencranz, *Acid Rain in Europe and North America*, 1983, pp. 150–3.

22. *Materials* includes sandstone and other building materials, all metal surfaces and all painted surfaces.

23. Conversation with Ted Williams, US Department of Energy, 5 November 1985.

24. The US Mid-west has numerous heavily polluting older power plants which are all *exempt* from the strict 'New Source Performance Standards' of the Clean Air Act. These standards apply only to plants built after 1970.

25. *The Economist*, 21 September 1985.

12

Toward resolution of
the acid rain controversy

Göran Persson

Swedish Environmental Protection Agency,
Solna, Sweden

1   A first step taken

The condition for a resolution of the acid rain controversy is reduced emission to a level that is acceptable from the environmental point of view to the net receivers of acid substances.

Under the terms of the Convention on Long-range Transboundary Air Pollution, states recognize the acidification problem and make a general commitment to take countermeasures. With the adoption of the Convention it is no longer a question of *whether* measures are to be taken to reduce emissions, but of what measures to take, when and on what scale.

No country can be expected to accept large-scale environmental damage caused by emission of pollutants in another country. That principle was formulated in the 1972 UN Conference on the Human Environment in Stockholm, and it has now been endorsed in the Convention. Accordingly, the primary reason for working, under the auspices of the Convention, toward a reduction of sulphur and nitrogen oxides emission is that these substances lead to acidification damage at points far from the emission sources.

Nevertheless, there are also great environmental advantages to be gained in the immediate vicinity of these sources, primarily in the form of ameliorated health effects, reduced corrosion and less damage to plants. Far-reaching measures are justified on socio-economic grounds. This is especially so if it is accepted that the acidification problem did not arise overnight and cannot be solved overnight. There is a need to take measures step by step according to a long-term plan.

An important first step was taken in Helsinki, Finland in July 1985 when 21 signatories to the Convention agreed to reduce sulphur emissions by at least 30 % in the period 1980–93.

2   By how much must emissions be reduced?

2.1   *To avoid acidification of surface waters?*

Lakes and watercourses in acidification-susceptible areas are the most vulnerable parts of our ecosystem. Today, given the knowledge that we now have, there are several ways of formulating what might be an 'acceptable' level of deposition, that is to say, how much the sensitive ecosystems can stand without suffering cumulative damage.

Acidification in Norway and Sweden, as we know, developed progressively mainly after the Second World War. The deposition level prior to that might thus be regarded as 'acceptable', even if occasional cases of acidification had been reported earlier.

On the Scandinavian peninsula the deposition declines as one moves from south to north. Even though there are large acidification-susceptible areas in northern Sweden, for example, the lakes there (with some few exceptions) are not acidified. The deposition levels that do not cause acidification in northern Scandinavia should thus be 'acceptable' in southern parts as well.

There are also models, developed in Canada, Norway and Sweden, which describe the relationship between deposition and lake acidification. These models can be used to calculate an 'acceptable' deposition.

All these bases of calculation give similar results. A sulphate deposition of about 0.5 grams of sulphur per square metre per year could be tolerated without entailing any risk of large-scale acidification damage. To achieve this level of deposition a reduction of 75–80 % of European sulphur emissions is required.

The deposition of nitrates, as yet, is of markedly less significance than the sulphate deposition, but nitric acid deposited in snow contributes significantly to low pH-values of 'acid surges' during snow melt. This contribution is important as it is not the average year-round pH of a given lake or watercourse that shows how far the water is threatened by acidification. The critical level, the figure that determines the biological effects, is instead the lowest pH – probably in combination with a certain aluminium concentration – to which the organisms are subjected during the most sensitive part of their life cycle, usually the initial stage. This critical level is often reached during snow melt.

2.2   *To avoid acidification of soil and groundwater?*

Compared with surface water, the soil has a greater resistance to acidification, but the properties of the bedrock and the type of soil produce great regional differences in sensitivity. Soil is acidified not only by acid precipitation but also by silviculture and agriculture. On ploughland, the harvest that is extracted and the use of nitrogenous fertilisers are decisive as regards acidification and the resultant need for liming.

The acid that reaches coniferous forest comes in part from precipitation and in part from biological processes in the ground. Seen over one forest generation, the acid increments from these two 'sources' are of the same magnitude. Here, too, however, there are differences in the distribution from place to place, depending on the amount of precipitation and the productivity of the soil.

Soil acidification due solely to biological acid formation does not normally lead to large-scale acidification of lakes and watercourses. This becomes evident when one considers that the acidification of forest land by biological processes has been going on for thousands of years without any widespread acidification of surface waters. Even so, there is a close inter-relationship between the acidification of land and that of water. In general, it is only lakes in areas with acid soils that suffer acidification. The explanation is that sulphate and nitrate, deposited from the atmosphere on acid ground, are transported together with hydrogen and aluminium ions to surrounding waters. It is above all the size of the sulphate deposition – and thus indirectly the size of the sulphur emissions – that determines this acid transport to the water. The nitrate is to a large extent absorbed by vegetation, at least up to a certain point.

Sulphur deposition also leads to the acidification of groundwater. So far, acidification has been found in the groundwater reservoirs that are relatively close to the surface, but just as with surface water, the acidification is gradually penetrating deeper into the ground and spreading to larger areas, with increasingly serious effects on groundwater. Acidification like this increases the mobility of metals, which are leached out of the ground and end up in the groundwater. Acid groundwater can suffer additional metallic contamination from corroded water pipes.

Cadmium is one of the heavy metals that are beginning to 'migrate'. If groundwater with increased cadmium concentrations is used as drinking water, then the population, which is already heavily burdened with cadmium, gets another unwelcome increment, albeit a relatively small one.

Weathering is the process in the soil that counteracts acidic deposition. The weathering capacity varies considerably with the type of soil. Our limited knowledge of the weathering processes of different soils does not allow us to put a figure on the 'acceptable' sulphur deposition. We do not know, therefore, if the most threatened areas are the sensitive soils receiving moderate depositions or the less sensitive ones with high depositions.

In southern Scandinavia, in areas of high sulphate and nitrate deposition, important nutrients (basic cations such as calcium, magnesiu and potassium) are being progressively leached out. Within one or two decades the situation may be that forest production is limited by lack of nutrients other than nitrogen.

2.3   *To avoid forest damages?*

It was not until the early 1980s that dramatic forest changes were clearly recorded. Currently, some 7 million hectares of European forest land has suffered damage. In West Germany an official 1984 forest survey indicated that about 50 % showed clearly visible damage.

There is a broad consensus that forest die-back is currently ascribable to direct leaf or needle damage from deposition. There is, however, some debate as to which pollutant is the main cause – ozone, sulphuric and nitric acids, ammonia, etc., with a good case being made for ozone. The balance of evidence indicates that the interactive effects between all these pollutants are probably so complex that this debate is largely irrelevant. In addition drought, frost and fungal attacks contribute to the observed damages.

Reductions in the emissions of sulphur oxides, nitrogen oxides and hydrocarbons is the only way of preventing direct leaf or needle damage from gaseous pollutants. The lack of knowledge of the detailed mechanisms behind the forest die-back makes it difficult to estimate an acceptable air quality and to calculate necessary emission reductions. The serious nature of the damages indicate, however, that radical reductions will be needed.

3 Countermeasures at the receiving end are inadequate

Lakes and watercourses can be limed, groundwater can be processed to remove metals before being used as drinking water, nutrients can be supplied to forestland by fertilisation, and various other negative effects of acidification can be countered by measures in the environment, i.e. at the receiving end. Such views are often asserted, since the other type of countermeasure, the stringent limitation of sulphur- and nitrogen-oxide emissions at the source, is regarded as very costly.

But such arguments do not stand up. Liming is not a wholly adequate solution to the problem of lake and watercourse acidification. The first thaw water in the spring can be many times more acidic than the snow as a whole. This so-called chemical 'acid surge' also affects lakes with a long water-turnover time, since the inflowing thaw water collects under the ice along the shores. This means that the thaw water, which has high metal concentrations as well as being acidic, affects the most important fish-reproduction area of the lakes. The effects are often devastating, and they can occur even if the lake has been limed.

When the snow melts right away during a short period in the spring, the flow of water in the smaller watercourses may increase a hundred times over, assuming almost the same composition as the thaw water. This so-called hydraulic acid surge is difficult to eliminate by liming.

The liming of land has been suggested as a method of countering the acidification of great areas of land. But land liming as a general method is unrealistic on both practical and environmental grounds. It has also been shown that forest trees do not grow so well on limed lands.

We cannot come to terms with acidification by countermeasures in the enviroment – when the negative effects have already become apparent. It is not the symptoms but the causes of acidification that we have to tackle. However, the liming of lakes and watercourses is needed as a defence until such time as we achieve a meaningful reduction in the deposition of the sulphate and nitrate.

4   Technical solutions are available

When it comes to limiting the emissions of sulphur and nitrogen oxides we are not without the technical means. The simplest way to reduce sulphur emissions is to increase the use of fuels naturally low in sulphur. Supplies of such fuels are, however, limited and there is therefore a need for ways of desulphurising oil and coal, especially for use in small-size combustion plants. In the case of oil there are effective desulphurising processes that can be employed at moderate cost. High-grade desulphurization of coal is more difficult to achieve.

Fuel-gas desulphurization and denitrification have been developed in recent years to the point of being commercially available techniques. Scientists have succeeded in increasing operational reliability while at the same time reducing the costs. With new coal-fired power plants, flue-gas desulphurization puts the production costs up by 10–15 %. What effect this will have on the price of electricity will depend on what proportion of the generated power is produced by plants fired with fossil fuels and employing desulphurization. In the case of new power plants fired with normal, i.e. high sulphur fuels, fuel-gas desulphurization should be seen as an integral part of the production process.

Today we are witnessing the breakthrough in a new technology, the fluidised bed, whereby the sulphur is fixed at the time of the combustion. The incremental costs of this desulphurization are small, and there is a bonus in that emissions of nitrogen oxides are also substantially reduced. It ought to be possible to control the emissions of organic substances as well. The technology is commercially available for small and medium-sized plants and the costs are comparable with those of conventional combustion.

Efficient technologies exist for the reduction of emissions of nitrogen oxides and hydrocarbons from motor vehicles; these are applied in the US and Japan.

Energy saving is an attractive method of limiting pollutant emissions; the smaller the amounts of fuel we use, the smaller will be the emissions of sulphur and nitrogen oxides. The steep rises in energy costs since 1973 have spurred interest in energy-saving technology. Looking ahead a little, there is ample scope for bringing about lower energy consumption.

5   Some arguments and answers

The following three arguments are commonly used by large emitters:

(i) If abatement of sulphur and nitrogen oxides emissions were embarked upon, it is impossible to measure its effectiveness.

(ii) The abatement technologies are improving and if we wait a few years we shall almost certainly have more cost-effective solutions by then.

(iii) The costs needed to abate pollution are greater than the damage done to the receptors.

Regarding (i) above, we know that over a large industrialized region such as Europe, deposition is proportional to emission when averaged over a few years. Hence any emission abatement would be expected to produce a corresponding reduction in deposition. This suggests that it is a waste of time to put the blame on *one* emitter or *one* type of industry or even on *one* country. Both emission strategies and deposition goals must be worked out collectively. If this could be managed, a lot of temporizing, useless effort and evasion would be avoided.

Regarding (ii) above, given the direction and tempo of research on this topic, it is now unlikely that further work will provide totally revolutionary abatement management. And, further delay may mean that we shall be forced to deal with the problem when it has assumed crisis proportions.

One major difficulty with argument (iii) is that it begs a fundamental question – what moral, economic or legal right has an emitting country got to dump pollutants, whatever the level of nuisance or damage they cause, onto a second party? At best it is uncivilized behaviour and, at worst, an unwarrantable interference in the private affairs of another state, tantamount to a hostile act.

6   Clear-cut goals for European emission reductions are needed

Reduced sulphur emissions in Europe, to a level that is acceptable from environmental and health points of view, should be the long-term goal for a sulphur reduction programme within the framework of the Convention. Maximum deposition of sulphur in susceptible regions should then be below $0.5 \ g/m^2/year$. The question is whether a programme of this kind should be drawn up with uniform rules for the whole of Europe.

If the acidification in Scandinavia were the only motivation for reducing sulphur emissions, it would certainly be more effective, in economic terms, to direct the initial step to those emission areas that make the biggest contribution to the deposition in Scandinavia. But it has to be recognised that acidification is not an exclusively Scandinavian problem. Large forest areas in Central Europe are seriously threatened both by acid precipitation and by direct gas damage. Added to this are health effects, corrosion and direct plant damage in areas of large sulphur emissions. When all the effects of sulphur emission are taken into account, then, the overall conclusion is that we must regard Europe as one area with one common airspace, in which uniform rules governing emissions must apply. In the continued work within the framework of the Convention, however, there are good reasons for considering various principles by which the problems might be solved, for example the formulation of uniform rules for more limited areas.

Since the combustion of oil and coal is the wholly preponderant source of sulphur emissions in Europe, the measures we take should make reduction of those emissions their first aim. A programme of action might adopt the objective of gradually reducing the sulphur emissions per unit of energy to a level that would be common to all the countries involved and would be determined with reference to the environmental effects. The acceptable sulphur emissions per unit of energy will depend on the total consumption of fossil fuels within the region. It is therefore also important to use all possible ways of saving energy and to exploit possible alternative sources of energy, notably those that are renewable.

If a programme is drawn up according to these principles it could be left to each country to choose the methods that are most cost-effective from the standpoint of that country. Countries that currently have a low energy consumption would thus be free to increase it to the extent that is necessary to achieve national goals in various sectors.

Other principles could of course be taken as the basis for agreements, and it is important to explore various possible lines of progress within the framework of the Convention.

At the same time, all the countries that share this common airspace must accept the position that common sacrifices will be necessary if the intentions of the Convention are to be realised. Our generation does not own the lands and water amidst which it lives. We merely have them on loan, and we must therefore prepare to pass them on, unspoiled to coming generations.

Part IV

The case of marine pollution

13

Marine pollution agreements: successes and problems

Douglas M. Johnston

Faculty of Law, Dalhousie University, Halifax, Nova Scotia, Canada

1   The output

One of the most conspicuous features of modern diplomacy is the volume and variety of environmental agreements (or perhaps more properly 'arrangements') which have been negotiated in recent years. Liberally defined, 'environmental management' has become one of the most frequently negotiated sectors of treaty-making. The total number of environmental agreements in existence may exceed 500.[1] Because of the widening spread of non-local environmental concerns, and the accumulating evidence of 'systemic environmental damage',[2] most environmental arrangements today are *multilateral*. In this area of treaty-making 'environmental management' may now rank ahead of any other sector.

Marine pollution is not the oldest sub-sector of environmental treaty-making. International arrangements in the fields of wildlife protection and fishery conservation have had a much longer history.[3] But since 1954 marine pollution has attracted a remarkable quantum of diplomatic energy, and the treaty-making output has been fairly prodigious. The most recent listing of marine pollution agreements[4] includes over 70 multilateral instruments of one kind or another, organized in 40 'clusters' of related treaty arrangements. Frequently the first instrument negotiated in a designated subject area generates a number of 'satellites' in the form of protocols, amendments, rules, revisions or other types of ancillary arrangements, which are separate in form though dependent in function. These 40 'clusters' are divided into six categories: (i) general law-making conventions and other global non-treaty instruments designed in part to promote international legal development (six in number); (ii) global marine pollution conventions of general application (four); (iii) regional marine pollution arrangements (thirteen); (iv) intergovernmental liability and compensation schemes (seven); (v) industrial liability and compensation schemes (three); and (vi) general maritime safety conventions (seven). Some of these instruments are only indirectly related to the prevention and control of marine pollution, but on the other hand it might be possible to add a few more of an unconventional sort, such as the 1984 Ottawa Guidelines on Land-Based Marine Pollution recently negotiated under UNEP auspices.

The diversification which has occurred in this area of environmental treaty-making can be attributed to the multi-faceted character of the marine pollution problem. The variety of 'sources' of the problem was recognized at the Third UN Conference on the Law of the Sea (UNCLOS III), and six categories of marine pollution were included in the environmental provisions of the final text, the 1982 UN Convention on The Law of the Sea (hereafter, the UNCLOS III Convention): (i) vessel-source (or ship-generated) pollution; (ii) land-based marine pollution; (iii) dumping; (iv) marine pollution related to offshore petroleum development (exploration and exploitation of the resources of the continental shelf); (v) marine pollution related to mineral resource development in the international area of the deep ocean floor (beyond the limits of natioal jurisdiction); and (vi) marine pollution arising from the atmospheric transportation of pollutants. Only the first three of these six categories of marine pollution have given rise to official, multilaterally negotiated arrangements, and by far the largest number fall into the category of vessel-source pollution. Significantly, however, the trend in recent years has been to an increasing number of multilaterally negotiated arrangements in the field of land-based marine pollution. The concerns reflected in this field have risen to a level that seems to have deflected diplomatic attention from the last three of the UNCLOS III categories of marine pollution, and on present evidence it seems unlikely that the international community will wish to assign comparable priority to them in the coming years.

2 Six family portraits

The listing of these agreements reflects also a wide variety of approaches to the multifaceted problem of marine pollution. In each of the three negotiated sectors – vessel-source pollution, land-based marine pollution, and dumping – an assortment of tasks and techniques have begun to be developed. The diversity is striking as we survey the distinctive characteristics of the six families.

The first family (*general law-making conventions* and other global non-treaty instruments designed in part to promote international legel development) tends to emphasize *normative* development, not only through the traditional task of establishing and developing legal rules and principles ('obligations') but also through the promotion of less 'binding' norms and criteria designed to govern environmental action ('responsibilities'). In these instruments legal recognition is given to the responsibility of states and international agencies to participate in the setting of international standards and to promote the internationalization of 'recommended practices'. The legal task also includes the definition or re-definition of crucial concepts, the stipulation of conditions and exceptions, and increasingly the elaboration of legal 'regimes' of norms, procedures and institutions with which future negotiated arrangements will be required to conform.

The second family (*global marine pollution conventions of general application*) consists of more specific arrangements which might be said to constitute distinguishable 'regulatory systems'. The London Dumping Convention (LDC), for example, clearly has created a system or regime to which every state either does or does not 'belong'. Each such regime is intended to evolve, almost organically; but from this perspective the international community is seen to be sharply divided between participants in the system ('contracting parties') and non-participants ('third parties'). The principle that consent should govern the (horizontally structured) international community has divided the world into "dos" and "don't's" in this area of environmental management. The traditional requirement of treaty ratification has split the human biosphere into two kinds of states, insiders and outsiders, and it threatens to create two divergent groups, the legally responsible and the legally irresponsible. Through the convenient device of withholding consent, under the law of treaties, any state, developed or developing, may enjoy the comparative advantage of immunity from the legal impact of specific systems of environmental management.

The third family (*regional marine pollution arrangements*) consists of more tentative instruments designed to promote legal and institutional development at the *regional* level: more tentative, either because they precede legal or regulatory commitments in the first or second category of agreements, or because the parties are not yet ready to move swiftly from the 'soft law' to the 'hard law' end of the spectrum of environmental responsibilities accepted within the first and second categories. The most recent of these regional agreements are, however, firmly linked with the newest members of the first and second families, so that many parties to these regional agreements, once they are more fully developed through specific protocols, may be brought into conformity with the responsibilities articulated in these other global instruments without being formally 'bound' to them, at the global level, under the law of treaties. Because most of these regional agreements in recent years have emerged from UNEP's Regional Seas Programme, which is designed almost exclusively for the benefit of developing countries in the eleven designated 'regional seas', this third family of environmental agreements seems likely to split into two groups of contracting states: the 'have nots' of Africa, Asia, Latin America, the Caribbean and the South Pacific; and the 'haves' of Europe. On the face of things, this is likely to create disparities in the scope and character of regional commitments accepted or in the rate of acceptance and implementation, or both, holding out the prospect of inter-regional asymmetry in this context of environmental management.

The fourth family (*intergovernmental liability and compensation schemes*) is more closely associated than the first three with the traditional seafaring countries, countries with ancient customs protective of commercial interest such as that of liability limitation afforded to shipowners and the successful practice of underwriting marine perils through private insurance. The public as well as private need for compensation for marine pollution damage caused to coastal interests in modern times has resulted in treaty-based commitment to the principle of strict liability, albeit within the traditional maritime framework of limited liability. This family of arrangements is clearly distinguishable from the first three, and the sixth, by reason of its preoccupation with *remedial principles and procedures*, instead of preventive measures. It lives on the opposite side of the street. The states which accept this sort of treaty commitment are likely to be those that dominate the shipping, marine insurance, and energy industries and best understand the need to reconcile state and corporate interest in this context of environmental policy and management.

Located next door, as it were, the fifth family (*industrial liability and compensation schemes*) maintains a love–hate relationship with the fourth. Both focus on remedial principles and procedures, and deal with 'practical' rather than normative or political considerations. They also purport to be on good terms with each other and to some extent the relationship between the two families is based on a pledge of mutual support. But in practice the relationship is often competitive rather than cooperative, and in some instances commitments accepted within this fifth family are incompatible with commitments accepted by the fourth.[5] With the backing of the state apparatus, the intergovernmental agreements may seem likely to prevail over the industrial, as the cat seems likely to prevail over the mouse in the longer run of things. But the game is complicated, and industry's control of technology and most of the relevant information tends to balance the odds.

The sixth and last of the families (*general maritime safety conventions*) consists of highly detailed provisions on technical standards and procedures. Based on a technological or operational approach to *problem-solving*, they reflect the newest and best ideas of those expert in vessel construction and design and navigational practices. It is the least provocative family on the block.

3   The Input

The record of environmental diplomacy is difficult to evaluate, even in the well-documented context of marine pollution. Precisely because of the impressive volume and variety of outcomes in the form of negotiated agreements and arrangements, it may seem carping to question the effectiveness of this sector of environmental treaty-making. Yet most participants in the process, as well as thoughtful observers, readily concede that the long-term effects, as distinguished from the immediate outcomes, of marine pollution diplomacy are, on the whole, disappointing. On or off the record, many marine pollution specialists are prepared to admit that the treaty-making record is highly misleading. With relatively few exceptions, it has proved difficult to induce a substantial majority of states to sign and ratify the *global* agreements. Most of these instruments take five to ten years to come into force. Not infrequently, the economic and technological assumptions underlying the text are open to question, if not clearly invalid, ten years after conclusion of negotiations. More often than not, the language of commitment is sufficiently general, if not vague or equivocal, to support diverse interpretations of what was agreed to – usually by design rather than by accident. Often a ratified commitment in treaty form remains meaningless in practice, in the absence of any serious effort to 'implement' the provisions through appropriately effective 'measures' at the national level. It is not yet clear that *regional* marine pollution arrangements will fare much better.

Admittedly, the incidence of oil pollution from vessels seems to have abated in the last fifteen years or so. But much of the credit for this improvement must be due to technological innovation supplied by industry and to the upvaluing of oil in the market place in the period after 1973. To the extent that industrial innovation is forced by government pressure, it can be questioned whether that pressure would be significantly less effective in the absence of these treaty commitments. In the case of hazardous susbstances, it will be interesting to see whether effective pollution controls can be implemented, after the general acceptance of appropriate treaty commitments, without an upvaluing of chemicals and nuclear energy similar to what took place in the case of petroleum.

Heretical as it may seem, especially to those trained in international law, the *process* of marine pollution diplomacy may be more important than the *product*. A clearer evaluation of the process may emerge from a study of the *input* rather than from a textual analysis of the *output*. The input into most types of marine pollution diplomacy is chiefly technical in nature. It is virtually impossible to make an *effective* contribution to marine pollution treaty-making without possessing, or having direct access to, a sophisticated understanding of the technologies related to the problem of marine pollution and to the alternative solutions available. At the risk of giving offence, it should be said that the effectiveness of this kind of environmental diplomacy depends, above all, on the interaction of the relevant *technical elites*. At the risk of giving further offence, it might be added that effective marine pollution diplomacy depends also on the ability of these technical elites to de-politicize the process. In some circumstances, it may even depend on their skill in deflecting political (national sovereignty) sentiments from the field of environmental management. One would wish to back 'los tecnicos' in their constant, if understated, struggle with 'los politicos'. Even lawyers, trained to focus on the output of the treaty-making process, may be inclined to focus on the input. Clues to the 'successes' and 'problems' of marine pollution agreements are to be sought within the processes of making and maintaining treaties of this kind.

4　　　Back to neo-functionalism

By this reasoning, success in marine pollution diplomacy depends essentially on the political skills of the appropriate technical elites. These elites operate on transnational circuits or networks, including not only those of intergovernmental organization, both global and regional, but also various kinds of international non-governmental associations of a scientific or technical character. To put one's trust in this kind of circuitry or networking is to return to 'functionalism', or at least to the more modern ideas of the 'neo-functionalists', in political science.[6]

Very few of us today look forward with any confidence to the imminent collapse of the nation-state system. Yet many of us, in our own modest way, wage a tiny war each day against the forces of nationalism and political sentiment. We may hesitate to place all our eggs in the UN basket. It may seem unwise, as well as unfashionable, to invest our fondest aspirations in *global* bureaucracy. But 'regime-building' at the *regional* level seems to be in process, offering new outlets for impressive accomplishments in cooperative management, not least in the multisectoral context of ocean resource management.[7]

In this neo-functionalist vein, it might be suggested that the *primary* emphasis in the field of marine pollution diplomacy should now be placed on the *integration* of existing treaty-based arrangements at the regional level, rather than on the resort to new global treaties. The prospect of regional integration of this kind depends on the ability of the relevant technical elites to re-organize existing arrangements rather than on the will of political elites to accept new commitments. Instead of attempting to sell individual treaties as blocks of legal obligations, they should attempt to present regionally defined clusters of arrangements for coordination with a view to increasing the potential environmental benefits available to participating members of the regional community.

Finally, however, two concessions should be offered. First, it must be acknowledged that there is a continuing need to generate new treaties in certain areas of marine pollution, especially perhaps in that of the transportation, storage and disposal of hazardous substances. Second, the task of regional integration of existing marine pollution control arrangements cannot fairly be assigned to the secretariats of global organizations, whose loyalties are directed to the world community as a whole. Accordingly, the *second*, if not secondary, requirement is that the secretariats of the global organizations amass the appropriate technical information, and coalitions of technical experts, to impress on the political elites the need for new and meaningful commitments to the control of the most hazardous uses of the ocean environment.

Notes

1 This estimate is based on the number of environmental agreements listed in collections edited by Burhenne, Rüster, Simma and others.

2 For a recent overview see Douglas M. Johnston, 'Systemic Environmental Damage: The Challenge to International Law and Organization', 12 *Syracuse Journal of International Law and Commerce* 255 (1985).

3 Douglas M. Johnston, 'The Environmental Law of the Sea: Historical Development' in Douglas M. Johnston, *ed.*, *The Environmental Law of the Sea* (International Union for Conservation of Nature and Natural Resources, 1981), pp. 17–70.

4 Edgar Gold, *Handbook on Marine Pollution* (1985).

5 On the tensions between intergovernmental and industrial approaches to liability issues in the context of ship-generated marine pollution, see R. Michael M'Gonigle and Mark W. Zacher, *Pollution, Politics and International Law: Tankers at Sea* (1979), *passim*.

6 A. J. R. Groom and Paul Taylor, *eds.*, *Functionalism: Theory and Practice in International Relations* (1975).

7 See, for example, Oran R. Young, *Resource Regimes: Natural Resources and Social Institutions*, University of California Press (1982).

14

Issues and problems in the protection of the marine environment

Satu Nurmi

Legal Counsellor for International Environmental Affairs
Ministry of the Environment, Helsinki, Finland

In publication, in conferences, in international units the matters are generally divided into air pollution, land pollution and water pollution. In fact there is only one pollution because every single thing, every chemical whether in the air or on land will end up in the ocean *Jacques-Yves Cousteau*

1   General aspects

The marine environment is made up of the shores and the rolling waves, of the archipelago and broad expanses of water, both deep and shallow, of lush bays. This environment embraces the flora and fauna of the coastal or deep-sea areas, sandy beaches and boulders, the inner archipelago and the most distant rocky skerries, the tides and currents. The marine environment is one of the main components of the natural environment and is closely linked to the others: inland water resources, air, land and living natural resources. The marine environment, because of the diversity and quantity of its biological resources plays a crucial role in the equilibria of the biosphere. The health of the sea is of utmost importance because man derives part of his food from the seas through fishing and aquaculture. The sea is vital also for transport and for many recreational activities. Exploitation of the mineral and energy resources of the oceans is a challenge for the future.

The marine environment is also important from the political point of view. The importance attached to the sea by different countries has been demonstrated on many occasions, in their attempts to secure an outlet to it in order to safeguard political independence and their desires to extend their control over coastal waters and areas of the high seas. For many years, these aspects have been central to the United Nations Convention on the Law of the Sea.

2   Notion of marine pollution

The most cited definition of marine pollution is that proposed in 1969 by the joint group of Experts on the Scientific Aspects of Marine Pollution (GESAMP) and thereafter adopted in the following, slightly amended form by the Intergovernmental Oceanographic Commission (IOC) of UNESCO:

> Introduction of man, directly or indirectly, of substances or energy into the marine environment (including estuaries) resulting in such deleterious effects as harm to living resources, hazard to human health, hindrance to marine activities including fishing, impairment of quality for use of sea-water and reduction of amenities.

The GESAMP definition was endorsed by the Stockholm Conference on Human Environment in 1972 and has thereafter been adopted, subject to variable though slight changes, *inter alia*, in the 1974 Helsinki Convention on the Protection of the Marine Environment of the Baltic Sea Area, the 1974 Paris Convention for the Prevention of Marine Pollution from Land-Based Sources, the 1976 Barcelona Convention for the Protection of the Mediterranean Sea against Pollution, and the 1978 Kuwait Regional Convention for Cooperation in the Protection of the Marine Environment from Pollution. The formulation has also been cited – closely resembling but not completely identical to the GESAMP text – in the text of the 1982 United Nations Convention on the Law of the Sea. The GESAMP text is basically of 'action oriented' nature: its operative point of departure is the 'introduction' of something e.g. polluting substances into the marine environment. At the same time, however, it also presupposes that such introduction is to result in 'deleterious effects' to marine life. Without such effects no 'marine pollution' would occur.

Polluting substances may cause changes in the physical–chemical environment, e.g. in temperature, salinity, pH, gas content, chemistry, colour or turbidity of the water, which in turn may influence the marine life in different ways. They may also cause direct damage to organisms, e.g. on physiological processes, including alimentation and reproduction, after having reached a certain threshold concentration.

Pollutants have spread enormously, especially since the early 1950's, and no part of the seas, even at great depths, seems now to be completely free from them. Nobody knows how many pollutants there are, but already the pertinent new chemical compounds can be counted in tens of thousands.

3 Monitoring and assessment of the state of the sea

3.1 *Monitoring*

Monitoring is an important method to observe, measure, evaluate and analyse the risks or effects of pollution of the marine environment. Monitoring data form a part of the background information for an appropriate assessment of the state of the marine environment and for a forecast of possible man-induced changes. In order to register such man-induced changes, the natural changes of different elements of the ecosystem must be known. Therefore, monitoring will often include registration of more or less 'natural' conditions. In its more restricted sense, the term is applied to the regular measurement of pollutant levels in relation to set standards or in order to judge the effectiveness of a system of regulation and control.

During the 1970s considerable advances were made in scientific understanding of the physical and chemical properties of the oceans, and of the circulation of their waters. However, the monitoring of water quality and of sediment and living organisms is in general quite recent and is not yet sufficiently developed to show whether pollution is increasing or decreasing, except in specific cases where vigorous pollution control measures have been applied. Efforts to harmonize marine environmental monitoring methods are of special importance. Further problems are that available data on the state of the seas are often limited, difficult to compare and not widely published. According to the United Nations Environment Programme (UNEP) assessment the best data is recorded from the Baltic Sea, the North Sea, some North American and Australian estuaries and coastal waters, and the Mediterranean. The Regional Seas Programme of the UNEP is collecting information about other seas as well.

In the case of the Baltic Sea the Contracting Parties to the Helsinki Convention have elaborated a coordinated Baltic Monitoring Program (BMP). The programme is intended for implementing in several stages. The first stage, which took five years, had an experimental character and served as a pilot programme comprising a limited number of stations and measurements but, nevertheless, providing a basic coverage of the major aspects concerned. The objective of the second and further stages is an optimization of the programme according to experience gained and knowledge available in order to provide data for more comprehensive assessment of the state of the Baltic marine environment. The duration of the second stage will be five years, starting in 1984. Guidelines for the third stage of the BMP, starting in 1989, are being developed. It was agreed to implement the program on a moderate basis with a few strategic stations in different parts of the Baltic Sea, but with enough determinants to give a reasonable overall picture of the ecological changes in the sea.

This year the Helsinki Commission considered the establishment of an operative Data Bank for the BMP data at the Finnish Institute of Marine Research. The information concerns hydrographic, hydrochemical and biological data since 1979. The monitoring and study of radioactive materials in the Baltic Sea is not included in the present BMP proper, but will be conducted separately in association with the expertise of the International Atomic Energy Agency (IAEA).

The monitoring programme on airborne pollution has started on 1 January 1985. Modelling of the origin of transport of air pollutants for the Baltic Sea Area will be the subject of a seminar next year sponsored by the German Democratic Republic. The meeting of the Scientific Committee has recently expressed its concern of the insufficient knowledge of the effects to the Baltic Sea caused by the harmful substances carried by the air, in particular atmospheric transport and deposition of organic compounds such as the polychlorinated hydrocarbons. A recommendation concerning monitoring of airborne pollution load will be presented to the Helsinki Commission in 1986.

3.2   *Assessment*

The state of the marine environment and changes to it over time are not easy to understand in general terms with any degree of certainty. Although the deterioration of certain specific geographical areas has been well documented and understood by scientists, our knowledge of the general state of the marine environment still has numerous gaps.

According to the UNEP review there were serious deficiencies in knowledge of the state of the oceans and seas in 1970–80, although information about some shallow seas and estuaries was increasing rapidly. While the general characteristics of the world oceanic circulation, seawater composition and biological production have been broadly established, the monitoring of pollutants and ecosystems has been highly localized and time series data are lacking for most areas. Existing data on pollutant concentrations obtained by different laboratories are not always comparable because methods, standards and sampling techniques differ. Intercalibration exercises on contaminants in biota and sea water carried out by the International Council for the Exploration of the Sea (ICES), the Inter-Governmental Oceanographic Commission (IOC) and the International Laboratory of Marine Radioactivity of the International Atomic Energy Agency (IAEA) have demonstrated the seriousness of this problem. Trends in the concentration of pollutants between 1970 and 1980 can therefore only be established in a few limited areas, such as the Baltic or the North Sea.

Similarly, biological changes in the major oceans cannot be ascertained because of insufficient monitoring. Fishery and whaling statistics do, however, allow comments on the state of species and stocks in some regions. More general evaluations have been made by some international groups of experts such as the Group of Experts on Scientific Agriculture Organization of the UN (FAO).

As to the Baltic Sea the first interntionally coordinated assessment of the effects of pollution on the natural resources of the Baltic Sea, carried out under the auspices of the Helsinki Commission with scientific and technical assistance from the ICES, has been published in 1981.

A first so-called periodic assessment of the state of the Baltic Sea is being published in 1986. There are underway also a number of so-called specific assessments in the Baltic Sea Area, such as assessment on fish carried out in 1985–6, assessment on sediments carried out by 1987, and coastal assessments, which are already well under way.

4   **The main sources and forms of pollution –
          problems in their control and abatement**

Pollutants affecting the marine environment may originate from land, reach the sea waterborne, airborne or directly from the coast, from the operation of ships or pleasure craft, from seabed activities or through disposal at sea of waste or other matter.

Pollutants vary not only in the manner in which they enter the marine environment, but also in their chemical composition and behaviour. Some sources of marine pollution can be pinpointed, others are for all practical purposes untraceable. Some marine pollutants present a clear and immediate threat to marine life; others may only be dangerous in the long term, and the precise nature of these threats may still be unknown.

In its various forms land-based pollution may contain pollutants of virtually every composition. On the basis of guidelines established by GESAMP the main classes of marine pollutants may be as follows:

  (i)   halogenated hydrocarbons;
  (ii) petroleum and its derivatives;
  (iii) other organic chemicals;
  (iv) nutrient chemicals;
  (v)   inorganic chemicals;
  (vi) suspended solids;
  (vii) radioactive substances;
  (viii) thermal waste.

The main sources of marine pollution are usually identified as land-based pollution, vessel-based pollution, pollution from dumping and incineration at sea, pollution from exploration and exploitation of the sea-bed and from other marine activities.

4.1   *Land-based pollution*

Land-based pollution usually denotes any activity which, directly from coast to sea or as waterborne or airborne, introduces polluting substances or energy into the marine environment. The Montreal Guidelines of 1985 on the Protection of the Marine Environment Against Pollution from Land-Based Sources adds to the previous sources also 'Sources of marine pollution from activities conducted on offshore fixed or mobile facilities within the limits of national jurisdiction, save to the extent that these sources are governed by appropriate international agreements'. The inclusion of fixed or mobile offshore activities amongst the land-based pollution sources constitutes the latest dimension of the definition.

It is estimated that the greater part of marine pollution is caused by landbased activities. Their exact contribution to the total load of marine pollution remains difficult to determine but a proportion from 50 to 90 % has been estimated. It has further been estimated that while some 35 % of the overall release of petroleum into the sea comes from vessels, land-based activities account for some 54 % of the oil reaching the marine environment. And the proportion of land-based releases may prove even larger depending on the quantities of vapourized petroleum reaching the ocean surface through air.

Pollution from such land-based sources as port, industrial, urban and tourist activities has put pressure on the marine environment of estuaries and has sometimes had dangerous effects on coastal ecosystems. Estuaries are usually areas of intensive breeding for many marine species. These zones are therefore particularly important for coastal ecosystems.

In areas where industrial activities and modern agriculture are only developing their polluting capacities, domestic waste, as multiplied by rapid growth in population, poses the principal threat to marine purity. Discharges of domestic waste water consist essentially of dissolved or suspended organic matter. The danger from this type of pollution, however, is rather limited to the area immediately around the point of discharge. Although seawater would not be used for human consumption, shellfish living close to major waste water discharge sites become contaminated through their filtration of the water and retention of microbes. In the developed world advanced methods of sewage treatment mitigate such adverse effects but in these countries industrial waste emerges as the major cause of concern. Effluent discharged by industry consists of toxic chemicals either in pure or compound form. The most toxic chemicals are often the least biodegradable or non-degradable. Chemical compounds that are present in the water in the form of trace elements, tend to accumulate in living matter that forms part of the food chain. A distinct effect of these pollutants has been the reduced shell thickness of the eggs of some seabirds or the impairment of the reproductive capacity of some sea mammals, such as the grey seal in the Baltic and three species of whales. In extreme cases, regular consumption of contaminated fish can affect human health.

In the Baltic Sea context high priority has been given to the abatement of so-called hazardous substances such as DDT and PCB in the first place.

Surveys show that the limitations on DDT and PCB from land-based sources have had intended effects. These substances have diminished in the organisms in the Baltic Sea, even if harmful effects still remain.

Regarding other hazardous substances, such as mercury, cadmium, lead, copper, zinc and oil, comprehensive work is going on in the individual countries to find solutions to minimize the discharges. For example, discharges of mercury have diminished, so that several areas earlier blacklisted due to high mercury content in fish are no longer blacklisted. The main goal in the abatement policy in the Baltic Sea countries is to demonstrate the effects of the substances in the environment, and to find possible ways to reduce discharges of these substances to the environment. The discharges into the Baltic Seas from industries, municipal sewage treatment plants, water courses and atmospheric deposition of each country shall and have been reported and compiled annually. Difficulties have revealed in each country to obtain all necessary information. The compilation has so far covered organic material, phosphorous and nitrogen. It has been observed that to be able to succeed in a relatively accurate estimate of the total pollution load to the Baltic Sea, essentially more resources and commitment is required. In order to ensure better results in the abatement efforts, it is important that the work on most dangerous substances is directed towards various kinds of technical measures to minimize discharges both from point sources and diffuse sources. Furthermore, additional measures are needed to minimize pollution from different types of sources such as agriculture, urban areas and heavy industries.

It seems today that the most significant reductions of many industrial effluents have already been achieved due to the application of modern technology to water protection measures. However, further measures aiming at reducing the load of oxygen-consuming substances and phosphorous are still necessary as well as decisions on further technological development, including rationalization and intensification of agriculture and forestry, and the changes in the structure of industry.

Land-based pollution is a problem with particularly strong national overtones inescapably linked to industrial growth and economic development.

4.2   *Vessel-based pollution*

Although land-based activities are responsible for the main flow of marine pollution, vessel-source oil is no doubt the most documented enemy of the marine environment. According to the OECD calculations, roughly 1.5 million tonnes of oil annually ar discharged into the sea by shipping: 1 tonne for every 1000 tonnes transported by sea. Estimates suggest that shipping is the source of less than half of all the oil reaching the oceans and that tanker accidents account only for some 10 % of the input from shipping. The largest source of oil discharges is of non-accidental origin and results from routine operations such as tank clearing deballasting and bilge discharges. Accidental oil spills, however, very often have a substantial impact on the particular locality when they occur in bays, estuaries or land-locked seas.

While carriage of oil has proved to be a critical hazard to the marine environment, recent years have also witnessed considerable progress in the promotion of environmental safety through better vessel construction, equipment and operational techniques. Modern remote monitoring techniques also provide accurate information on the location of oil slicks, most of which are found along the main tanker routes around Africa, Europe and Japan and between the US and Europe. Efforts both at national and international levels have recently improved the surveillance of tanker traffic and promoted the control of accidental spills. Problems still remain in many countries in practical oil combating operations. Furthermore, far too little is known about the consequences of discharging oil at sea. Impacts on fish have been assessed lately, but no assessments exist so far of the damage to marine ecosystems as a whole. Opinions and calculations are, if available, neither reliable nor comparable. It is generally agreed that much work still has to be done before the effects of oil spills on the high seas can be evaluated accurately.

Damage to ecosystems may also have very serious economic consequences. Considerable progress has, however, been made in recent years in evaluating the cost of damage caused by oil spills, both by OECD and under the auspices of different regional organizations. OECD has for example estimated that the damage and clean-up costs resulting from accidental oil spills total about US$ 500 million worldwide every year, which means roughly 3 % of the average cost of transporting 1 tonne of oil. However, calculations concerning more or less immaterial objects such as the extent of loss of amenities in the region, losses to natural resources or damage caused to ecosystems are less developed.

Besides oil, tankers may carry other environmentally harmful cargoes. Accordingly, tank cleaning operations may also result in the discharge of residues of various liquid substances other than oil. In case of accidents the multitude of such cargoes constitute a polluting factor of a quite unpredict-able nature. So far, at least, this type of releases have, however, remained of a relatively slight effect.

As regards the non-oil threats from maritime traffic, particular concern has been expressed over vessel-source radio-activity. The problem is twofold: radio-active substances carried as cargo may be accidentally released into the marine environment or contamination may be inflicted by the use of nuclear-powered vessels, mainly as a result of collisions or other accidents. Although no major damage due to such causes has, as yet, been reported, the risks involved will no doubt grow with the number of nuclear ships in operation. Incidents constituting serious warnings of potential disaster have already taken place.

As regards marine transportation of radio-active materials, similar inci-dents have appeared to be rare enough, which, of course, is not to exclude the possibility of future accidents. It would seem, however, that such dangers are fairly well guarded against, since effective precautions, based on international standards and recommended practices, are being taken for the safe carriage of such cargoes.

Apart from substances used for vessel propulsion or carried as cargo, pollution may also be caused by daily ship routines, producing variable amounts of sewage and sanitary wastes, all potentially for release into the sea.

About 20–25 million tons of oil per year are transported into the Baltic Sea by tankers. An enclosed sea with often very complicated shore lines and archipelagos such as the Baltic Sea is very sensitive to oil pollution. According to rough calculations 30 000–60 000 metric tons of oil is annually discharged into the Baltic Sea.

Matters related to pollution from ships have been efficiently handled from the start of the cooperation. A great number of recommendations have been adopted. All Baltic Sea states have in their ports established reception facilities for oil. It has been possible to comply to a considerable extent with provisions laid down within the International Maritime Organization (IMO). On the other hand the Baltic Sea States have been able to influence the course of matters dealt with by IMO. That organization has thus far adopted recommendations specifically concerning the Baltic Sea. Provisions con-cerning the carriage, discharge and reception of noxious liquid substances in bulk will be applied from 1 January 1986.

Combatting marine pollution by accidental spillages of oil and other harmful substances is a field where progress has been rapid. A machinery for cooperation has been agreed upon. The procedures and guidelines for join actions have been included in an extensive manual issued by the Commission which is of considerable practical importance.

4.3 *Dumping and incineration of waste at sea*

Dumping – and to a lesser extent incineration – of land-based wastes at sea such as radio-active materials, chemical weapons and highly toxic industrial waste has contributed to the release of potentially polluting substances into the marine environment.

Though particularly offensive in character, as a whole dumping provides a relatively modest addition to marine pollution by now. According to some estimates, the amount of waste dumped at sea in recent years constitutes no more than 10 % of the total load of marine waste disposal. At the same time, international efforts to curb dumping particularly within the framework of the London Dumping Convention and the Oslo Convention of 1972, have been intensified and the public at large has also come to deplore the use of the sea as a dumping ground. On the other hand, the constant increase in the total volume of world waste places increasing pressure on the various means and methods of waste disposed, dumping included. Already for this reason alone it is important to continue keeping an eye on developments in the field of waste disposal options to ensure that alternative land-based methods be utilized and increased wherever possible.

Four main types of waste have been dumped at sea: dredged material, industrial waste, sludge from waste water treatment plants and radioactive waste. It is estimated that dredged material removed from the sea bottom in connection with dredging operations constitutes nearly 80 % of what is dumped at sea. But it is not only mud and gravel that are thereby disposed of. Since most dredging is carried out in estuaries, harbours and other areas of coastal vicinity, the sediments dredged often contain considerable quantities of pollutants from municipal, industrial and agricultural sources. Accordingly, a load of dredged material may have an environmental effect similar to that of deliberate disposal of industrial chemicals.

Industrial waste makes up the second major category of materials subject to dumping operations. The composition of such waste varies widely due to type of source industries and production processes. Since a great many of these substances are highly toxic, disposal thereof may constitute the gravest hazard in dumping activities.

The disposal of sewage sludge produces a critical problem in large metropolitan areas. This type of dumping covers a wide range of waste products containing organic and inorganic chemical matter. It is difficult to quantify the impacts of these types of discharge – which should be better controlled or even prohibited, as part of the implementation of international conventions – in view of the fact that the material is dumped rapidly and completely destroys the flora and fauna in the area concerned. Some countries also dump the sludge from waste water treatment plants. Such sludge may contain heavy metals such as mercury, cadmium and lead. To construct treatment plants and then to discharge into the sea the water plus the contaminated sludge that has been separated out cannot be considered a proper solution. Many countries now dispose of this sludge on land, either by incineration or landfill or by using it for agricultural purposes.

Particular concern has been expressed over dumping of radioactive materials. Due to the rapid increase of nuclear activities especially in energy production, the disposal of radio-active waste has emerged as a crucial environmental problem still awaiting a final solution. For some time dumping in the deep ocean was widely employed as the best practicable means to hide the radio-active debris. Gradually, however, protests were raised warning of the hazards of such policies. Although the waste to be dumped was usually well packed in concrete-filled metal containers, it was pointed out that under the corrosive conditions of the sea-bed the lifetime of any container is limited. It may be hoped that the decomposition of the containers would occur slowly enough to allow their contents sufficient time for de-activation or, at least, for safe dilution in the surrounding waters, but clearly no guarantees of this are possible. Besides, unpredictable factors, such as earthquakes on the ocean floor, may break open even the strongest containers. Quite apart from safety considerations, it was also submitted that in many cases economic reasons argued in favour of land-based storage. These arguments have resulted in partial reduction of dumping operations.

The OECD Nuclear Energy Agency has supervised such dumping in accordance with the requirements laid down by the IAEA in the Multilateral Consultation and Surveillance Mechanism adopted by the OECD Council in 1977. According to OECD estimates, between 1967 and 1982 the tonnage dumped annually remained roughly the same while the radio-activity level of the waste increased. The dumping of radio-active waste was temporarily halted in 1983 and 1984 due to recommendations adopted by the Consultative Meeting of the London Dumping Convention. In September 1985 the permissibility of dumping of low and medium level radio-active waste was considered again. On the basis of a scientific-technical review some countries assumed that such disposal on land was safer and more controllable while others considered that the marine environment is a suitable recipient for such waste and that sea dumping options could be pursued. The former option was chosen by vote at the Ninth Consultative Meeting of Contracting Parties to the London Dumping Convention. This means that an open-ended moratorium will continue and an extensive body of additional studies and assessments are to be carried out in different international scientific fora. Arguments behind the decisions taken were *inter alia* geological formations on land would secure a more adequate isolation from the biosphere than dumping at sea; the long-term effects are difficult to evaluate while the short-term effects on marine organisms are still unreliable; and there is need for further assessments to examine the issues of comparative land-based options and to consider the costs and risks associated with these options.

With regard to the prevention of dumping in the Baltic Sea Area, dumping operations generally are prohibited by the provisions of the Helsinki Convention. There are, however, two exceptions to this general prohibition: dumping of dredged material subject to a prior special permit and so-called emergency dumping when the safety of human life is endangered or a vessel or aircraft is threatened by destruction or loss.

4.4   *Other marine pollution sources*

Among the more novel uses of the seas, there is particular environmental significance in the exploration and exploitation of the sea-bed's non-living resources. In a few decades the sea-bed, earlier virtually beyond human reach, has turned into a scene of intense industrial activity with ever bolder prospects envisioned for the future.

At the outset, petroleum and gas were not merely the most attractive but the sole object of industrial sea-bed operations. The first off-shore wells were drilled at the end of the nineteenth century but it was not until the 1940s that commercial production, in a proper sense, got under way. With the help of technological developments ever greater depths of the continental shelf areas – which embrace most of the known reserves of off-shore oil and gas – have since been subjected to exploitation.

Following upon the rapid increase in oil and gas activities, other sea-bed minerals have lately attracted industrial interest, in particular, mineral nodules. Since most of the nodules rest far from land, in the deep ocean floor, it is only recently that their economic exploitation has been even remotely possible. Today, however, marine technology in certain countries has developed to the point where industrial exploitation of the nodules could be commenced in the near future.

The possible environmental impacts of sea-bed exploration and exploitation have been only partially disclosed. Since deep-sea mining is still at an initial stage of operation, no comprehensive data exist regarding its effects on the surrounding ocean space. On the other hand, the decades of off-shore oil and gas production have provided abundant evidence of the dangers involved in these activities.

According to literature the following phenomena, at least, will have to be taken into account:

(i) Deep-sea operations will destroy benthic organisms and their habitats, to the extent they exist. Such organisms would include the life-forms in physical contact with the nodules and potentially playing a significant role in their formation.

(ii) Since the nodules are often partly buried in the ocean floor, their elevation will produce scarring and scraping of the bottom soil. As a result, sea-bed sediments will be stirred up and the geological pattern of the top layers of the ocean floor will be altered.

(iii) In various phases of the mining operations sedimentary material, associated bottom organisms and bottom water may be introduced into the different layers of the water column. Very little is known of the effects that such 'doses' may have on commercial fish stocks.

Further problems will result from processing activities which may take place either on land or at the mining site. Operators will have to face, for instance, the question of sea disposal of the non-exploitable components of the nodules being processed.

Since 1981 commercial interest in the polymetallic sulfides has been aroused. The sulfide deposits are formed in areas with a volcanic activity and thus far have been found inside the 200 mile exclusive economic zone. Thoughts on exploitation are thus encouraged not only because of the magnitude but also the commercial value of these resources. We have every reason to believe that exploration of sulfide deposits will be intensified in the coming years and that they will become subject for commercial exploitation in the course of a decade.

Oceans are also exposed to sources of potential pollution which cannot readily be included in the categories so far mentioned. A timely example is the 'superport' constructed in the open sea to receive supertankers too big to enter shallow coastal waters. Similarly, environmental harm may be caused by the multitude of scientific devices scattered over the oceans to collect data or otherwise to promote man's knowledge of the marine phenomena. In rough seas such devices may be lost, adding to the oceans' man-made waste. Potential threats may also be posed by scientific experiments in underwater 'sealabs' or by the loss or disposal at sea of persistent plastics, fishing nets and lines.

It can be predicted that further uses of the seas will evolve in the future. It has already been envisaged that such developments may include floating airports and nuclear power plants anchored to the sea-bed as well as various subsurface installations for military purposes. It has also been observed that cuts and sores have healed exceptionally well in under-water conditions. This might lead to the establishment of sea-bed hospitals and sanatoria. Finally, recreational activities in marine areas are likely to expand in the future. All such measures and projects may have environmental implications.

The marine environment is further affected by such physical pollution as warm-water effects caused by discharge of warm cooling water from nuclear power plants, military waste due to accidental loss of bombs and torpedoes, mines and war gases. Extraction of sand and gravel on a large scale as well as erosion and leaching of mineral organic substances may change the bottom structure, and fish spawning grounds may be destroyed. There is also another kind of physical pollution, namely acoustic pollution, caused by noise of machines of ships and motorboats, and from underwater operations such as oil prospecting and certain military operations and experiments, a pollutant certainly felt by many fish and marine mammals.

5   Effects on marine life

Although marine life has proved to be more resilient than had been expected, aquatic ecosystems have been severely damaged near some industrialized areas, and their produce near some coastlines has become unfit for human consumption.

Destruction of marine ecosystems by irrational exploitation soon revealed to have implications in real economic terms. Although the world oceans are large, their productivity is enormous, and this pattern did permit enormous growth in the world fish catch until quite recently. By the 1970s in fact, nearly every major species traditionally sought in the northern Atlantic waters was overfished, and some stocks had collapsed. The same trend in catch was marked all over the world: around the waters of Africa, the Far East and South America. Now, in many areas, newly responsible and effective regulation of fishing will hold down catches; elsewhere, fully exploited or overexploited stocks will not support higher catches anyway. The FAO calculates that the catch of conventionally fished species could in theory be increased by 20–30 million tons over its current level. Perhaps half this increase would result from restored productivity of stocks now depleted by overfishing, the rest from harvesting the few remaining under exploited stocks.

The whales have a story of their own. Although the history of the commercial whaling is a sad one, recent developments point to a happy ending. Controls are not being applied that should prevent extinction and permit the eventual restoration of many whale stocks. If the past destruction of whales is a symbol of humanity's failures in relation in nature, the current progress in salvaging these mammals should inspire hope for the future. Much has still to be done for the proper protection of other species of marine mammals, such as seals and sirenians. Apart from fishes and marine mammals, sea turtles form a heavily exploited group of species also in need of urgent protection measures.

6   Management options and problems

The goals of the protection of the marine environment are, at large, almost equivalent to those adopted for environmental policy in general: to prevent, as far as possible, further environmental deterioration, and to restore already deteriorated parts of the environment to safeguard and maintain ecological balance for future generations. Against this background the protection of the marine environment is a manifold and complex matter and it thus requires expertise in many fields and the cooperative efforts of numerous branches of administration research institutes and organizations. Careful management can limit disturbances and minimize conflicts, but it also demands thorough scientific analysis and contact between all types of users of the marine environment. Furthermore, efforts to solve the problem of marine pollution have been made – and are being made – in various directions: at national level, by bilateral agreements, on a regional basis, through multilateral action.

The major burden of marine pollution control is, however, entrusted to national strategies and policies.

6.1 *Policies and measures at national level*

Waste disposal as well as water pollution control management is a national responsibility and can be best achieved through appropriate administrative measures and legal enactments. Efficient control measures are compromised of such strategies and instruments as water protection requirements, environmental planning, impact assessments, permissibility rules, licensing procedures, exemption procedures, emission standards or marine environmental quality standards, government subsidies and economic incentives, supervision and inspection at local, sub-regional and national levels. Water pollution control technology, methods and their application, on the other hand, constitute the other important field of action.

As far as water legislation is concerned, legal enactments controlling various aspects of sea pollution tend to be dispersed among laws and regulations intended primarily for other purposes. They often are incorporated into legislation concerned with navigation, fisheries or other uses of marine resources or with port authorities. Sometimes the only effective and enforceable control is that available under planning legislation. In some countries the control of landbased discharges into the sea is motivated by the need to protect the local environment only. Sea water has not traditionally played any major role in the overall management and planning of national water resources. Furthermore, when means are limited they are employed where the need is most urgent and where the return expenditure is most significant and immediate. In consequence the measures for the control of the pollution of sea water have, at least in the past, tended to be subsidiary to those adopted to safeguard the quality of inland freshwater.

This background explains why legislation on marine pollution control is unsystematic and sometimes does not have an autonomous character. Quite often marine pollution legislation has first been enacted to control internal waters and is only later extended to the control of sea waters. Problems may also arise if there is no appropriate integration between inland water and marine pollution control measures. The lack of interaction may also easily derive from the fact that in recent times at international level, in particular, an extensive and rapid development takes place in the field of the law on marine pollution – not least due to the adoption of the United Nations Convention on the Law of the Sea. Therefore, efficient and expeditious implementation of the decisions *inter alia* by the International Maritime Organization (IMO) on establishment and operation of reception facilities for noxious liquid substances or by the Consultative Meeting of Contracting Parties to the London Dumping Convention on dredged material disposal provide a well-established legal regime at national level. Expeditious entry into force of the existing conventional regime would seem to offer not only an encouraging but also a rather well-balanced scheme of pollution abatement.

However, there has not as yet been such effective implementation. Consequently, it is of utmost importance in the coming years to pay more attention to securing the broadest possible accession to the present body of international treaties in the field of marine environment protection.

The use of the sea as the recipient of unlimited amounts of society's waste is definitely not justified even if controlled and in compliance with a multitude of different national regulations, standards and development options. There is no doubt that further measures are needed for the truly effective protection of the marine environment. New means and measures such as technology transfer concerning alternatives to sea-disposal call for attention. A greater effort should be made to develop and apply land-based methods of waste disposal. The waste disposal problem could be accomplished technologically by using processes which do not produce wastes and by the recycling and re-use of waste produces to the extent feasible. When wastes cannot be safely utilized by recycling or re-using them, they should be destroyed at source if possible, or else treated in such a manner as to render them harmless in the environment or effectively isolated from the ecosystem as in the case of radio-active waste. Such treatment should be directed toward the entire waste and not consist of merely purifying one waste stream at the expense of producing a more toxic residue. To diminish considerably and gradually eliminate the disposal at sea of industrial wastes including sewage sludge requires further efforts to develop waste diposal methods and alternate disposal routes.

The recent policies tend to place emphasis on preventative measures in nearly all pollution categories, such as provisions for cargo handling and safe navigation or reception facilities in ports. This approach should be maintained and developed as such technologies already exist for most types of industries and wastes. In the short run the problem of their application might be economic, although improved technological and waste management treatment processes pay off in the long run.

6.2 *International action for environmentally sound marine development*

Cooperation between coastal states is essential in developing and harmonizing their national management measures for the protection of the marine environment. Regional cooperation has proved to be the best and most efficient way of dealing with enclosed or semi-enclosed seas as well as with geographic areas covered by states with similar and/or mutually interdependent problems. Such cooperation exists in the framework of the ICES, the Helsinki Commission, the Oslo and Paris Commissions and in the framework of UNEP's Regional Seas Program. The latter was initiated in 1972 and includes ten regions (the Mediterranean, the Kuwait Action Plan Region, the West and Central Africa, the Wider Caribbean Coast, the Asian Seas, the South East Pacific, the Red Sea and the Gulf of Aden, the East Africa and the South West Atlantic). Over 120 coastal states participate in it. Each regional action plan is designated according to the needs of the region as perceived by the governments concerned. It is to assess the quality of the marine environment and the causes of its deterioration with activities for the management and development of the marine environment in the region. The action plans promote the parallel development of regional legal agreements and of action oriented program activities. Coordinated international projects or control organizations such as regional commissions provide a useful forum for continuous international cooperation and share mutual abatement responsibilities. Multinational control has clearly resulted in better compliances with environmental objectives, which quite often benefit areas beyond national jurisdictions.

Many marine pollution problems also require a global approach and concerted international action. There are also questions that can ultimately be solved only within a global context, such as the development of rules on state responsibility for environmental damage.

References

Baltic Marine Environment Protection Commission – Helsinki Commission: 1983, *A Report of the Seminar on 'Review of Progress Made in Water Protection Measures'*, Baltic Sea Environment Proceedings No. 14, Helsinki, p. 17–23 and 44–85.

Baltic Marine Environment Protection Commission – Helsinki Commission: 1985, *A Report on the Activities of the Commission 1984*, Baltic Sea Environment Proceedings No 15, Helsinki, pp. 5–14.

Baltic Marine Environment Protection Commission – Helsinki Commission: 1985, *A Report of the Sixth Meeting of the Commission*, Helcom 6/16, Helsinki.

Baltic Marine Environment Protection Commission – Helsinki Commission: 1985, *A Report of the 12th Meeting of the Scientific-Technological Committee*, ST C 12/18, Helsinki.

Brown, E.D.: (1983), 'Pollution from Seabed Mining: Legal Safeguards', *Environmental Policy and Law* **10**, pp. 122–34.

Cooper, C. (1981), *'Economic Evaluation of the Environment'. A Methodological Discussion with Particular Reference to Developing Countries'*, Hodder and Stoughton Educational, pp. 50–7.

Delegation of Finland (1984), *Written Statement at the International Conference on the Protection of the North Sea by the Observer*, Helsinki, Finland.

Dybern, B.I. and S.H. Forselius (1981), 'Pollution', in A.Voipio (ed.), *The Baltic Sea*, Elsevier Scientific Publishing Company, Amsterdam, pp. 351–76.

Frank, R.A. (1987), *A Report of the Working Group on Environmental Regulation of Deepsea Mining*, The American Society of International Law, Studies in Transnational Legal Policy No 10, Washington D.C.

FAO (1971), *Pollution: An International Problem for Fisheries*, No 14, Food and Agriculture Organization, Rome.

GESAMP (1969), A Report of the First Session, UN Doc. GESAMP I/11, London, p. 5, para 12.

GESAMP (1982) 'The Health of the Oceans', *UNEP Regional Sea Reports and Studies*, No 16, UNEP.

Goldberg, E.D. (1976), *The Health of the Oceans*, Paris.

Hakapää, K.: 1981, 'Marine Pollution in International Law, Material Obligations and Jurisdiction With Special References to The Third United Nations Conference on The Law of The Sea, *Annales Academiae Scientiarum Fennicae Dissertationes Humanarum Litterarum*, **28**, Helsinki, pp. 31–58 and 289–98.

Hayward, P. (1983), 'The Role of Regional Pollution Conventions', *International Ocean Disposal Symposia, Special Symposium on Waste Management*: Policy and Strategies, Secretary of the Oslo and Paris Commissions, London.

Hodges, J.W. (1974), 'International Law and Radioactive Pollution by Ocean Dumping', *San Diego L. Rev.*, pp. 757–75.

Hulm, P. (1983), 'A Strategy for the Seas', *The Regional Seas Program: Past and Future*, UNEP.

IAEA (1961), 'Radioactive Waste Disposal into the Sea', *International Atomic Energy Agency Safety Series*, No 5.

IMO (1985), *Report of International Activities Relating to the Disposal of Radioactive Wastes at Sea*, Including the Final Report of the Scientific Review, International Maritime Organization, LDC 9/WP.5 and Resolution.

International Union of Local Authorities and United Towns Organization Association of Finnish Cities (1979), *Documents of the Intermunicipal Baltic Sea Protection Conference*, Helsinki.

IOC (1969), '*Comprehensive Outline of the Scope of the Long-Term and Expanded Programme and Oceanic Exploration and Research*, UN doc. A/7750, Annex p. 25.

Keckes, S., 'Protecting the Marine Environment', *Ambio*, 12, No. 2, pp. 112–14.

Leuch, H. and Masseron, J. (1973), 'Economic Aspects of Offshore Hydrocarbon Exploration and Production', 1 *Ocean Management*, pp. 287–325.

Mac Neill, J. (1984), 'Impacts of Oil Pollution', *Environmental Policy and Law*, 13/3/4, pp. 87–96.

Markussen, J.M. (1985), 'Polymetallic Sulfides – Perspectives on Commercial Exploitation', *Special Issue on Deep Seabed Mining*, Newsletter, The Fridtjof Nansen Institute No. 2, Norway.

OECD (1982), *The Cost of Oil Spills*, Paris.

OECD (1982), *Combatting Oil Spills*, Paris.

OECD (1983), *Review of Fisheries in OECD Member Countries*, Paris.

OECD (1985), *The State of the Environment 1985*, Paris, pp. 70–88.

Oslo and Paris Commissions (1984), *The First Decade – International Co-operation Protecting our Marine Environment*, in C. van den Burgt (Editor in Chief), The Chameleon Press Limited, London, pp. 14–34.

Papadakis, N. (1977), *The International Legal Regime of Artificial islands*, Leyden.

Rotkirch, H. (1984), 'Ten Years of Environmental Co-operation in the Baltic Sea, An Evaluation and a Look Ahead', *Aqua Fennica* 14, No 1, Helsinki, Finland.

Schachter, D. and Serwer, D. (1971), 'Marine Pollution Problems and Remedies', *UNITAR Research Reports* No. 4, New York.

Secretary General of the UN (1971), *The Sea. Prevention and Control of Marine Pollution*, U.N. doc. E/5003.

UNEP (1982), '*The World Environment 1972–1982*', 8, Report, ed. by M. Holdgate, M. Kassas, G. White, E. El-Hinnawy, Tycooly International Publishing Limited, Dublin, Ireland, pp. 74–120.

15

Review of the status of implementation and development of regional arrangements on cooperation in combating marine pollution

David Edwards

Head, Environment Programme Section,
Marine Environment Division,
International Maritime Organization, UK

1 Introduction

The International Maritime Organization (IMO) and the United Nations Environment Programme (UNEP) and other organizations have for many years actively cooperated in encouraging the development of regional arrangements for combating marine pollution in cases of emergency. This cooperation has resulted in the development of intergovernmental regional agreements which commit groups of states to cooperate in responding to major incidents of marine pollution which are likely to affect more than one state. This commitment is in several regions reinforced by the establishment of regional and sub-regional contingency plans and in two regions by a regional centre. To date there are 13 regions in the world where a regional intergovernmental agreement on cooperation in combating marine pollution incidents is either in effect or under development (see Table 1). Clearly, there are considerable benefits to be gained by exchanging experience and information between countries participating in and developing regional

Any views expressed in this article are those of the author alone, and are not to be attributed in any way to IMO or its Secretariat.

Table 1   Regional arrangements for cooperation in combating pollution in cases of emergency

Region	Legal instrument	Date of entry into force	Organization responsible for secretariat duties	States/territories involved
North Sea Region	Agreement for Cooperation Dealing with Pollution of the North Sea by Oil (Bonn Agreement, 1969)	August 1969	Bonn Agreement Secretariat, London	Belgium, Denmark, France, Federal Republic of Germany, Norway, Sweden, United Kingdom – Contracting Parties
Nordic Area	Agreement between Denmark, Finland, Norway and Sweden concerning Cooperation in Measures to Deal with Pollution of the Sea by Oil (Copenhagen Agreement)	September 1971	Direction co-operation between the Governments concerned	Denmark, Finland, Norway, Sweden – Contracting Parties
Baltic Sea Region	Convention on the Protection of the Marine Environment of the Baltic Sea Area (Helsinki Convention, 1974): Annex VI – Cooperation in Combating Marine Pollution	May 1980	Baltic Marine Environment Protection Commission, Helsinki	Denmark, Finland, German Democratic Republic, Federal Republic of Germany, Poland, Sweden, USSR – Contracting Parties
Mediterranean Region	Protocol concerning Cooperation in Combating Pollution of the Mediterranean Sea by Oil and Other Harmful Substances in Cases of Emergency (Barcelona Emergency Protocol, 1976)	February 1978	UNEP (Coordinating Unit for the Mediterranean Action Plan, Athens)	Algeria, Cyprus, Egypt, France, Greece, Israel, Italy, Lebanon, Libya, Malta, Monaco, Morocco, Spain, Syria, Tunisia, Turkey, Yugoslavia, EEC – Contracting Parties to the Protocol

Region	Legal instrument	Date of entry into force	Organization responsible for secretariat duties	States/territories involved
Kuwait Action Plan Region	Protocol concerning Regional Cooperation in Combating Pollution by Oil and Other Harmful Substances in Cases of Emergency (Kuwait Emergency Protocol, 1978)	July 1979	Regional Organization for the Protection of Marine Environment (ROPME, Kuwait)	Bahrain, Iran, Iraq, Kuwait, Oman, Qatar, Saudi Arabia, United Arab Emirates – Contracting Parties to the Protocol
West and Central African Region	Protocol concerning Cooperation in Combating Pollution in Cases of Emergency (Abidjan Emergency Protocol, 1980)	August 1984	UNEP	Guinea, Ivory Coast, Nigeria, Republic of Cameroon, Senegal, Togo – Contracting Parties to the Protocol
South East Pacific Region	Agreement on Regional Cooperation in Combating Pollution of the South East Pacific by Hydrocarbons or other Harmful Substances in Cases of Emergency	Not yet in force (adopted in Lima, November 1981)	UNEP/CPPS	Colombia, Chile, Ecuador, Panama, Peru
Red Sea and Gulf of Aden Region	Protocol concerning Regional Cooperation in Combating Pollution by Oil and Other Harmful Substances in Cases of Emergency (Jeddah Emergency Protocol, 1982)	July 1985	ALECSO	Palestine (represented by the PLO), Arab Republic of Yemen, Saudi Arabia, Sudan – Contracting Parties to the Protocol

Region	Legal instrument	Date of entry into force	Organization responsible for secretariat duties	States/territories involved
Wider Caribbean Region	Protocol concerning Cooperation in Combating Oil Spills in the Wider Caribbean Region	Not yet in force (adopted in Cartagena in March 1983)	UNEP	Antigua and Barbuda, Bahamas, Barbados, Belize, British Virgin Islands, Caymen Islands, Colombia, Costa Rica, Cuba, Dominica, Dominican Republic, France, Grenada, Guatemala, Guyana, Haiti, Honduras, Jamaica, Mexico, Netherlands, Netherland Antilles, Nicaragua, Panama, Puerto Rico, St. Christopher and Nevis, St. Lucia, St. Vincent and the Grenadines, Surinam, Trinidad and Tobago, Turks and Caicos Islands, United Kingdom, United States and Venezuela
South Asian Seas Region	Draft Agreement concerning Cooperation in Combating Marine Pollution by Oil and Harmful Substances in Cases of Emergency in South Asia	To be considered later	To be decided later	Bangladesh, India, Maldives, Pakistan and Sri Lanka

Region	Legal instrument	Date of entry into force	Organization responsible for secretariat duties	States/territories involved
South Pacific Region	Draft Protocol concerning Cooperation in Combating Oil Pollution Emergencies in in the South Pacific Region	To be finalized by an Expert Meeting in 1986	To be decided later	American Samoa, Australia, Cook Islands, Federated States of Micronesia, Fiji, France, French Polynesia, Guam, Kiribati, Marshall Islands, Nauru, New Caledonia, New Zealand, Niue, Northern Mariana Islands, Palau, Papua New Guinea, Pitcairn Islands, Solomon Islands, Tokelau, Tonga, Tuvalu, United Kingdom, United States, Vanuatu, Wallis and Futuna and Western Samoa
Eastern African Region	Protocol concerning Cooperation in Combating Marine Pollution in Cases of Emergency	Adopted in Nairobi in June 1985	UNEP	Comoros, France, Kenya, Madagascar, Mauritius, Mozambique, Seychelles, Somalia and United Republic of Tanzania
East Asian Seas Region	ASEAN Contingency Plan	1976	ASEAN	Indonesia, Malaysia, Philippines, Singapore and Thailand

This table has been prepared on the basis of information provided by the United Nations Environment Programme (UNEP).

anti-pollution arrangements. In addition, in view of the international character of maritime transport, there may be elements of regional arrangements amenable to harmonization (e.g. pollution incident reporting).

The IMO Marine Environment Protection Committee (MEPC), through its Working Group on International Marine Oil Spill Contingency Planning, has developed Guidelines for International Marine Oil Spill Contingency Planning which have been widely circulated and used as the basis for the development of sub-regional contingency plans aimed at ensuring that general legal agreements such as the protocols adopted at an intergovernmental level are given effect at the operational level. Recognizing that it would greatly assist those States developing regional arrangements to participate in discussion and exchange of information on the development and operation of international contingency plans, the IMO Secretary-General and the UNEP Executive Director recently agreed to convene a joint meeting of experts on regional arrangements for cooperation in combating major incidents of marine pollution. It was also recognized that such a meeting could usefully identify problems common to the different regions, the ways and means to surmount these problems and make recommendations for future inter-regional cooperation and international assistance. This paper was prepared for submission to the meeting which took place at the IMO Headquarters in London from 19 April–3 May 1985 and has been updated to reflect recent developments.

2   Main elements of regional arrangements

As mentioned above, what amounts to nearly all the coastal states of the world are involved in executing or considering the development of regional agreements or arrangements on cooperation in combating marine pollution. Before reviewing the status of these arrangements it may be useful to recall the elements common to them. In general these agreements possess some, if not all, of the following main obligations which are briefly discussed below.

2.1   *Pollution reporting*
A feature of fundamental importance common to all the regional agreements is the obligation to notify contracting states of marine pollution incidents or

threats thereof likely to affect them. Consequent to that obligation is that of establishing pollution incident reporting procedures and, where necessary, standard message formats to ensure that information regarding such incidents are reported as rapidly as possible. The existing regional agreements include the undertaking that contracting states will issue instructions to the masters of ships flying its flag, pilots of aircraft and in some cases those in charge of offshore facilities under its jurisdiction to report to it or contracting parties likely to be affected by marine pollution incidents. The contents of such reports are often included in an annex to the agreement and follow closely the requirements of Article IV of Protocol I of the International Convention for the Prevention of Pollution from Ships, 1973 and the Protocol of 1978 relating thereto (MARPOL 73/78), 'Provisions Concerning Reports On Incidents Involving Harmful Substances'.

It is important to note that much attention has been paid to the possibility of harmonizing pollution reporting formats under different regional agreements. However, mention should be made of the distinction between pollution reporting systems for exchanging information between contracting parties of regional agreements, such as the POLREP system adopted by the Bonn, Helsinki and Copenhagen Agreements, and the mandatory reporting system and reporting format under MARPOL 73/78, which is primarily a ship reporting system relating to the obligation of the master of ship to report without delay incidents in which his ship is involved. Guidelines for reporting incidents involving harmful substances have been agreed by the IMO Marine Environment Protection Committee.

2.2   *Mutual assistance and cooperation*

The essence of all the regional agreements is the commitment to cooperate with other states in combating marine pollution incidents and to render assistance to other contracting parties which request such assistance to deal with such incidents. The obligation to render assistance is in general qualified to mean that a state will 'use its best endeavours', 'do its utmost', or will render assistance 'within its capabilities'. This latter phrase is of particular relevance to the majority of regions composed of contracting states which have only very limited national pollution response capability. Most agreements require a state responding to a marine pollution incident to make a preliminary assessment of the situation, promptly determine its ability to deal with it and any assistance that may be required and consult with other contracting parties concerned in the process of determining the necessary response.

2.3   *National response capability*

It is widely recognized that a nationally-based capability to respond to a marine pollution incident is of fundamental importance and provides the necessary underpinning of regional agreements. Regional agreements should therefore be considered as a 'supplement to' rather than a 'substitute for' a national response capability. Indeed, there are those who feel that the existence of a national contingency plan is a prerequisite for the development of a regional agreement or contingency plan. However, experience has shown that in several regions the development of regional agreements and contingency plans has served to encourage a more rapid development of national contingency plans by focusing on the problems of marine pollution combating at high government level. Indeed, many of the regional agreements oblige contracting states within their capability to establish and maintain the means of responding to marine pollution incidents, including the development of national contingency plans.

2.4   *Exchange of Information*

In addition to the obligation to report marine pollution incidents, the regional agreements provide that contracting parties keep each other informed of their national organization for dealing with pollution incidents, in particular the identity of the competent authority responsible for operational aspects of the implementation of the agreement.

Contracting parties also undertake to exchange information on technological developments, operational procedures and laws and regulations relating to the prevention, control and combating of marine pollution incidents.

2.5   *Institutional arrangements*

The regional intergovernmental agreements, either directly or by virtue of their inter-relationship to a framework convention of which they form a part, provide for periodic meetings of contracting parties. The purpose of these meetings by and large is to monitor the implementation of the agreements, consider questions of amendment, provide guidance to the secretariat and decide on financial matters related to the implementation of the agreement and its support.

The secretariat functions in the main tend to be provided by the sponsoring organizations, e.g. UNEP in the case of the Barcelona, Cartagena, and Abidjan Conventions, or by a regional organization either established or designated by the convention, e.g. Helsinki Commission, Regional Organization for the Protection of the Marine Environment (ROPME) and the Permanent Commission of the South Pacific (CPPS).

Operational or technical functions specific to the support of the regional anti-pollution agreements or protocols are in some instances provided by a regional centre or coordination unit. These functions include, for example, collecting and disseminating information, maintaining current inventories of emergency response equipment, materials and expertise available in the region, assisting contracting parties upon request in matters such as contingency planning, encouraging technological cooperation and training programmes for combating marine pollution. In establishing these regional centres, governments concerned clearly decided not to provide the centres with an operational capability to either conduct or actively coordinate an on-scene response to a marine pollution incident. However both Resolution 7 of the Barcelona Convention and the Kuwait Protocol provide that the relevant centre's functions may be expanded to include initiating operations to combat pollution by oil and other harmful susbstances after consideration and approval by governments. Given the expense and logistical difficulties involved it is considered that such functions could most likely be best undertaken at the bilateral or sub-regional level.

At least two regional agreements have established expert groups on cooperation in marine pollution combating matters which meet periodically to consider operational, technical and scientific questions concerning the implementation of these agreements. Such specific topics as pollution reporting, spill detection, monitoring and surveillance, alarm procedures and exercises, and dispersant use are discussed at the periodic meeting by government experts.

3   **Regional, sub-regional and bilateral contingency plans and anti-pollution manuals**

Governments in several regions have adopted bilateral and multilateral arrangements and detailed anti-pollution manuals in order to ensure that intergovernmental regional agreements are given effect at the operational level or deal in a more direct way with a sea or coastal area of primary concern to two or three states.

IMO has circulated Guidelines for International Marine Oil Spill Contingency Plans which were, to a great extent, followed in the development of the Sub-Regional Oil Spill Contingency Planning for the Island States and Territories of the Wider Caribbean Region. The Contracting Parties to the Agreement on Regional Cooperation in Combating Pollution of the South East Pacific have adopted a supplementary Protocol dealing *inter alia* with cooperative mechanisms in the event of oil spills and have developed a comprehensive regional contingency plan. Pollution combating manuals have been developed under the aegis of the Helsinki and Bonn Agreements which contain, for example, operational guidelines for cooperation in the event of a pollution incident as well as information on national pollution response capability.

4   **Review of regional agreements on cooperation in combating marine pollution**

4.1   *Non-UNEP regional seas areas*

4.1.1   North Sea   The forerunner of the regional agreements to combat marine pollution incidents is the Agreement for Cooperation in Dealing with Pollution of the North Sea by Oil (Bonn 1969) which entered into force in August 1969 for the eight States which surround the North Sea. A revised version of this agreement was signed in September 1983 extending its application to harmful substances other than oil polluting or threatening to pollute the North Sea area and including provisions governing the financial arrangements for combating pollution. In addition, the new Agreement provides that the European Economic Community (EEC) may become Party thereby bringing it into line with the Barcelona and Cartagena Conventions. Since 1977 the Contracting Parties have met annually and have established a working group on operational, technical and scientific questions. A Bonn Agreement Counter Pollution Manual has been developed which describes inter alia the operational arrangements for joint spill response and is kept up to date at regular intervals taking into account experience gained from combating operations as well as from joint exercise and technological developments.

The Bonn Agreement is perhaps unique in that, unlike the regional agreements which followed it, the sea area of application, i.e. the North Sea, is divided into zones in which a particular contracting party is obliged to take initial response action. Zones of joint responsibility are also defined which are subject to special technical arrangements concluded bilaterally.

The following is a succinct listing of the achievements of the Bonn Agreement since 1977:

(i) development of an agreed command structure for joint combating operations;

(ii) development of an agreed procedure for radiocommunications in joint combating operations;

(iii) development of a pollution reporting form (POLREP) for communication between contracting parties in the event of a pollution incident;

(iv) development of procedures for alarm exercises to test the readiness of contracting parties to respond in pollution incidents;

(v) definition of the response problem represented by oil pollution incidents and means of assessing cost-effectiveness of different response techniques;

(vi) development of guidelines for exchange of information on pollution incidents and the effectiveness of response;

(vii) establishment of principles for the use of dispersants;

(viii) establishment of principles for the use of safe havens;

(ix) identification of suggested methods for the development of response capability in incidents involving hazardous substances other than oil.

4.1.2 Nordic Sea area The Agreement between Denmark, Finland, Norway and Sweden concerning Cooperation in Measures to Deal with Pollution of the Sea by Oil (Copenhagen Agreement) came into force in

October 1971 and since that time contracting parties have met annually and established technical working groups which have prepared operational guidelines for implementation of the Agreement.

These working groups have developed command structures, communications schemes, alarm procedures and exercise programmes as well as an exchange of information on equipment and national combating organizations. All these procedures are contained in a manual on cooperation which is updated periodically based on actual experience and exercises.

The Copenhagen Agreement treats together both multilateral cooperation in dealing with oil pollution incidents and cooperation in ensuring compliance with international and national regulations relating to the prevention of marine pollution from ships. This latter aspect is reflected in the obligation to furnish information of any offence against such regulations and assist in investigation of such offences. With respect to combating pollution, it introduces the obligation on contracting parties to establish the means to deal with a major oil spill and provides for cooperation in combating activities and mutual assistance upon request. As all the Contracting Parties to the Copenhagen Agreement are Contracting Parties to the Bonn Agreement or the Helsinki Agreement, or both, there has necessarily been a good deal of experience of harmonization, in particular with respect to pollution reporting systems.

The following is a summary of the obligations under the Copenhagen Agreement:

    (i) to inform other contracting parties of the national contingency organization and stocks of oil combating equipment;

    (ii) to inform on experience gained during past response operations;

   (iii) to inform on observed oil spills which may threaten other parties;

   (iv) to inform on action taken in response to large oil slicks at sea;

    (v) to respond to requests for assistance;

   (vi) to inform on recorded violations of national and international oil pollution regulations;

  (vii) to assist in investigation of alleged violations of oil pollution legislation covering territorial or adjacent waters of the contracting parties;

 (viii) to exchange information on reception facilities for oily residues from ships;

   (ix) to exchange information on national legislation;

    (x) to exchange information on national contact addresses.

4.1.3 Baltic Sea area The Convention on the Protection of the Marine Environment of the Baltic Sea Area (Helsinki Convention) was signed by the seven Baltic coastal states in 1974 and the Convention came into force in 1980. This Convention deals comprehensively with the prevention and control of pollution from land-based sources, disposal of wastes at sea, ships and exploration and exploitation of the seabed including their resources and marine life as well as regional cooperation in combating marine pollution.

A separate annex to the Convention contains the provisions relating to regional cooperation in combating marine pollution which cover the main elements of regional anti-pollution agreements mentioned above. It is interesting to note that the specific obligation to maintain an ability to combat spillages of oil and other harmful substances is given more specificity in a recommendation that national contingency arrangements should aim at combating oil spillages of up to 10 000 tons of oil for a period not exceeding ten days, initiating a response within two hours of alert and reaching any part of a spill that may occur in the response region of the country in question within six hours.

Although the Helsinki Convention does not divide the Baltic Sea area into zones of national responsibility, it does call on states to agree bilaterally or multilaterally on the delimitation of response regions for combating marine pollution.

The Convention established the Baltic Marine Environment Protection Commission (Helsinki Commission) to carry out the secretariat functions connected with implementation of the Convention. The contracting parties of the Commission meet annually to review the implementation of the Convention as a whole and make appropriate recommendations. In addition, an expert group on cooperation in combating matters meets regularly and has developed *inter alia* guidelines in the form of a manual on marine pollution combating operations. The manual, similar in contents to that developed for the Bonn Agreement, contains guidelines for cooperation and details of national capabilities. The following lists the topics dealt with under guidelines for cooperation:

   (i) introduction (including glossary of terms used);
  (ii) the Helsinki Convention (Articles 9, 10 and 11 and Annexes V and VI);
 (iii) HELCOM recommendations on combating matters;
 (iv) response regions;

    (v) reporting procedures
- (a) general guidelines for reporting
- (b) information scheme
- (c) communication scheme
- (d) pollution report Baltic (POLREP BALTIC) description of system
- (e) pollution report Baltic (POLREP BALTIC) detailed information on the system
- (f) position reporting system (BAREP);

   (vi) guidelines for requesting and providing assistance;

  (vii) operation cooperation;

 (viii) radiocommunications;

   (ix) exercises
- (a) exercise types
- (b) exercise schedule;

    (x) finance, general guidelines (lease, costs, etc.);

   (xi) mutual assistance in investigating violations of discharge and dumping regulations.

4.2   *UNEP Regional Seas areas*

4.2.1   Introduction   At present, in accordance with the decisions of the Governing Council, the Regional Seas Programme covers 11 areas where regional action plans are operative or are under development: the Mediterranean Region, the Kuwait Action Plan Region, the West and Central African Region, the Wider Caribbean Region, the East Asian Seas Region, the South East Pacific Region, the Red Sea and Gulf of Aden Region, the South Pacific Region, the East African Region, the South West Atlantic Region and the South Asian Region.

The substantive aspect of any regional programme is outlined in an 'action plan' which is formally adopted by an intergovernmental meeting of the governments of a particular region before the programme enters an operational phase. In the preparatory phase leading to the adoption of the action plan, governments are consulted through a series of meetings and missions about the scope and substance of an action plan suitable for their region. In addition, with the cooperation of appropriate global and regional organizations, reviews on the specific environmental problems of the region are prepared in order to assist the governments in identifying the most urgent problems in the region and the corresponding priorities to be assigned to the various activities outlined in the action plan. UNEP coordinates directly or, in some regions, indirectly, through existing regional organizations, the preparations leading to the adoption of the action plan.

All action plans are structured in a similar way, although the specific activities for any region are dependent upon the needs and priorities of that region. An action plan usually includes the following components: environmental assessment, environmental management, environmental legislation, institutional arrangements, and financial arrangements.

IMO has been actively involved in the Regional Seas strategy, in particular with respect to the environmental management and environmental legislation components of the action plans in the regions. Through such involvement IMO has been able to promote regional anti-pollution arrangements in accordance with its own mandate in this field and to ensure an important degree of harmonization of the relevant provisions of regional legal instruments dealing with pollution from ships, dumping of wastes, and cooperation in combating major incidents and threats of marine pollution.

The regional approach to the development of environmental legislation usually takes the form of a comprehensive umbrella or framework agreement for the protection and development of the marine environment. It lists the sources of pollution which require control: pollution from ships, dumping, land-based sources and sea-bed activities together with airborne pollution. It also identifies environmental management issues for which cooperative efforts are to be made, e.g. specially protected areas, cooperation in cases of emergency, environmental impact assessment and scientific and technical cooperation. There is also an article on liability and compensation.

By ratifying a protocol, a party accepts more specific obligations to control pollution from a discreet source, or to cooperate in a specific aspect of environmental management. Under these agreements no state or, in certain cases, regional economic integration organization may become a contracting party to the Convention without also becoming a contracting party to at least one protocol and it is usually foreseen that additional protocols will be developed in the future. In every region where such framework agreements have been adopted a protocol concerning cooperation in combating marine pollution incidents has been adopted simultaneously.

4.2.2   Mediterranean Sea   A Conference of Plenipotentiaries took place in Barcelona, Spain, early in 1976 at which the 16 participating States and EEC adopted the Convention for the Protection of the Mediterranean Sea against Pollution, a Protocol for the Prevention of Pollution of the Mediterranean Sea by Dumping from Ships and Aircraft and a Protocol concerning Cooperation in Combatting Pollution of the Mediterranean Sea by Oil and other Harmful Substances in Cases of Emergency. This became known as the Barcelona Convention and entered into force in 1978. UNEP was designated as the Secretariat of the Action Plan and the Barcelona Convention. The Convention includes articles on monitoring, cooperation in emergencies, scientific and technological cooperation, and liability and compensation.

Pursuant to Resolution 7 adopted at the Barcelona Conference, the Regional Oil Combating Centre (ROCC) was established in Malta in 1976 by UNEP and IMO to further the objectives of the Protocol on Cooperation in Combating Pollution of the Mediterranean Sea by Oil and Other Harmful Substances in Cases of Emergency. The objectives of ROCC are to facilitate cooperation among the Mediterranean states in order to combat massive pollution by oil, to assist the states in the development of their own national capabilities, and to facilitate information exchange, technological cooperation and training. ROCC has a small staff which is technically and administratively supported by IMO.

The work of ROCC, as well as the implementation of the Protocol on combating pollution, are monitored within the context of an overall review of the Barcelona Convention and the Mediterranean Action Plan through regular meetings of Contracting Parties. Whilst no special technical working groups have been established, as under the Bonn and Helsinki Agreements, ROCC has established focal points in each of the coastal states which have on occasions met to discuss the work of ROCC and the implementation of the Protocol. Although the Protocol applies to harmful substances other than oil, the scope of ROCC activities has been limited to oil pollution incidents. It is envisaged that the contracting parties will consider in future extending the information and training activities of ROCC to include combating pollution incidents involving harmful substances other than oil.

In line with the general objective that each action plan of the Regional Seas Programme should become financially self-supporting, a trust fund was established in 1979 which currently provides the funding of the operation of ROCC as well as other elements of the Mediterranean Action Plan.

ROCC, which has no operational role, confines its activities to the exchange of information through designated focal points in each of the coastal states by means of publication of information bulletins and inventories of equipment and expertise available in the region, and the provision of training and technical advisory services in cases of emergency and for the development of national contingency plans.

The most recent review of ROCC's activities by the contracting parties has resulted in the recommendation that greater emphasis be placed on encouraging the development of sub-regional agreements or contingency plans for combating marine pollution. ROCC has recently developed a guide for oil pollution combating, similar in scope to those developed under the Bonn and Helsinki Agreements, only with more emphasis on providing basic information on the means available for combating marine pollution and criteria for selecting the most appropriate.

4.2.3   Kuwait Action Plan   The Kuwait Regional Conference of Plenipotentiaries on the Protection and Development of the Marine Environment and the Coastal Areas was convened by UNEP in 1978. The Conference adopted the Action Plan, the Kuwait Regional Convention for Cooperation on the Protection of the Marine Environment from Pollution, and the Protocol concerning Regional Cooperation in Combating Pollution by Oil and Other Harmful Substances in Cases of Emergency.

Although modified somewhat to cater for the particular needs of the region, the Kuwait Convention bears a marked resemblance to the Barcelona Convention. It was developed as an umbrella convention and provides for specific protocols dealing with various types of sources of pollution. Its relatively rapid entry into force (in 1980) and essential independence from UNEP must in part at least be a reflection of the similar rapid state of development of the eight states involved and the ready availability of funding within the region.

The Kuwait Convention provided for the establishment of the Regional Organization for the Protection of the Marine Environment (ROPME) to *inter alia* oversee the implementation of the Convention and its Protocols and the Action Plan for the region. ROPME was formally set up in Kuwait in 1981 and the contracting parties composing the ROPME Council meet regularly to pursue the implementation of the Convention and its Protocols and the Action Plan.

The Kuwait Protocol Concerning Regional Cooperation in Combating

Pollution by Oil and Other Harmful Substances in Cases of Emergency contains all the basic elements of regional agreements mentioned above and provides for the establishment of the Marine Emergency Mutual Aid Centre (MEMAC) which was formally set up in March 1983 in the host state, Bahrain. The functions of MEMAC are similar to those of the Malta Centre and are focused on strengthening the capacities of the contracting states to combat pollution through technical assistance, training and information exchange. The coordination functions of the Centre are strengthened by the obligation placed on contracting parties to the Protocol to provide the Centre with information pertinent to the implementation of the Protocol as well as reports of pollution incidents and the steps undertaken to combat and mitigate the effects of pollution.

As in the case of ROCC, initiating operations to combat pollution is not one of the functions of MEMAC; however, provision is made in the Protocol for future consideration of including this activity as one of the functions of the Centre.

Since its establishment in Bahrain early in 1983, MEMAC has been receiving technical assistance through a cooperative arrangement between IMO and UNEP. It has, in particular, dealt with the Nowruz oil spill incident and development of the work programme of MEMAC. It is of interest to note that the Third Meeting of ROPME *inter alia* decided that the Secretariat should convene Technical Working Group meetings to set up regional criteria for the selection and use of dispersants in the sea area.

MEMAC's activities are currently confined to the exchange of information through the circulation of inventories of equipment and expertise, marine casualties, sensitive areas and national training programmes. Training, through the provision of workshops, seminars and equipment demonstrations, is organized by MEMAC. Technical advice has been arranged for all Contracting Parties to assist them in the development of national contingency plans.

4.2.4   West and Central Africa   In 1981, UNEP convened in Abidjan, Ivory Coast, a Conference of Plenipotentiaries on Cooperation in the Protection and Development of the Marine and Coastal Environment of the West and Central African Region. The Conference agreed upon the Action Plan and adopted two legal instruments:

(i) Convention for Cooperation in the Protection and Development of the Marine and Coastal Environment of the West and Central Africa Region; and

(ii) Protocol Concerning Cooperation in Combating Pollution in Cases of Emergency.

The Convention and Protocol entered into force in August 1984.

The Abidjan Convention is a comprehensive, umbrella agreement for the protection and management of the marine and coastal areas. Like the Barcelona and Kuwait Conventions, it foresees the development of additional protocols which will elaborate upon detailed obligations for the control of pollution and management of resources. A trust fund was proposed and UNEP was entrusted with its management and was designated as the Secretariat of the Convention.

A Steering Committee was established by the Conference which meets periodically to oversee the implementation of the Action Plan. At its first meeting in mid-1981 it identified four priority projects: establishment and coordination of national contingency plans, control of coastal erosion, monitoring of marine pollution, and various supporting measures, e.g. training, legislation, exchange of data and a public awareness campaign.

The Protocol Concerning Cooperation in Combating Pollution in Cases of Emergency, which entered into force in August 1984, contains all the basic elements of such regional agreements mentioned above. The Protocol applies to 'marine emergencies' which are broadly defined to include any incident, however caused, resulting in substantial pollution (by oil or other harmful substances) or imminent threat thereof. In addition, the Protocol uniquely cites the presence of oil or other harmful substances arising from the failure of industrial installations. UNEP has been designated as the Secretariat of the Convention and no special institutional arrangements have been made for the implementation of the Protocol other than review by ordinary meetings of the contracting parties to the Convention.

IMO is one of the executing agencies within the framework of a UNEP project entitled 'Institution and Coordination of National Contingency Plans in the West and Central African Region'. The main purpose of the project is to support the development and implementation of the Action Plan for the Protection and Development of the Marine Environment and Coastal Areas in the region and, in particular, to develop the capabilities of the countries of this region to respond to marine emergencies posing a threat to the environment and/or to the coastal population as envisaged in Article 1(2) of the Protocol Concerning Cooperation in Combating Pollution in Cases of Emergency.

Within the framework of the above-mentioned project, and in cooperation with the relevant national authorities, drafts of national contingency plans for marine pollution emergencies have now been developed for Benin, Congo, Ghana, Guinea, Liberia and Sierra Leone. A report on Arrangements for Combating Marine Oil Pollution in the West African Sub-Region (Nigeria, Cameroon, Equatorial Guinea, Gabon, Sao Tomé and Principe) has also been prepared, and a regional workshop on contingency planning was held in 1985 to review the status of national contingency planning and explore the feasibility of developing sub-regional contingency plans.

Pending the establishment of a regional coordination unit, there is a need for UNEP or IMO to collect and circulate information on how to contact national focal points designated to receive pollution reports and lists of resources available in the region.

4.2.5   Wider Caribbean   In March 1983 a Conference of Plenipotentiaries met in Cartagena de Indias, Colombia, and adopted the Convention for the Protection and Development of the Marine Environment of the Wider Caribbean Region and the Protocol Concerning Cooperation in Combating Oil Spills in the Wider Caribbean Region.

The Cartagena Convention, like the Barcelona, Kuwait, and Abidjan Conventions, is a comprehensive, umbrella agreement for the protection and development of the marine environment and it is foreseen that additional protocols to it will be developed in the future.

The Cartagena Protocol includes all the basic elements of the regional agreements mentioned above. Although the Protocol does not specify zones of responsibility, it provides that Contracting Parties should conclude bilateral or multilateral sub-regional arrangements.

The Protocol calls for cooperation in taking all necessary measures, both preventive and remedial, for the protection of the marine environment and places an obligation on Contracting Parties to establish and maintain or ensure the establishment and maintenance of the means to respond to oil spill incidents. The enactment of legislation as well as the preparation of contingency plans are included in such means.

Although the Protocol refers only to oil spills the contracting parties commit themselves, in an annex thereto, to prepare, at their first meeting, the changes necessary to extend the Protocol to regional cooperation to combat spills of hazardous substances other than oil. Pending the preparation and entry into force of these changes the Protocol is considered to apply provisionally to such substances. Specific provision is made in the Protocol for meetings of the contracting parties to be held in conjunction with those of the Convention and that such meetings should *inter alia* review its operation and to consider technical arrangements and other measures to improve its effectiveness.

As is the case of most Conventions and Protocols developed under aegis of the UNEP Regional Seas Programme, the Secretariat functions of the Convention and Protocol are assigned to UNEP. However, the Cartagena Protocol specifically refers to IMO in respect of the functions related to implementation of the Protocol to be carried out by UNEP through a Regional Coordination Unit, to be established in Jamaica to coordinate the implementation of the Caribbean Action Plan. These functions are similar to those undertaken by ROCC and MEMAC and include technical assistance, coordination and liaison, training and information and communication related functions.

Although the Convention and Protocol have not yet entered into force there exists in the region an extremely high level of cooperative activity related to the development of national and regional contingency planning. IMO, the Organization of American States (OAS) and UNEP have, since 1978, cooperated in a number of activities aimed at enhancing the national capability of the states and territories of the region to combat marine pollution and encouraging regional or sub-regional cooperation. Such activity has taken the form of expert missions, overview studies, workshops or seminars and expert meetings and has benefitted from financial support from the UNEP Caribbean Trust Fund, OAS, the United States Agency for International Development (USAID) and the Swedish International Development Authority (SIDA).

A significant landmark has been reached with the adoption of the afore-mentioned sub-regional contingency plan for the island States and the territories by a Government Experts Meeting, convened jointly by IMO, UNEP and OAS in St. Lucia in May 1984.

This plan provides a framework under which island States and territories may cooperate at the operational level in responding to oil spill incidents, as required by Article 8 of the Cartagena Protocol. The objectives of the plan are to:

    (i) promote and implement regional cooperation in oil spill contingency planning, prevention, control and clean-up;

    (ii) develop appropriate measures of preparedness and systems for detecting and reporting oil spill incidents within the area covered by the plan;

    (iii) institute prompt measures to restrict the spread of oil; and

    (iv) identify resources to respond to oil spill incidents.

The plan contains sections on the following: introduction, policy and responsibility, response operations, report and communications, administration and logistics. The plan will in fact resemble the combating manual developed under the Helsinki and Bonn Agreements in that it will include the following annexes and appendices: information on the response capability of each participating island, pollution reporting format (CARIPOL-REP). In addition, technical information annexes will be included on such matters as high risk and sensitive areas, documentation and cost recovery and hazardous spill response.

The Island States and territories have asked that the Secretary-General of IMO undertakes the Secretariat functions connected with the implementation of the plan and it is envisaged that this will be carried out through the IMO Regional Consultant on Marine Pollution based in Puerto Rico. This post was established by IMO in 1983 and is funded by USAID and filled by an individual seconded to IMO by the US Coast Guard.

The plan recognizes that one of the essential prerequisites to sub-regional contingency planning is that all of the participating states and territories develop and implement national oil spill contingency plans. The activities of the IMO Regional Consultant have, to a large extent, been focused on assisting the states and territories of the region in developing their plans which will contain a number of common basic elements to ensure maximum benefit from participation in the plan.

Turning from the islands of the Caribbean to Mexico and Central America, IMO, using the consultant services of the International Tanker Owners Pollution Federation (ITOPF) and with funding from the Marine Industry Group (MIRG), carried out a survey of the risk of major oil spillages and the resources vulnerable to oil pollution damage and an analysis of the capabilities for combating major oil spills and scope for regional co-operation in June/July 1983. The survey covered the Caribbean coastlines of Mexico, Panama and the Central American countries and was considered by a Sub-Regional Workshop convened by OAS, IMO and UNEP in Panama in October 1983, principally to consider the possible development of bilateral and multilateral sub-regional arrangements pursuant to Article 8 of the Cartagena Protocol.

The Workshop *inter alia* agreed that, based on studies conducted by each country, the preparation of bilateral agreements should be considered in the first instance and that each country should develop a national plan along similar lines to facilitate integration with a comprehensive sub-regional contingency plan to be considered at a later date. At the governments' request, an IMO/OAS consultant followed up the workshop with visits to each of the countries rendering advice on formulating a national plan. It is anticipated that in 1986 or 1987 a meeting of government experts could be convened to review the status of national contingency planning and consider the adoption of such a plan.

A similar series of activities which focuses on the needs of Colombia, Venezuela, Guyana, Suriname and French Guiana as well as the contiguous island countries of Trinidad and Tobago and the Netherlands Antilles in respect of risk assessment and oil spill response preparedness has been undertaken. Such activity would concentrate on the oil pollution risks faced by these states and territories, analyse their capability and specific problems, assist in the development of national contingency planning and explore the feasibility of formulating sub-regional arrangements for cooperation in the event of a marine pollution emergency compatible to the Cartagena Protocol.

As can be seen from the above, regional oil spill contingency planning has been accorded a high priority and it is anticipated that future activity in the region will concentrate on training including periodic simulated oil spill exercises, assistance in the development of national legislation for the prevention, control and combating of marine pollution, the development of regionally applicable guidelines for dealing with incidents involving oil and other hazardous substances and assistance in determining the suitability of oil dispersant chemicals for use in the Caribbean region.

4.2.6 South East Pacific The Conference of Plenipotentiaries on the Action Plan for the Protection of the Marine Environment and Coastal Area of the South East Pacific was convened jointly by the Permanent Commission of the South Pacific (CPPS) and UNEP in Lima, Peru, in November 1981. The Conference adopted the Action Plan for the Protection of the

Marine Environment and Coastal Area of the South East Pacific together
with the following two legal agreements:

(i) Convention for the Protection of the Marine Environment and
Coastal Area of the South East Pacific; and
(ii) Agreement on Regional Cooperation in Combating Pollution of the
South East Pacific by Hydrocarbons or Other Harmful Substances
in Cases of Emergency.

Subsequently, the first meeting of the General Authority of the Action
Plan for the Protection of the Marine Environment and Coastal Area of the
South East Pacific was convened jointly by CPPS and UNEP in Quito,
Ecuador, from 20–22 July 1983. The meeting adopted the following two
protocols:

(i) Supplementary Protocol to the Agreement on Regional Cooperation in Combating Pollution of the South East Pacific by Hydrocarbons or Other Harmful Substances; and
(ii) Protocol for the Protection of the South East Pacific against
Pollution from Land-Based Sources.

All four legal agreements have been signed by the five coastal states of the
South East Pacific. The CPPS has been designated as responsible for the
depository and secretariat functions of the agreements and liaison with
national focal points to facilitate the implementation of the agreements.

The Agreement on Regional Cooperation in Combating Pollution contains the basic elements of regional agreements mentioned above. The
Supplementary Protocol to the Agreement specifies in more detail the
cooperation mechanisms that would come into play in the event of a 'massive
oil spill' and outlines the basic elements to be included in national
contingency plans.

A Regional Contingency Plan for the Combating of Oil Pollution in the
South East Pacific in Cases of Emergency has been developed to provide an
operational basis for cooperation within the context of the Agreement on
Regional Cooperation in Combating Pollution of the South East Pacific by
Hydrocarbons or Other Harmful Substances in Cases of Emergency.

The Regional Contingency Plan is extremely comprehensive including
eight annexes containing, for example, each national contingency plan, list of
experts and equipment available in each country, vulnerability indices,
proposed fees and charges for personnel and equipment, etc. The countries

which will participate in the plan are Colombia, Chile, Ecuador, Panama and Peru. The Secretariat functions associated with the Regional Plan are also assigned to the CPPS which coordinates activities in the following areas: exchange of information; contingency planning assistance and assistance in emergencies; development of common approach to risk analysis; evaluation of damage, civil liability and compensation; and use and testing of dispersants etc. and training.

A joint IMO/CPPS/UNEP Training Course on Oil Spill Control and a Workshop of Legal and Technical Experts on the Contingency Plan for the Combating of Oil Pollution in the South East Pacific in Cases of Emergency were held in March 1985 in cooperation with the Government of Panama. The course involved participants in a simulated oil spill response escalating from local to national, regional and international response designed *inter alia* to identify areas for improving integration of national and regional contingency planning. The Experts Meeting reviewed the Regional Contingency Plan and formulated an appropriate strategy for implementation and suggested possible improvements in the operational arrangements.

4.2.7   Red Sea and Gulf of Aden   A Plenipotentiary Conference convened by the Arab League Educational, Cultural and Scientific Organization (ALECSO) and held in Jeddah, Saudi Arabia, in February 1982 adopted a Regional Convention on the Protection of the Marine Environment of the Red Sea and Gulf of Aden and a Protocol concerning Regional Cooperation in Combating Marine Pollution arising from Emergencies as well as an Action Plan for the Protection of the Marine Environment of the Region.

The Protocol is closely aligned to that adopted in the Kuwait Action Plan region and includes all the basic elements of regional agreements mentioned above. For example, it provides for the establishment of a Regional Commission for Conservation of the Red Sea and Gulf of Aden and a subsidiary Marine Emergency Mutual Aid Centre to strengthen the capacities of the contracting parties. However, it is not known when such a Centre will be setup. The Red Sea and Gulf of Aden Environment Programme (PERSGA), an arm of ALECSO, operating out of Jeddah, provides the secretariat support and technical backstopping for the implementation of the Protocol as well as the Convention and the Action Plan.

A general conference convened in late 1985 discussed programme activity for 1986/87 and it is envisaged that consideration will be given to the framework for regional cooperation for combating marine pollution and the requirements and role of a regional or sub-regional centre. The assistance of IMO has been requested in this matter as well as the conduct of surveys of coastal oil pollution to the coast of Sudan, Democratic Republic of Yemen, Arab Republic of Yemen, and possibly Somalia.

4.2.8   South West Pacific   In March 1982 a Conference on the Human Environment in the South Pacific, held in Rarotonga, adopted an Action Plan for the Region which includes the environmental assessment, management and legal components and institutional and financial arrangements common to action plans adopted in other regional seas. Although it was recognized that the South Pacific region is not traversed by major tanker routes, the great majority of the countries of the region reported concern about the effects on their resources of a major spill from vessels delivering oil supplies in the region and expressed great interest in contingency planning. This interest is reflected in the components of the Action Plan. The 'impact of marine oil spills on sensitive coastal environments of the region' has been identified as one of the initial areas requiring environmental assessment and the 'development of national contingency plans integrated with a regional control plan to minimize the effects of major oil spills' was cited in the environmental management component as an area regarded as regionally important.

By the end of 1985 a total of four expert meetings had been held on a convention for the protection and development of the natural resources and environment of the South Pacific region and related protocols on the prevention of pollution by dumping and cooperation in combating pollution emergencies with the expectation that they would be adopted by a Plenipotentiary Conference in early 1986. The later protocol includes all the basic elements of regional marine pollution combating agreements mentioned above.

As in several protocols, the contracting parties are encouraged to develop and maintain appopriate sub-regional arrangements, bilateral or multilateral. In view of the vast distance between the parties to the protocol the development of such arrangements, in particular with respect to reporting of pollution incidents, would appear particularly important.

The Protocol provides that the South Pacific Commission will carry out, through the South Pacific Region Environment Programme (SPREP) secretariat, a number of specific functions relating to the implementation of the Protocol normally assigned to a regional combating centre or coordination unit. These include such activities as technical assistance training, programme development, dissemination of information related to prevention, control and combating of marine pollution, identifying or maintaining emergency response communication systems, etc.

A Workshop on Marine Pollution Prevention, Control and Response was convened jointly by the South Pacific Commission, South Pacific Bureau for Economic Development, IMO and UNEP, in cooperation with the US Coast Guard, in Fiji in November 1984. 26 participants from 17 countries in the South Pacific region attended this Workshop and a number of recommendations were made regarding further training in the following areas:

  (i) handling, storage and transportation of dangerous goods in packaged form;
 (ii) response procedures for spills of noxious liquid susbtances;
(iii) practical exposure to deployment of oil spill response equipment;
(iv) contingency planning on a national, sub-regional and regional basis;
 (v) on-scene commanders oil spill management course.

4.2.9 South Asia In January 1982, prior to the inclusion of this region in the UNEP Regional Seas Programme, IMO convened a meeting of government legal and technical experts in Colombo, Sri Lanka, the purpose being to consider cooperative arrangements for dealing with pollution arising from marine emergencies.

The meeting based its work on a draft agreement concerning cooperation in combating marine pollution by oil and other harmful substances in cases of emergency in South Asia, prepared by the IMO Secretariat. The meeting agreed in principle that it would be desirable to have a legal instrument and considered that the draft prepared by the IMO Secretariat could be regarded as a suitable model.

The meeting invited the Secretary-General of IMO to take further steps leading to the convening of a Plenipotentiary Conference of the countries of the region (Bangladesh, Burma, India, Maldives, Pakistan and Sri Lanka) at which the final agreement on emergencies could be prepared and adopted. Efforts to convene such a conference have not yet reached fruition but it is still hoped that sufficient support will be forthcoming from governments for a conference to be held in the near future. Now that preparatory work for development of an Action Plan for the region has been initiated by UNEP, a regional agreement on marine pollution combating may take the form of a protocol to a framework convention on the protection of the environment.

In view of the pressing nature of the problem concerning cooperation in combating marine emergencies in South Asia, the meeting has already made the following recommendations for consideration by the governments of the region pending the conclusion of a regional agreement:

(i) that countries of the region which still do not have a national contingency plan should initiate action to do so at the earliest possible time, giving such action the necessary legal and administrative backing required;

(ii) that respective governments should designate a person, body or authority in such national contingency plans who will, as the need arises, participate and act as focal points in the regional programme of action;

(iii) that governments shall advise others of their focal points or contact and agree to establish direct contact/communication in case of major spill/pollution;

(iv) that governments shall exchange data/information relating to existing legislation, administrative and other arrangements specially relating to resources both in respect of training and equipment;

(v) that any sighting or detection of spillage on the high seas should immediately be communicated to all such countries of the region which are likely to be affected;

(v) that governments should, with proper and prior arrangement with respective immigration and custom authorities, ensure fast passage of men and material for combating pollution;

(vii) that governments should, through prior consultation, arrange for meetings from time to time and should at a later stage review the need for any institutional set-up or secretariat;

(viii) that donor countries and other international agencies may be approached for technical and financial assistance both in respect of national as well as regional programmes; and

(ix) that, in the event that governments eventually agree to cooperate on the development of regional anti-pollution arrangements, training of personnel at the regional level should be given high priority.

It is currently envisaged that a meeting of experts on the Action Plan will be held in November 1985 for the purpose of reviewing country studies on environmental protection priorities with a view to developing priorities for regional cooperation and action.

4.2.10 Eastern Africa In June 1985, a Conference of Plenipotentiaries met in Nairobi, Kenya, and adopted an Action Plan, a Convention for the Protection, Management and Development of the Marine and Coastal Environment of the Eastern African Region, a Protocol concerning Protected Areas and Wild Fauna and Flora in the Eastern African Region and a Protocol concerning Cooperation in Combating Marine Pollution in Cases of Emergency in the Eastern African Region.

The Protocol is similar in scope and content to those developed in other regions and includes all the basic provisions mentioned above. As in the case of the Cartagena Protocol, UNEP will carry out, in cooperation with IMO, functions related to the implementation of the Protocol as specified in the Protocol. These functions include technical assistance, information dissemination, identifying and maintaining means for marine emergency response communication, encouraging research on marine pollution related matters, etc.

4.2.11 East Asian seas A regional action plan was first drafted in 1979 and was eventually adopted by the five Association of South East Asian Nations (ASEAN) states in early 1981 at an intergovernmental meeting convened by UNEP in Manila, Philippines. The action plan consists of environmental assessment and environmental management components, the latter concentrating on control of pollution from oil and from land-based sources. Subsequent to the adoption of the action plan, a trust fund was established and UNEP was entrusted with its management. The East Asian Seas Action Plan does not include a legal component nor has it a regional framework convention on environmental protection, nor has a protocol on regional cooperation in the combating of marine pollution been adopted. However, as participation in the East Asian Seas Action Plan currently includes only the member states of ASEAN, that organization has provided a general framework for cooperation in marine pollution incidents in the form of an ASEAN Contingency Plan which entered into force in 1976.

Cooperation between IMO and ASEAN on oil pollution problems

developed in the first place through IMO's involvement with the ASEAN Experts Group on Marine Pollution, which has responsibility for administering the ASEAN Oil Spill Contingency Plan.

There are two principal tanker routes through the ASEAN region: firstly, the VLCC route through the Malacca and Singapore Straits and, secondly, the VLCC route through the Lombok/Makassar Straits and the Celebes Sea. In recognition that the latter route is less well served by contingency plans and anti-pollution measures, in January 1980 an IMO/UNEP expert meeting was convened in Jakarta to consider the development of sub-regional oil spill arrangements in the Celebes Sea. On the basis of a risk analysis and evaluation of existing oil combating capabilities in the sub-region, the meeting concluded that support should be sought from funding agencies for procurement of major items of equipment and that training should be provided in its maintenance and operation. Subsequently an IMO/United Nations Development Programme (UNDP) project has been implemented which has resulted in the upgrading of the capabilities of an existing sub-branch of the National Operations Centre for Oil Pollution (NOCOP) of the Philippines Coast Guard in Davao, in terms of both equipment and trained personnel, so that an at-sea response can be initiated in the event of a tanker accident in the sub-region. Approximately $360 000 has been expended by IMO from UNDP funding on dispersant spray equipment, pumps, containment boom, radio communication sets and a work boat for the Centre.

Practical training has also been provided and operational procedures for surveillance of oil spills, inter-country communication and operation and maintenance agreed between the three countries cooperating in the project (Indonesia, Malysia and the Philippines).

4.2.12 South West Atlantic   Development of a regional seas action plan in this area is still at an early stage. The UNEP Governing Council in 1980 tentatively delineated the area as including the Atlantic coastal waters and adjacent coasts of Argentina, Uruguay and Brazil.

At the request of the Governments of Argentina and Uruguay, IMO has prepared a draft 'Agreement of Cooperation between the Argentine Republic and the Republic of Uruguay to Combat Pollution in the Marine Environment Caused by Spills of Oil and Other Noxious Substances' including annexes dealing with operational aspects of a joint response. The geographic scope of the Agreement is the River Uruguay and the Rio de la Plata including its maritime limits and the adjoining shorelines. It was anticipated that the existence of three joint technical commissions dealing with the River Uruguay and the Rio de la Plata would provide the institutional framework for the implementation of the Agreement.

5   Other regional arrangements

5.1   *The role of the EEC*

The European Economic Community participates actively in the implementation of two regional agreements which are in force, namely the Bonn Agreement and the Barcelona Convention. In addition, provision is made in the Cartagena and Nairobi Conventions for the Community to become a Contracting Party. Such participation is viewed by many states as desirable from the standpoint of the financial contribution which can be made by the EEC to the trust funds established for the implementation of the agreements and action plans.

In 1978 the Council adopted an action programme on the control and reduction of pollution caused by hydrocarbons discharged at sea. This programme provided a mandate to the Commission of the European Communities to undertake studies and to make the appropriate proposals in different fields. Within the framework of the Action Programme several achievements can be listed as follows.

The Community information system arising from a decision of the Council in December 1981 consists of the following:

(i) inventory of the means, both equipment and personnel, existing in the Community to deal with pollution of the sea by oil;

(ii) catalogue of the means of combating pollution containing short but comprehensive descriptions of all the different types of clean-up facilities listed in the inventory;

(iii) compendium of hydrocarbon properties which was compiled by CONCAWE (the Oil Companies International Study Group for the Conservation of Clean Air and Water in Europe). This compendium contains a wealth of facts on the principal physical and chemical properties of hydrocarbons, on how they change in the course of natural processes such as evaporation and oxidation and on how they react to specific types of treatment;

(iv) compilation study on the different impacts of hydrocarbons on fauna and flora, depending on the characteristics of the oil and the area concerned.

A Council directive on contingency plans is now under consideration. This proposal envisages an inter-related set of contingency plans at local, regional, national and Community level. The intention is that all the related plans should be compatible so that they can protect the Community's seas in an effective manner. This is to be achieved by fixing the minimum components which all the national plans must contain and by presenting a method for assessing the effectiveness of the plans after serious accidents. At the request of the European Parliament, the Commission has amended the original proposal to include harmful substances other than oil.

The Advisory Committee on the Control and Reduction of Pollution by Hydrocarbons (ACPH) was set up by the Commission in June 1980. This Committee, consisting of highly qualified experts, gives the Commission advice on all subjects relating to oil pollution.

A new Community budget item was established in 1982 for the protection of the marine environment. The proposed allocation for 1985 for this budget item is ECU 900 000.

At the end of 1985, more than 50 studies and pilot projects for the development of combating means and techniques will have been achieved. A total of approximately ECU 2 million has been used to promote these studies and projects. In addition, marine environmental research programmes are also sponsored by the Commission's Directorate General for Research. This programme ranges from studies concerning basic coastal and marine ecosystem processes to specific research on oil pollution. Attention is also being given to methods for the detection of spilt oil and other pollution by remote sensing techniques from aeroplanes and satellites.

On 25 March 1985 the Commission of the European Communities decided to extend its policy on combating pollution by oil to other harmful substances. To achieve this objective the Commission established a plan which comprises three elements.

The legal framework, which includes:

(i) a decision by the Commission of the European Communities to extend the competence of the ACPH and a proposal to the EEC Council to extend the EEC's information system.

The action programme consists of a series of projects started in 1985, the aim of which is to develop intervention capability and enhance cooperation through:

   (i) elaboration of a list of priority hazardous substances based on a synthesis of existing lists;

   (ii) development of a decision-making system;

   (iii) simulation models of the effects of hazardous substances, dispersion of gases, dispersion in the water column, etc;

   (iv) an inventory of the means of combating pollution;

   (v) elaboration of a contact point network for specialist advice.

Training under which the following options are being considered:

   (i) a high-level seminar for those responsible for the combating operations;

   (ii) a course at an intermediate level for scientists and technicians aimed at the use of the information systems, databases, etc;

   (iii) at the level of the combating crews and personnel, who may have to work on board a vessel in difficulty.

5.2   *Oil company regional arrangements for combating major oil spills*

In several regions, oil company cooperatives have been established to facilitate a rapid and efficient response to an oil spill beyond the immediate capabilities of one company and in an area of joint concern.

In the Caribbean and Gulf of Mexico there are two equipment-owning cooperative industry groups. The Marine Industry Group (MIRG) is an 11-company regional cooperative concerned with the US coastline and the Gulf of Mexico. The Clean Caribbean Cooperative is a 15-company international group covering several Caribbean islands. A proposal for an industry oil spill response capability in the Malaysia/Indonesia/Singapore region is in the final stage of development. This proposal is for an industry organization owning oil spill response equipment. An inter-company arrangement is being developed at Southampton, England, which will be an equipment-owning arrangement using an already well-established equipment base developed by BP as part of its own oil spill response capability.

The Gulf Area Oil Companies Mutual Aid Organization (GAOCMAO) Agreement of 1972 was perhaps the first of its kind in which the concept of mutual assistance in times of emergency is the keynote. Member companies are obliged under the terms of the GAOCMAO Agreement to maintain in readiness at all times defined minima of oil spill response equipment and oil dispersant chemicals for use in emergency situations, if required. These equipment/materials minima must be made available to a requesting member company when required by the latter for pollution response. In addition, member companies are expected to render such supplementary assistance as they are able when so requested by a member company which is experiencing an oil pollution emergency. The terms and conditions of this assistance are clearly laid out in the GAOCMAO Agreement and it is only in instances where the standard provisions are varied that further negotiations between member companies are necessary. The existence of these 'ground rules' greatly facilitates the mobilization of equipment and materials in times of emergency. The original Agreement has been revised three times, the most recent revision being in 1984 when a wholly rewritten and more comprehensive Agreement was adopted by the member companies.

Probably the most significant feature of the GAOCMAO Agreement is the provision for voluntary liability, up to a total of US$20 million, for the oil spill response costs of other member companies when a member company is itself responsible for oil pollution which affects, or threatens to affect, others. This liability provision has been a unique characteristic of GAOCMAO Agreements since the Organization was first formed. It has no known parallel in any other cooperative agreement between oil companies. The companies of GAOCMAO operate in seven different countries of the Sea Area. Thus, pollution generated in one country by a member company may adversely affect another member company operating in a neighbouring country. In the absence of established procedure, such a situation could be very difficult to resolve and, depending on the damage caused and expense involved, might generate political embarrassment between the countries concerned. However, through the liability provision of the GAOCMAO Agreement, an agreed claims procedure is available whereby the 'innocent' party is able to obtain recompense. All this is done at an inter-company level, transcending the international boundaries concerned and, above all, without involving national governments. The recompense available encompasses only reparation for costs directly incurred by the member company in responding to the pollution; it does not address the question of consequential damage in any of its forms.

The Sea Area referred to is that sub-tropical sea shelf lying between latitudes 25 °N and 30 °N and centred on longitude 52.2 °E. Its western boundary is the Arabian Peninsula, whilst in the east it is deemed to terminate at the median line between Iran and the Arab Gulf States. In addition to the water just defined, the Sea Area also includes the coastal waters of the Sultanate of Oman as far south as Muscat.

The objectives of GAOCMAO can be briefly stated as:

(i) to provide a means for joint response to oil pollution by the member companies;
(ii) to establish and maintain effective inter-company communications, especially during oil pollution emergencies;
(iii) to develop member companies' basic spill response capabilities;
(iv) to provide a forum for information collection, dissemination and exchange on all subjects relevant to the oil industry in the Sea Area, with special emphasis on matters relating to oil spill prevention, control and response.

6 Elements of regional arrangement amenable to harmonization

As may be seen from the foregoing review of existing regional agreements, there already exists a considerable degree of similarity between them. This situation has arisen more from one text being used as the basis for the other and the continuity of UNEP and IMO involvement in the preparation of the 'first draft text' than from a conscious decision to harmonize the texts. On the contrary, in the areas of the Regional Seas Programme, governments were often urged to formulate their agreements and action plans to meet regional requirements but the effect of precedent, in particular with respect to the preparation and adoption of international treaties, was as always compelling. This is not to say that each new agreement simply duplicated previously adopted agreements. There are differences and doubtless the government experts who participated in the drafting of the agreement would agree that the differences are substantive and a real improvement on earlier variations on the basic theme.

The most compelling argument for harmonization exists firstly where the provisions of the agreement relate to matters already the subject of international agreements and affect for example the legitimate activities of non-contracting parties within the sea area covered, and secondly where the geographic scope of one agreement is contiguous to another and where one or more contracting parties may be a common member of more than one regional agreement.

All the conventions which have been prepared under the United Nations Environment Programme's Regional Seas Programme include an article dealing with pollution from ships. The relevant article generally requests that contracting parties shall take all appropriate measures in conformity with international law to prevent, reduce, combat and control pollution in the convention area caused by normal or accidental discharges from ships, and shall ensure the effective application in the convention area of the internationally recognized rules and standards relating to the control of this type of pollution.

All of the regional agreements provide for pollution incident reporting in one form or another. In general they require coastal states receiving a report of an incident to notify all other contracting states thereof to be affected. The primary source of reports of this nature will be from the vessel or offshore platform either involved in or aware of an incident. Most of the agreements includes an obligation that each contracting party will require masters of all ships flying its flag to report to it incidents involving its ships. In addition, there exists the global mandatory reporting requirements of MARPOL 73/78 relating to reporting requirements on violations, casualties and pollution incidents.

Where pollution incident reporting involves obtaining information from the ship it is essential that procedures should be agreed internationally within IMO and that any regional scheme should comply with these procedures. The revised Protocol I of MARPOL 73/78 concerning reports on incidents involving harmful substances will be adopted at the IMO Assembly in November 1985 and it contains detailed procedures and standard message formats requiring vessels involved in incidents as well as those ships assisting including the salvor to report to the nearest coastal state.

With respect to interstate communication within a regional agreement, a common pollution reporting system (POLREP) has been adopted by the Bonn Agreement, the Copenhagen Agreement and the Helsinki Commission and could form the basis of regional harmonization for other regions. In those areas where regions are contiguous or one country may be a common member of more than one regional agreement it would be particularly useful to agree on a common reporting scheme based on the POLREP system.

Although not the subject of regional arrangements for combating marine pollution, there is a trend towards adopting protocols to framework conventions concerning specially protected areas wherein contracting parties undertake to take all appropriate measures with a view to protecting those marine areas which are important for the safeguard of *inter alia* the natural resources of the sea area. Among the protection measures included in such protocols is regulation of the passage of ships and the prohibition of any stopping or anchoring. Clearly it would be advantageous to ensure the harmonized approach at the international level of operational procedures which may be adopted at the regional level dealing with the regulation of shipping in such specially protected areas.

7   **Sources of technical assistance on developing national and regional contingency plans**

As perhaps is well known, IMO has over the years provided technical asssistance in the field of national and regional contingency planning. Such assistance is either provided direct to individual governments upon request or in cooperation with, for example, UNEP and regional organizations such as OAS and CPPS within the context of a regional programme. The assistance primarily takes the form of advisory services which are carried out by IMO staff members, both regional and head-quarters based, or by IMO appointed consultants. Such assistance can involve the organization of national or regional seminars or workshops as well as advice on the preparation and improvement of national or regional contingency plans. Aside from the advisory services provided by the regular staff of IMO such technical assistance activities of this kind are funded from a variety of sources. Where such assistance is rendered in the context of a regional environment programme or action plan, it is funded by UNEP or a regional trust fund. Other sources include UNDP, SIDA, NORAD, USAID and OAS. In terms of personnel which can readily provide technical advice in this field, IMO has an Adviser on Marine Pollution based at IMO Headquarters, a Regional Consultant on Marine Pollution for the Wider Caribbean Region, based in Puerto Rico and funded by USAID, a Regional Adviser on Marine Pollution for Latin America, based in Santiago, Chile, and funded by UNDP, and in the near future a Regional Adviser on Marine Pollution for Asia and the Pacific based on Bangkok, Thailand, funded by NORAD.

A particularly important means of providing technical assistance is through bilateral cooperation. Such assistance can often be arranged through normal diplomatic channels either as part of a bilateral aid programme or on the basis where the out-of-pocket costs (e.g. per diem, airfare, etc.) are paid by the recipient government. In this regard it may be recalled that IMO Resolution A.448(XI) on Regional Arrangements for Combating Major Incidents or Threats of Marine Pollution, adopted by the IMO Assembly in 1980, invites those Governments which have resources and expertise available to assist in developing and implementing national and regional contingency plans.

As previously mentioned, several of the regional agreements make provision that the function of the regional centres include the provisions of technical support in the development of national contingency plans. In the Mediterranean, ROCC is staffed to provide such technical assistance to the countries in the region requiring it. In the Kuwait Action Plan region it is understood that MEMAC is developing its capability to arrange for technical advisory services to its participating states. Where such regional centres can provide or arrange for technical assistance, it would appear desirable that they should be approached in the first instance.

There are universities and national research institutes which have developed expertise and training programmes in the field of marine pollution prevention, control and combating. These services have on occasion been used by IMO and UNEP with satisfactory results. Naturally, the services provided have to be paid for but, because of the nature of such organizations, the fees charged may be less than purely commercial enterprises.

There are aspects of contingency planning which may benefit from obtaining expertise from, for example, the Food and Agriculture Organization (FAO) and the International Union for the Conservation of Nature and Natural Resources (IUCN). FAO and IMO have cooperated in the past in arranging for assistance in evaluating the environmental impact of an oil spill and in particular its effects on living marine resources. Recognizing the importance of knowing beforehand precisely what living resources are at risk for protection, mitigation and claims purposes, FAO should be able to assist countries on cooperation with IUCN in, for example, marine resource mapping and the identification of particularly vulnerable zones. These organizations were particularly instrumental in the development of protocols on specially protected areas.

Mention should also be made of the role of the oil industry in the development and implementation of national contingency planning. For instance, whilst originally having been set up as an oil tanker owners' pollution liability insurance 'clearing house', ITOPF has over the years developed a high level of expertise in the field through attendance at spills and working as IMO consultants in several regions. Also, in several regions oil company cooperatives have been established to facilitate a rapid and efficient response to an oil spill beyond the immediate capabilities of one company and in an area of joint concern. Such cooperatives would most probably be in a position to provide technical advice on the development of national contingency plans.

9   Response to major marine pollution incidents beyond regional capability

9.1   *Availability of international assistance*

IMO has in the past been involved in providing timely technical assistance in the event of a major spill. Organizations such as UNEP, UNDP and the United Nations Disaster Relief Organization (UNDRO) may mobilize limited funds for technical assistance in dealing with an oil spill which can be seen as a disaster having a particular acute economic and environmental impact on the limited resources of a developing country. However, to the extent known, such assistance in the past has been limited to funding the visits of technical experts and has not been utilized to lease oil spill clean-up equipment or pay contractors. For those states members of the International Oil Pollution Compensation Fund (IOPC Fund), i.e. as set up under the 1971 International Convention, provision is made for the extension, in certain circumstances, of reasonable credit facilities to enable a contracting state which is in imminent danger of substantial oil pollution damage to initiate or continue to take adequate preventive measures. This aspect of pre-financing oil pollution defence measures should be explored further.

A key role is played by ITOPF and ITOPF personnel provide advice and assistance at most major oil spills primarily on behalf of the tanker owners and insurers. Consequently, the technical staff have gained a substantial experience of the most effective clean-up techniques. ITOPF staff also carry out post spill surveys again normally for the tanker owner and his third party insurer. The Oil Companies Institute for Marine Pollution Compensation Services Ltd (the Administrators of CRISTAL – the oil cargo owners voluntary compensation agreement) and its intergovernmental counterpart, the above-mentioned Fund, also employ the ITOPF services. The post spill surveys have two main components: evaluation of the technical reasonableness of the clean-up response and assessment of the extent of any pollution damage caused by the spill.

As previously mentioned with respect to contingency planning, bilateral assistance requested through normal diplomatic channels can be a viable source of technical expertise in the event of a major spill.

In November 1985 the IMO Assembly adopted a resolution (A.587(14)), the operative paragraphs of which are as follows:

1 INVITES the Secretary-General of IMO, in cooperation with UNEP, UNDP and other organisations concerned, as appropriate, to undertake on a priority basis an evaluation of the problems of countries faced with the threat of major marine pollution from spillages of oil and other hazardous substances, taking into consideration the roles of the respective organizations in dealing with these problems;

2 REQUESTS IMO's Marine Enviroment Protection Committee on the basis of this evaluation to take steps and to make recommendations, as appropriate and as soon as possible;

3 REQUESTS FURTHER the IMO Council and the Secretary-General to take all possible steps to implement these recommendations and to report to the Assembly at its fifteenth session.

It is anticipated that one of the actions arising from this resolution is that IMO will undertake the preparation of a directory that would contain information provided by governments, international and regional intergovernmental and nongovernmental organizations and industry on the type of assistance that might be made available in the event of a major marine pollution incident and how a request for such assistance should be made. This document could as well briefly describe the role and function of the various entities which could be involved in a marine emergency and its aftermath. It could also include valuable information provided by potential requesting States such as the identification of a national focal point and arrangements for receit of material resources and personnel which would facilitate the provision of assistance in an emergency.

9.2   *Facilitation of the provision of international assistance in the event of a major spill*

Many of the regional agreements or protocols contain provision that each contracting party shall facilitate the movement into, through and out of its territory of technical personnel, equipment and material necessary for responding to oil spill incidents. Notwithstanding this proviso and the obvious interest of states in facilitating the provision of such assistance in the event of a major spill, it is not unknown for difficulties to arise in the timely clearance of, in particular, material and equipment. Whilst it is basically a national responsibility to make the appropriate arrangements with custom and immigration services for the rapid entry of equipment and personnel, there is a need for governments to be encouraged to make such arrangements. For example, an IMO Assembly Resolution could be addressed to governments as well as relevant international organizations such as the Customs Cooperation Council calling for the attention of, for example, customs services to be drawn to the need to develop arrangements for the rapid clearance and in some instances the temporary importation of oil spill clean-up equipment.

It may be of interest to note that the IMO Convention on Facilitation of International Maritime Traffic contains provision that public authorities should, to the greatest extent possible, facilitate the entry and clearance of persons and cargo arriving in vessels engaged in natural disaster relief work. Although a major oil spill is usually a man-made disaster, its effect may in certain circumstances be as severe as a natural disaster. Consideration could be given to including at least a recommending practice in the Facilitation Convention on this subject and in this connection the Facilitation Committee is undertaking a comprehensive review of the Technical Annex to the Convention with a view to its revision. As most personnel and material need to arrive by air in the event of an oil spill, a similar recommendation should also be considered by ICAO in respect of their Facilitation Convention. However, this does not detract from the need for suitable provisions being contained in the IMO Facilitation Convention since equipment and possibly some personnel may be returned to the country of origin by sea.

Mention should be made of a draft convention on expediting the delivery of emergency assistance prepared under the aegis of UNDRO and under study by governmental experts. In this connection 'disaster' is broadly defined to include any natural, accidental or deliberate event as a result of which assistance is needed from outside the state. The draft convention *inter alia* provides that the state shall exempt relief consignments and equipment from all customs duties and charges and shall be cleared rapidly if necessary outside business hours and as a matter of priority by customs authorities. The convention also provides for free transit and the granting without undue delay of permission for the overflight, landing and departure of civil aircraft. It should be noted, however, that 'emergency assistance' is defined as relief consignments and services of an exclusively humanitarian character. It would remain a question of interpretation whether response to an oil or hazardous chemical spill was of a humanitarian character.

9.3   *Desirability of a clearing house for requests for international assistance*

IMO in cooperation with UNEP and other organizations, both governmental and nongovernmental, will continue to respond to requests from governments for technical assistance, including advice on the combating of marine pollution arising from emergency situations. Obviously such a function can only be carried out within the capabilities of the organization and any request to expand this function would have to be considered by the relevant bodies of the organization taking into account the overall work programme.

However it would appear that the present situation whereby IMO, UNEP, and e.g. FAO, regional organizations, oil industry cooperatives and organizations such as ITOPF and IPIECA, all play a role in responding to requests for assistance may be considered adequate notwithstanding the somewhat fragmented approach. The centralization of requests for assistance might create expectations which could not be readily satisfied unless specific budgetary provisions were made in this regard.

10   Conclusion

The similarity of stated purpose and content of the regional agreements adopted worldwide does not disguise the differences in the way in which they will be implemented at the national and regional level. The most obvious difference exists between those agreements involving the more developed and better equipped countries and those in which developing countries predominate. In the case of the Copenhagen, Bonn and Helsinki agreements the emphasis can be placed on joint operations and the development of agreed command structures, communications and pollution reporting formats and, to a certain extent, evaluation of the state of the art in oil combating, exchange of technology and development of common policy. Mutual assistance is also a very real possibility in these regions, however, only the rare and very large spills will be beyond the national capability of many of the countries participating in such agreements. In other regions, such as West and East Africa, the logic of joining forces to maximize limited national capability in facing a major spill remains. However, the concept of mutual assistance is less realistic as many of the states have little or no oil spill response capability or equipment themselves and for a number of practical reasons (transport infrastructure and political climate) would find it difficult to readily transfer such equipment in an emergency if they had it. In states in these regions the response to most major maritime casualties and related spills will have to come from outside the region. These states are acutely aware of their predicament and have suggested the establishment of an international fund to assist countries in the purchase of such equipment and/or the establishment of strategically-located stockpiles. It is however considered unlikely, given current circumstances, that donors, either government or industry, could be found for the establishment of a new fund.

In these regions the agreements, as previously mentioned, act as a catalyst for the development of national oil spill contingency plans and as a framework for cooperation in training and research. An unstated objective of the agreements in which developed and developing states participate (e.g. Cartagena, Barcelona, South Pacific) is to commit the developed or richer partners (e.g. United States, France, United Kingdom, Australia, etc.) to assist the less well-off partners through the treaty process. In the Caribbean, the expectation of a windfall United States contribution to the Caribbean Trust Fund was not however realised when the United States declared that it would not contribute to a 'blind' trust fund but would rather render support on a project by project basis. It also made a distinction between such trust fund contributions to which it would not contribute and contributing to the costs connected with the implementation of the Cartegena Convention and its protocols which it would. France, Mexico and Venezuela emerge as major contributors to this Trust Fund which finances projects but it is the assistance of the United States which is most likely to be immediately available in the event of the major oil spill. In the Mediterranean, the South looks to the Regional Oil Combating Centre and the Barcelona Convention and Protocol as a conduit or framework for technical assistance from the North. Here again, real on-the-spot assistance in the event of a major spill will be sought and probably obtained on a bilateral basis through normal diplomatic channels with the provisions of the Barcelona Convention and Protocol invoked only as an added impetus.

The regional agreements developed under the auspices of the UNEP Regional Seas Programme all emerged as part of a package including an Action Plan on the protection and development of the marine and coastal environment, the implementation of which was funded in the initial phase by the UNEP Environment Fund. This doubtless accounted for the enthusiastic way in which the agreements were welcomed by many countries and in a very practical way allowed for the participation in expert groups which drafted the agreements and now reviews them periodically. Once the Regional Agreement is adopted and the costs associated with its regional implementation and review are transferred back on to the states either directly or through the operation of a regional trust fund, it will be difficult, to say the least, for the participating States in many regions to maintain the same level of involvement. Indeed, there is a very real risk that the agreements will remain as yet another example of the triumph of hope over experience. The Mediterranean has maintained the impetus towards goals declared ten years ago and unattained today largely because of the success of the Mediterranean Trust Fund with France, Italy and Spain carrying over 90 % of the budget. Other regions will not be able to generate the funds required and it is unrealistic to think otherwise. UNEP often claims its role is only catalytic producing a change in the chemistry of decision-making among states without undergoing a change itself. If the poorer regions of the world are not to be left at the starting gate, UNEP will have to change its policy towards continued financial support of work they have initiated, and maintain substantial contributions to the costs of implementing the regional agreements and action plans.

Part V

16

Conclusion

The preceding chapters present a view of the industrialized world's diplomatic, political, legal and economic thinking relative to the definition, status, direction and resolution (or lack thereof) of international diplomatic problems of an environmental nature. The authors represent a cross-section of both scholars and practitioners of international environmental diplomacy living and working in the European or North American milieu, the milieu in which most transboundary environmental issues as defined have thus far arisen. Within these chapters we see a history of some success, much failure and, above all, countless challenges facing us in the future. In writing this concluding chapter, I have chosen to utilize the most tangible product of international environmental diplomacy, the treaty or convention, and as well the institution charged with its implementation, as the venue for presenting this volume's concluding thoughts.

Among the many things we learn from reading the preceding chapters is that our planet today has more international treaties, conventions and accords today than it has ever had before. And a great number of them are very recent – since 1970 to be exact. We have also learned that our planet is experiencing a greater number and more serious calibre of international

environmental problems than ever before. Is this great number of international agreements a result of the seriousness of our impacts on one another?
Perhaps, it certainly would be logical to think so. But is this mass of
international agreements solving the problems, making things better? The
optimist would like to think so. The realist may think otherwise. Are the
agreements of any help? Certainly, if we measure their role, and particularly
their *educational* role, against the complete absence of same. But no, they are
not helpful if we permit their existence to convince ourselves the problem is
in hand.

Let us view a few of the best of them, at least in the minds of students of
international environmental policy: North America's International Joint
Commission (IJC), created by the Boundary Waters Treaty between the
United States and Canada, and Europe's Barcelona Convention and
Mediterranean Action Plan in that part of the world. It is often said that the
IJC is very successful. It is certainly an enduring institution at over 75 years
of age. But whether or not it is successful depends on what it is measured
against. If measured against other similar attempts to achieve bilateral accord
in North America or elsewhere, we may certainly say it is successful. And I
think most would agree it has been successful in its very narrow technical
responsibility in water apportionment at the (US–Canada) border. But in
broader societal concerns of water and air pollution, it has achieved little of
significance *when measured against getting the problem solved*, and that should
be the only real measure. Further, it has been kept out of the single most
significant area of transborder environmental diplomacy in North America –
acid rain. And, its findings and calls for the clean-up of toxic pollution of
North America's Great Lakes goes unheeded. And once we argue that it is
beyond the scope of such diplomatic instruments as the IJC to perform those
broad but vital tasks, we then admit we have no agreement or convention to
resolve the problem, nor any institution to do the job. I suggest we must start
to measure such entities as boundary waters treaties and the institutions they
spawn not on the basis of how much they seek to accomplish nor in how
much they claim, but, in the final analysis, in the health of the environment
they are meant to protect, and that means the long-term economic and
political environment as well as the natural ecosystem – for they are all
ultimately one.

We might also consider the Barcelona Convention and Mediterranean
Action Plan of UNEP. Once again, this effort has been lauded for the speed
of its enactment, the speed of consensus it achieved in moving toward

ratification. But what about the bigger environmental problems facing the Mediterranean, the ones so nobly identified for us by Captain Jacques-Yves Cousteau and others? This multilateral action plan will secure for us a certain amount of research and monitoring in the Mediterranean, and perhaps somewhat curb vessel discharge, but will it tackle the really big problem of non-point source pollution by land-based run-off, including that which has its source far from the Sea and deep in the interior of France and other nations? Will it significantly reduce the continued dumping of raw sewage and industrial effluent from point sources along the coast? There are few signs that it will do so in the near-term, and perhaps not in the long-term either. Yet we tend to view this diplomatic instrument against other similar efforts (which are often bigger failures or perhaps I should say 'non-starters') and thus call it successful. Could we call it successful if we measured it against results in the water quality of the Mediterranean itself, as Captain Cousteau would have us do? I think not. I contend that the practice of self-delusion in which we engage in the face of contemporary environmental degradation will further inhibit our societal willingness to meet these problems head-on and resolve them. We may continue to manage, perhaps to contain, but never to resolve, while continuing to proceed along this path.

Even more cogent examples can be developed relative to tropical rain-forest destruction, desertification, loss of topsoil, all of which, while often occurring within rather than across national borders, nevertheless affects every one of us, and quite directly. No treaties or conventions are yet solving or even ameliorating these most serious of environmental problems.

And nature will continue to challenge our conventional definition of sovereignty, for there is more than a little evidence now to indicate that nature cannot and will not recognize our anthropocentric definitions of sovereignty, our political borders which defy reality. Nature will continue to challenge the system we have inherited, the system whose evolution we have witnessed, until we recognize more realistically the interrelations and interdependencies of that broad ecosystem within which we must survive.

Do we have conventions, agreements, treaties? Yes, we have many indeed. Do we have institutions, large and small, to carry out their mandate? Yes, we most certainly do. Do we have a global environment which is getting healthier? No! In fact, quite the contrary. Do we have a reduction in transborder environmental problems? Not at all.

In essence, what I am saying is that there is a very large gap between the *direction* of our efforts in international environmental diplomacy, namely, toward *more* treaties and other diplomatic instruments and certainly toward more publicity and more awareness surrounding them, and the *direction* of the environmental course of events in our modern world today, namely toward increased rapidity of environmental decay and degradation, even into crisis proportions. The extremely rapid destruction of tropical rainforest, sharp increases in the loss of topsoil, increased desertification, and, in the pollution area, no real reduction in massive pollution of air and water associated with large-scale industrial development all provide the evidence. Therefore, while we may wish to cheer the successful development and ratification of instruments like the ECE Convention on the Long-Range Transport of Air Pollutants, or the Amazon Basin Compact acknowledging the international importance of the rainforests in that Basin, let us not delude ourselves into thinking that these things are sufficient, or that the destruction of the planet has stopped or even slowed, for it has not. Let us not delude ourselves into thinking that so-called success stories such as the clean-up of Lake Erie in North America by the reduction of conventional sewage and industry waste in its water does anything at all to attack the great quantity of much less visible but much more insidious toxic substances in that water. Sadly, the environmental problems we face as a global society are much more fundamental. Many are now coming to believe that conventional incremental – some would say 'reformist' – approaches will never do the job. Not only is the gap between problem and remedy great, but the rate of growth in the size of that gap seems to increase in direct proportion to our attempts to fix it.

Some in North America argue for what they call 'deep ecology', a new environmental or ecological ethic. Europeans are becoming particularly aware of political movements akin to this ethic called 'green politics', a profoundly broad economic, political, ecological and even social philosophy. The evidence of this widening gap between the problems facing us and what some would call our 'band-aid remedies' is clearly feeding the call of the green movement toward rejection of the conventional way of doing business, rejection of incremental approaches, and an embrace and acceptance of much more fundamental change in our philosophy of governance, of economics, of the way we live. Such evidence supports the idea that the system itself is the problem. The message of the Greens, therefore, may require closer study.

When there is such a gap between the apparent effort of society to rectify problems and, simultaneously, such a tangible worsening of those problems, then we may very well not be asking the right questions. For no matter what kinds of claims we can make, legitimately and honestly, about how much we spend, about how much good faith and good will we apply, the story is told in the condition of the environment, the natural environment including the human environment, and it is there for all to see. Whither do we next turn?

A careful reading of the preceding chapters informs the reader of some of what has been done and is being done in international environmental diplomacy. The reader may wish to measure this work against the environmental challenges our society now faces, and to inquire as to what kind of change might be needed in what we do, in how we live and conduct our affairs, if we are ultimately to resolve these problems.

Our forebears, both those of thousands of years and as well those of more recent centuries, developed a compact with life on earth which enabled them to survive. We must do likewise.

Index